College Writing

Brian McCrea
University of Florida

Toni Lopez Kemmerle

Bobbs-Merrill Educational Publishing
Indianapolis A publishing subsidiary of ITT

A publishing subsidiary of ITT
Printed in the United States of America

The Bobbs-Merrill Company, Inc.
4300 West 62nd Street
Indianapolis, Indiana 46268

First Edition
First Printing 1985

Acquisition Editor: Paul E. O'Connell
Project Editor: Elsa F. Kramer
Editorial and Production Management: National Evaluation Systems, Inc.

Library of Congress Cataloging in Publication Data

McCrea, Brian.
College writing.

Includes index.
1. English Language—Rhetoric. I. Kemmerle, Toni.
II. Title.
PE1408.M3937 1985 808'.042 84-20451
ISBN 0-672-61632-7

CONTENTS

College Writing

Preface

Our goal in *College Writing* is a text at once compact and comprehensive, a text that is teachable. We move from the basics of sentence structure through paragraph organization, expository prose models, and argumentative prose models; these topics form the major subjects of this book. By linking all our discussions to the concept of agent prose, we can treat *all* our subjects compactly but in a way that will allow teaching assistants to build an entire course from the materials. Experienced teachers will find the concept of agent prose compatible with their own approaches to teaching composition; they can use the book without having to continually devise supplementary materials. Students who study this text should begin to see that writing is a process in which they have a role to play—a process in which they are agents responsible for making clear assertions with effective supports.

Our goals for this text—brevity, comprehensiveness, and teachability—are ones from which we believe many current composition texts have strayed. We would like *College Writing* to be judged in terms of these goals; we hope it will be seen as a text that refocuses on the real needs of teachers (both old and new hands) and of students in composition classes.

Acknowledgments

This book has gone through more perils than Pauline, and we want to thank Paul O'Connell for rescuing it at the last moment. Ralph McCrea provided important technical assistance for which we are grateful.

The sample essays included in this text mention a number of colleges and universities. This created a problem for us, because we could not substantiate in all cases the charges that our student writers were making. At the same time, we did not want to invent names and lose the specificity and power that reference to an actual university gives. Our solution was to take all the names of universities and colleges that we had and to use them randomly. That is, we would take from the entire group a substitute for the university the student mentioned. The essays that complain about registration procedures or dormitory conditions do not, then, reflect conditions at the universities they name.

We also gratefully acknowledge our debt to the philosopher Kenneth Burke, from whom we have borrowed the concept of the *pentad*. Mr. Burke presents this concept in *A Grammar of Motives* (Berkeley and Los Angeles: University of California Press, 1969).

Introduction

As authors of this text, we make few assumptions about the writing skills you possess. These skills will vary quite widely depending on your familial and educational background. Whatever your background, our goal is to make writing less difficult for you (we must note that all authors, from Nobel Prize winners to harried composition teachers, agree that writing is never easy). But we cannot achieve this goal by merely teaching you rules and giving you models. Just as people who drive while looking at instruction manuals inevitably crash, people who try to write by continually referring to grammatical rules inevitably produce stilted, ineffective prose. Our focus will be on the reasons for the rules and models rather than on the rules and models themselves. If this text is successful, you should, after studying it, be able to write successfully without continually referring to grammatical rules; you should have the same kind of confidence in your prose style that you have in your ability to drive a car.

Most expository prose that is vague, abstract, confusing—choose whatever pejorative term you like—suffers from one flaw. Such prose fails to define an *agent*. By this term we mean a doer for the actions the prose describes. Throughout our discussions of the rules of grammar, paragraph organization, and essay structure, we will direct your attention to the agent. We believe that if you write agent prose, you will no longer need the rules; you will conform to them naturally and automatically. The ability to write agent prose, however, is not easy to develop. We live in a culture that has minimized the importance of personal responsibility for actions, the importance of agency. In a world of big government, big corporations, big unions, and big universities, we often forget that individuals shape events, that individuals can act for good or ill. We become confused about who is responsible for situations.

Insofar as our writing mirrors this confusion, it is vague, abstract, and unspecific.

This text will require you to buck the current trend. We will ask you to make the definition of an agent the first and most basic step in your writing. We feel that this difficult first step will lead to great and manifest benefits—most specifically an active, direct prose style.

To write agent prose, you will need to work with your instructor. You should see that you and your instructor share a goal—overcoming agentless prose—and that you can reach that goal only by understanding your mutual responsibilities. Your responsibility is to master—to make second nature—a body of principles. Your instructor's responsibility is to help you understand how applying these principles contributes to the definition of an agent and results in a clear writing style. You should never accept a rule without such an explanation; your instructor should never propose a rule without one.

By understanding your mutual responsibilities and working together, you and your instructor can overcome the handicap you both face: the tendency toward agentlessness in our society. We hope this text can foster understanding and cooperation and guide you to a prose style that will be an advantage rather than a liability. You should remember, as we have tried to remember, that no text can make fine writers. All any text can do is help writers realize their full potential. What you bring to this book is as important as any of the lessons it contains.

I Sentences That Make an Assertion: Agent Prose

Many studies have shown that courses that give students intense instruction in grammar—in the rules of speaking and writing—largely fail to improve the students' writing. Yet most of the prose that we read and admire today is grammatical. Obviously, then, while mastery of English grammar is basic to effective exposition and argument, the study of grammar alone does not promote good writing.

In 1776, for example, rules of grammar probably were not on Thomas Jefferson's mind as he faced the awesome task of justifying the American Revolution to a world that viewed monarchy as, at the very least, a normal and proper form of government and, at most, a sacred office. To win support for the American revolutionaries, Jefferson wanted to portray as powerfully as possible the misdeeds of George III that had pushed men like Jefferson "to dissolve the political bands" with England. His catalog of the king's "repeated injuries and usurpations" is at the heart of the Declaration of Independence and is one key to the document's powerful influence. We quote Jefferson's first four charges.

> He has refused his Assent to Laws, the most wholesome and necessary for the public good.
>
> He has forbidden his Governors to pass laws of immediate and pressing importance, unless suspended in their operation till his Assent should be obtained; and when so suspended, he has utterly neglected to attend to them.
>
> He has refused to pass other Laws for the accommodation

> of large districts of people, unless those people would relinquish the right of Representation in the Legislature, a right inestimable to them and formidable to tyrants only.
>
> He has called together legislative bodies at places unusual, uncomfortable, and distant from the depository of their Public Records, for the sole purpose of fatiguing them into compliance with his measures.

This is powerful prose, prose that may well have shaped the course of human history. But what are the sources of its power? We would point to two. First is the specificity of Jefferson's sentence subjects—"he" (the king, George III). Jefferson leaves no doubt that "he" is responsible for "the long train of abuses" the Americans have suffered. Second is the clarity of Jefferson's predicates—*refused, forbidden, called together*. Jefferson specifies the bad acts "he" has performed. Other sources of power in this prose include its use of parallelism: the repetition of *he has* builds to a kind of literary crescendo. But in this chapter we want to talk mainly about subjects and predicates and urge you to follow Jefferson's lead; for while Jefferson's prose is grammatically correct, the power, the urgency, and the cogency of his complaint spring from his identifying the agent (doer) for a series of actions. With less specific subjects and predicates, the complaint could be equally correct but not equally powerful.

In this chapter we will urge you to find subjects and predicates like Jefferson's—subjects that name agents and predicates that call up mental images of specific acts.

Building Sentences Around a Specific Subject

Throughout your schooling, teachers have urged you to make your writing clear, specific, concrete, and direct. One way to achieve this is to develop what we call *subject specificity*. Specific sentence subjects actually *do* the action that a sentence describes. Weak, nonspecific sentence subjects stand in the subject place but cannot act. They confuse the reader because they hide the basic, fundamental fact of who or what is responsible for an action. No one reading the Declaration of Independence wonders who is oppressing the American people. Jefferson's achievement—naming a name—may seem relatively simple, but it is the first step to writing clear prose, a step that many student writers overlook.

EXERCISE 1

In the following sentences, mark with an *S* those subjects you feel are specific, with a *W* those you feel are weak. Remember, your first question should be: Does the subject actually do the action that the sentence describes? As you identify the weak subjects, observe how easy it sometimes is to lose sight of the doer.

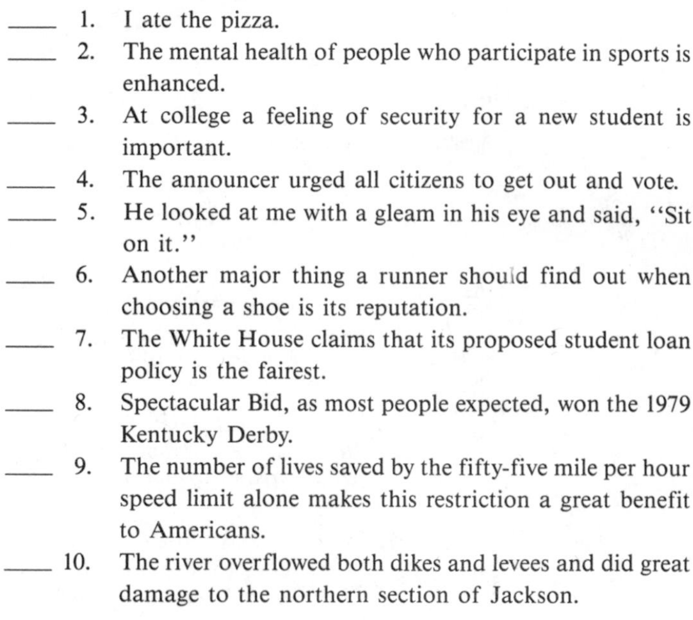

____ 1. I ate the pizza.

____ 2. The mental health of people who participate in sports is enhanced.

____ 3. At college a feeling of security for a new student is important.

____ 4. The announcer urged all citizens to get out and vote.

____ 5. He looked at me with a gleam in his eye and said, "Sit on it."

____ 6. Another major thing a runner should find out when choosing a shoe is its reputation.

____ 7. The White House claims that its proposed student loan policy is the fairest.

____ 8. Spectacular Bid, as most people expected, won the 1979 Kentucky Derby.

____ 9. The number of lives saved by the fifty-five mile per hour speed limit alone makes this restriction a great benefit to Americans.

____ 10. The river overflowed both dikes and levees and did great damage to the northern section of Jackson.

You can see that sentence subjects can be more specific or less specific. To test your subjects, try asking two questions about them. First, "Have I ever seen one?" Second, "Have I ever seen one walking down the street?" If the answer to both questions is no, you should recognize that your sentence has a subject but lacks an agent. You should then ask whether a more specific doer is available to serve as your sentence subject.

The meaning of subject specificity may become clearer if you study the following scale. The best, the most specific, subject will be a person, someone you can see walking down the street. Subjects will become weaker, less specific, as they become less personal and less animate.

SUBJECT SPECIFICITY SCALE

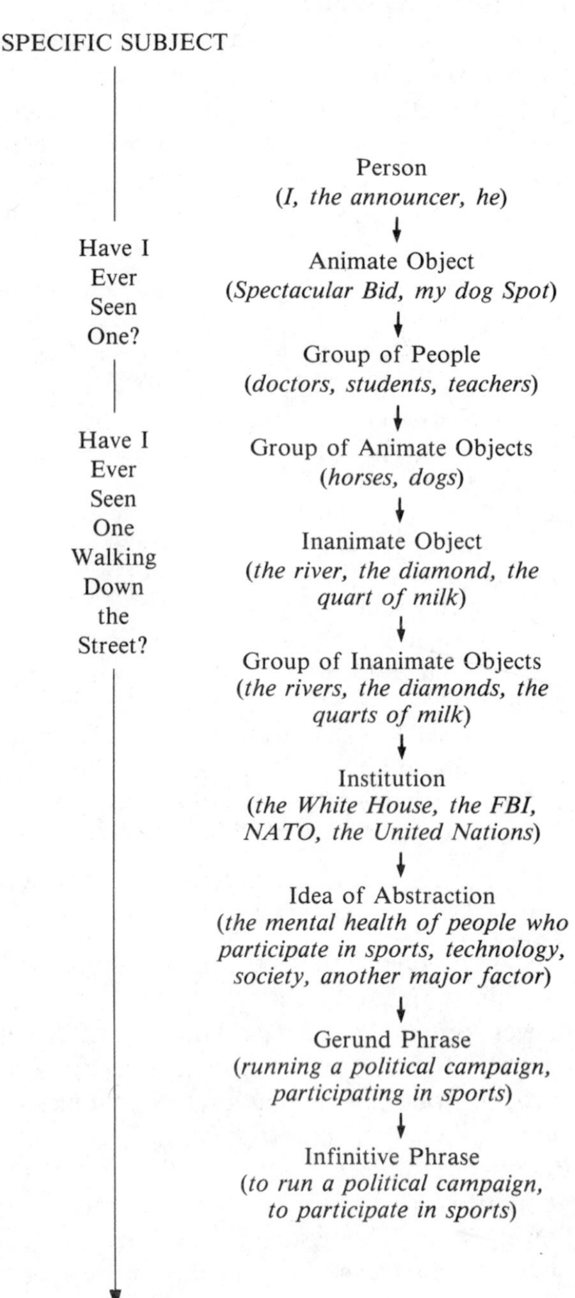

Of course, your answer to the two basic questions cannot always be yes. Sometimes you will inevitably make words like *technology, society,* and *the FBI* your sentence subjects. But if you cannot replace such unspecific subjects, at the very least you should always recognize them and realize the vagueness you risk. In addition to vagueness, such writing ultimately risks dishonesty. Contrast Jefferson's subjects and predicates to those in the following statement by former Secretary of State Alexander Haig, as he spoke about the killing in December 1980 of three American Catholic nuns and a lay worker in El Salvador: "Perhaps the vehicle that the nuns were riding in may have tried to run a roadblock, or may accidentally have been perceived to have been doing so, and there had been an exchange of fire." Although four people died, in Haig's sentence no one killed them; if anyone was at fault, it was the vehicle. This is a far cry from Jefferson's clear use of an agent.

Disguising the Subject: Latinate Diction

Never use a long word
where a short one will do.
George Orwell

Perhaps the greatest threat to subject specificity is the diction (choice of words) that George Orwell discusses in his famous essay "Politics and the English Language." Orwell points out that when authors of English prose use words of Latin origin, those words may blur our picture of an action and hide unpleasant realities: "Defenceless villages are bombarded from the air, the inhabitants driven out into the countryside . . . this is called *pacification*" (*Shooting an Elephant and Other Essays,* New York: Harcourt Brace Jovanovich, 1946). In his explanation of the death of the four American churchwomen in El Salvador, Alexander Haig's diction became so Latinate that he not only avoided naming the murderers but also made the fact of the murder disappear: "And this could have been at a very low level of both competence and motivation in the context of the issue itself." The murder becomes an "issue," the events surrounding it a "context"; *competence* and *motivation* usually belong to agents but here stand alone.

Latinate words tend to be long words because they add both prefixes (*de-, pre-, trans-, co-, bi-, super-,*) and suffixes (*-ology, -ment, -ize, -ion*) to word roots. In contrast to the basic Anglo-Saxon four-letter word, the Latinate word often stretches out to include ten or more letters. Of course, in some cases, Latinate words help us to avoid simpler but cruder words: *excrement, urine,* and *sexual intercourse* are all words that in certain situations most people will substitute for unacceptable Anglo-Saxon alternatives. Furthermore, a sophisticated writer like Thomas Jefferson can use Latinate diction without losing either power or precision. Recall another famous passage from the Declaration of Independence: "We hold these truths to be self-evident, that all men are created equal, that they are endowed by their Creator with certain unalienable Rights, that among these are Life, Liberty, and the pursuit of Happiness." However, when Jefferson

---

EXERCISE 2

Recently, Latinate diction has invaded sports reporting and broadcasting, overrunning a field in which clear, active prose was once fairly common. Study the following sentences, locate the Latinate words or phrases, and replace them with shorter, simpler Anglo-Saxon equivalents.

1. The middle guard made a great play and tackled the back for negative yardage.
2. No matter what you try, velocity is the one thing you cannot teach pitchers; they either have it or they don't.
3. While speed and strength are important, intestinal fortitude is what makes the truly great blocking back.
4. So far a surprising paucity of punts has characterized this game.
5. The rotation you put on the ball is the key to good shooting touch.
6. Gate Dancer's unruly behavior worried his trainer and fans.
7. The cacophonous clamor of the crowd drowned out the quarterback's voice.
8. Earvin Johnson's ability to manipulate the spheroid is equal to that of a small playmaker, even though he is 6′8″.
9. Almost knocked off his feet, the American Dream maintained his equilibrium and went on to pin his opponent.
10. Games of supereminent importance always seem to bring forth a maximum effort from Reggie Jackson.

---

uses the Latinate phrase *unalienable Rights,* he takes care to define those rights immediately. Thus, while you can use Latinate diction to good ends—to avoid vulgarity or to express complex ideas—in most cases the shorter Anglo-Saxon word will provide the more specific sentence subject, the agent you want.

The Latinate diction of the sports pages does not totally destroy clarity. It simply requires us to translate the sentences—to substitute *loss* for *negative yardage, rankness* for *unruly behavior, speed* for *velocity.* But Latinate prose is less evocative; *ability to manipulate the spheroid* calls up a much blurrier picture than *dribbling ability.* Latinate prose also requires more syllables and more words; it is less direct than plain English. *Games of supereminent importance* takes three times as much space as *big games; cacophonous clamor of the crowd* needlessly inflates *noisy crowd.*

Latinate diction becomes particularly dangerous when it allows writers to take vague nouns and use them as if they were agents. Consider the following examples cited by Robert Claiborne in his essay "Future Schlock."

> The increased rate at which situations flow past us vastly complicates the entire structure of life, multiplying the number of roles we must play and the number of choices we are forced to make.
>
> The speeded-up flow-through of situations demands much more work from the complex focusing mechanisms by which we shift our attention from one situation to another. (*The Nation* 212, 25 January 1971)

These sentences defy the kind of translation we made with the sports examples. *Situations* and *focusing mechanisms* (and their counterparts, *culture, technology,* and *civilization*) are intellectual conceptions so totally lacking in actual physical being that they stand near the very bottom of our sentence grid; they are abstractions. We cannot visualize the "speeded-up flow-through of situations," nor can we tell who is doing the "speeding up." The Latinate words destroy subject specificity and hide the agent.

When you analyze your prose for Latinate diction, you face a large and difficult task. Latinate words *are* part of our language and you cannot totally dispense with them, but you should focus on your sentence subjects and determine how many bear the telltale Latinate prefixes and suffixes. This study will tell you a great deal about the lack of agents in your prose. With Jefferson in mind, you should recognize that long words are not bad simply because they are long or because they have Latin roots. The words Orwell warns against become dangerous only when they hide agents. Noun subjects like *technology, civilization,* and *contingencies of reinforcement* sound impressive but ultimately say very little. They tell your reader nothing about the people who create the technology, the civilization, and the contingencies.

EXERCISE 3

Translate the following sentences into plain English. In all cases try to define an agent for the actions the sentence describes.

1. Our allocation program will distribute the surplus food as fairly as possible.
2. Cohabitation, commonly referred to as "living together," has an estimated 1,330,000 participants in the United States.
3. Culture controls the response of individuals to most stimuli, particularly through the influence of the family.
4. Advancing technology has left many unskilled and semiskilled workers with no hope of finding jobs.
5. Inadequate educational opportunity is the reason so few blacks are doctors.

In some cases revision of these sentences is easy. You need merely substitute an agent—a person or group of people—for the abstraction. Compare exercise sentence 1 to this revision: "Ms. Clark and I will distribute the surplus food as fairly as possible." But in some cases, the substitution is more difficult. You cannot make *advancing technology* or *inadequate educational opportunity* specific unless you define an agent who actually *advances* technology or *creates* inadequate educational opportunity. "Poor schooling is the reason so few blacks are doctors" is less Latinate, but does not solve the problems with sentence 5. Large numbers of Latinate subjects, then, are not merely a sign to rewrite. They also are a sign to rethink—to define an agent for the actions you are describing. The best revision will look something like this: "For years white educators and white legislators kept blacks out of good schools; as a result few blacks are doctors."

Latinate diction is avoidable, particularly if you remember that it is learned, not natural. As a child you lacked the vocabulary to speak abstractly. Your conversation probably was more fresh and surprising than it is today. You named things directly; you spoke in "Anglo-Saxon." But soon you learned, or your parents forced you to learn, some basic euphemisms—many of which rely on Latinate diction—to hide actions most people consider to be unpleasant or undignified. As you grew up, you learned that people do not *die;* rather, they *pass away* or are *lost.* Your mother and father did not *fight;* rather, they had *domestic discussions.* Finally, if you found yourself working at a worthy but unglamorous job as a cook, an auto mechanic, or a garbageman, you immediately changed your title to *culinary specialist, transportation supervisor,* or *sanitation engineer.* In everyday life these euphemisms are harmless enough, but in the office and in the schoolroom they often lead to vagueness.

EXERCISE 4

You will probably understand the following passage only with great difficulty. Locate the sentence subjects, and then analyze how they contribute to the lack of clarity.

> The difficulty is that although privacy may bring the knower closer to what he knows, it interferes with the process through which he comes to know anything. As we have seen, contingencies under which a child learns to describe his feelings are necessarily defective; the verbal community cannot use the same procedures for this that it uses to teach a child to describe objects. There are, of course, natural contingencies under which we learn to respond to private stimuli, and they generate behavior of great precision: we could not walk if we were not stimulated by parts of our own body. But very little awareness is associated with this kind of behavior. (B. F. Skinner, *Beyond Freedom and Dignity*)

Noun subjects like *privacy, contingencies,* and *verbal community* stand between us and a clear understanding of what this author means. They are abstractions rather than agents; they do not do the actions the sentences describe. They are the kind of subject you want to recognize and, if possible, replace.

Guiding the Reader with Clear Pronoun Reference

Do not use a pronoun
instead of a noun
if there might be
doubt about its antecedent.
College Handbook of Composition

Once you use a specific noun subject, you may choose to replace it with a pronoun in succeeding sentences. In doing so, you would be following Jefferson's example in his substitution of *he* for King George III. Pronouns, by definition, are small words that writers use to replace an earlier word or idea. They came into the English language as a convenience to help writers and speakers avoid needless repetition of lengthy words. (In this last sentence, *They* is a pronoun replacing the word *pronouns.*) But the convenience of the pronoun can lead to vague prose if the pronoun's *antecedent* (the noun or idea that it replaces) is not clear. We refer to the relation between the pronoun and its antecedent as *pronoun reference.*

You should be particularly careful about how you use two types of pronouns: the personal pronouns (*he, she, they,* and *it*) and the demonstrative pronouns (*this, that, these,* and *those*). In the following examples, note that only when the personal pronoun clearly replaces a noun, and the demonstrative pronoun an idea, is it—the pronoun—correct.

> The University of Florida has over 31,000 students. It also has a lovely campus.

Here *it* properly replaces the noun *University of Florida,* repetition of which would be both cumbersome and unnecessary.

> The University of Florida pays its faculty less than many other major state universities. That is why they have formed a union.

Here the personal pronoun *they* replaces the noun *faculty,* and the demonstrative pronoun *that,* rather than replacing a single noun, replaces the idea of low pay for faculty at the University of Florida. The demonstrative pronoun allows the second sentence to be shorter and more direct than it otherwise would be, but the pronoun reference is proper only because the idea of low pay is clear.

> Florida has superb athletic facilities, a fine faculty, and a beautiful campus. This is why the Gator teams are always among the nation's best.

Here the demonstrative pronoun *this* creates confusion because we cannot be sure what it replaces. Does it replace the idea that Florida has superb athletic facilities, or the idea that Florida has a fine faculty, or the idea that Florida has a beautiful campus; or does it somehow replace and combine all three of these ideas? To avoid imprecise pronoun reference of this sort, you must be alert for multiple antecedents; you must recognize when a sentence includes more than one noun or more than one idea that a pronoun might replace.

To determine if a pronoun is correct, locate its antecedent. If you cannot find an antecedent, the pronoun may lead to agentless prose. Writers who fail to specify antecedents give the impression that *it, this,* and *that,* in some mysterious way, work apart from human control.

EXERCISE 5

In the following paragraph, revise the sentences with weak pronoun reference. Replace with the appropriate pronoun those words or ideas that are repeated needlessly.

> Large lecture classes are one of the great enemies of education. Large lecture classes place very special and difficult demands on both teachers and students, and they sometimes overwhelm them. Large lecture classes crowd in five hundred students and they have to fight for a seat. Professors in large lecture classes cannot get to know their students personally, so they suffer from lack of attention. Students who need special help cannot get special help from their professors, so they really do not do their job. All in all, large lecture classes are a disaster for both teachers and students; they should be abolished.

Most of us have wide experience using vague pronouns. Because they can camouflage agents so well, vague pronouns are attractive (if you are trying to avoid responsibility) and frustrating (if you are trying to place it). As a child, after you broke your first window, and your parents responded to your claim "The window has been broken" with the obvious question "By whom?" you perhaps said, "They did it." In your childish wisdom, you, of course, were trying to avoid direct responsibility for your action—trying to claim that *they* should be blamed. Your parents' next question, of course, was "Who is *they?*" Your parents wanted to know the antecedent for your pronoun, the agent for the action. At this point in the conversation, you either had to lie (blame your friends or some mysterious strangers) or else you had to admit that the antecedent for *they* really was *I.* Most children favor the "mysterious strangers" antecedent.

Still, children only anticipate the more sophisticated use of vague pronouns that adults practice. Adults misuse both personal and demonstrative pronouns, but since the abuse of personal pronouns is more obvious, we will look first at the "truant they"—the *they* you perhaps turned to as a child. Particularly popular among bureaucrats, *they* is a great hider of agents and of truth. Thus when you finally reach the end of a long registration line only to discover that you are lacking one key signature and need to go through the entire process once again, the registration officials will treat you with great sympathy. The individual who tells you the bad news certainly bears you no ill will. He or she gladly would help you were it not for rules that *they* have made. People who do not question this *they,* who do not find out who is responsible for the rules, could spend their lives as victims. People who say, "Who is *they?* I want to talk to him or her" and do not budge until they receive satisfaction often spare themselves additional trips through lines. Actually, many of the recently popular and highly praised assertiveness training techniques are no more than lessons in pronoun reference. (Always get the name of the person to whom you are talking. Never be content to talk with a subordinate of the person who actually makes policies and decisions.) These techniques are successful because they teach one basic truth: Give a bureaucrat a *they* and he or she will beat you into submission with it.

In addition to the "truant they," the other personal pronoun that suffers great abuse is what Robert Claiborne calls the "evasive we." Speakers often use *we* to hide the personal motive behind their views or to obscure the agent for an action. Thus as a child, when you wished to do something which you knew your parents would not allow, you would claim expansively, "We all are going." Or, if you wanted to spread the blame for that broken window, you might claim, "We did it." Officials who want to give force to their personal views or who want to avoid direct personal responsibility can use the "evasive we" in infinite ways.

> We have decided to reject your application.
>
> We feel that your work has not been up to our standards.

> We all can agree that this nuclear testing is in the best interests of our nation.

Of course, all these "we's" could have very specific antecedents. To protect yourself, however, you will want to know whom *we* replaces. In your writing you should take the words *we* and *they* as signals to look back and make sure that you have provided an antecedent, an agent.

Even more susceptible to misuse than the personal pronouns are the demonstratives. This is so because (as in this sentence) the demonstrative pronouns do not have to replace specific nouns but instead replace ideas. While you can easily test a personal pronoun—locate the antecedent and make sure no other potential antecedents intrude—judgments of demonstrative pronouns inevitably involve more subjective considerations: Is the idea clear? Can a pronoun summarize it? Demonstratives, then, can lead to agentless prose, and you must use them with care.

Empty Subjects: Expletives

Expletives are words that function like pronouns but have no reference; lacking reference, they add needless words to sentences and destroy clarity. The two basic expletive expressions are *there is* and *it is.* In conversation you often use different varieties of these expressions—"there might have been," "it would be," "there will be," "it could have been"—to mark time, to give yourself an opportunity to think what you will say next. You thus signal to your listener that you are pausing and that something important will follow. Great writers have used expletives, particularly expletives repeated in a parallel series, to achieve both balance and power. Charles Dickens has Sydney Carton, who gives his life for another, utter the famous final words: "It is a far, far better thing that I do, than I have ever done; it is a far, far better rest that I go to, than I have ever known." By repeating the expletive *it is,* Dickens gives dignity and emphasis to Carton's statement.

Expletives are useful in long parallel sentences and are perfectly fine in conversation; try talking without using them and you soon will learn how much we rely on them. In your writing, however, expletives may indicate that you have not thought out your topic clearly; as in conversation, you are inventing as you go along rather than following a plan. Expletives not only add meaningless words to sentences, they can also hide the agent. By standing in the place of a sentence subject, they delay the reader's encounter with the true subject. In some cases, when they are the sentence's only subject, they contribute to prose that is completely agentless. A sentence like "It is obvious that she will have to be committed" gives no information about who is making the decision.

Exercise 6

In the following sentences, underline the expletives. Notice that you need merely delete them and their complement *that* to shorten the sentence by at least three words without changing its meaning.

1. There are many other well-accepted festivities in our state that have much worse side effects than the bluegrass music festival.
2. The National Football League's records show that there is an average of twenty-seven arrests per game because of unruly conduct.
3. There seems to be a strange disease that affects young men when the time comes to pick a college.
4. It is true that the dorms are in poor condition at the University of Georgia.
5. It seems pretty clear in my view that the Tarheels need to pass more on the first down.

Exercise 7

Expletives are bad not only because they add words but also because, in many cases, they hide or replace agents. In the following examples, try to find the agent the expletive hides, and then rewrite the sentence.

1. In their view there are several reasons for the problem.
2. There must be no lowering of standards, no acceptance of mediocrity, in any aspect of our private or public lives.
3. It was true the evidence seemed to be against them.
4. It is my hope that someday the university will win a nationwide reputation for academic excellence.
5. There may have been twenty reasons for such strange behavior.

As a rule of thumb, unless you, like Dickens, are trying to highlight repetition within a sentence, you should use *it* only as a pronoun, not as an expletive. You want to make sure the word *it* always has an antecedent. Similarly, you should omit meaningless variations of *there is*. Of course, many fine writers have used expletives for purposes of balance and emphasis, and you may want to do the same. But you should do so with a full awareness that expletives, except in idiomatic expressions like "It is raining" or

---

EXERCISE 8

Identify the personal and demonstrative pronouns and the expletives in the following sentences. Rewrite the sentences to improve their pronoun reference, and replace all expletives with agents.

1. It is too bad that students feel so many pressures that they cheat on exams.
2. In a large lecture class, it is rare to establish a close student-teacher relationship.
3. The student could feel that since he has sixteen weeks for one class it would be all right to skip a few classes.
4. In addition, it is very important to find a thesis that you can believe in; for if you cannot convince yourself, it is improbable that you could persuade someone else.
5. It was through these methods that Professor Twitchell taught us to construct sound sentences.
6. Fortunately, because they were only living together and they had no children, it was easier for John and Rita to call the whole thing off without all the pain and ugliness of a divorce.
7. I left the food for the dog on the table. Please break it into bits.
8. Deregulation means higher prices for the consumer and more exploration; this should be considered an advantage.
9. The truth is that, despite all of President Carter's warnings, almost all Americans still dream of big, speedy cars. That is why they have not succeeded.
10. What is the better academic calendar? The semester system or quarter system? Students, teachers, and administrators all have different opinions, and this is my topic.

"It is five o'clock," essentially are meaningless pronouns that can lead you to write agentless prose. In general use the word *it* to refer to a thing, the word *there* to refer to a place.

Agentless Subjects: Participles, Gerunds, and Gerund Phrases

Avoid dangling modifiers.
Harbrace College Handbook

Participles are another threat to subject specificity; they are words that refer to an action, have some characteristics of verbs (for example, they can be in present or past tense), but function as adjectives in the sentence. The present participle ends in *-ing,* and the past participle, if it is regular, ends in *-ed.* If you say, "I was running," the word *running* is part of the verb. But if you say, "Running up the hill, I saw a bird," *running* is a verb form used as an adjective—a participle. When the subject of the main clause to which the participle is attached is not the agent of the action the participle describes, composition teachers say the participle dangles. Look at this sentence:

> After considering the appearance, location, size, and facilities of the rooms, Dickenson Hall is not the most desirable place to live.

Dickenson Hall is the fairly specific subject of the sentence (the writer has seen it, although he probably has not seen it walking down the street), but it is not the agent of *considering*. The participle dangles. The sentence "Running up the hill, I saw a bird" is correct, because its subject *I* is doing the running. To avoid misuse of participles, you must be clear about the agent of your sentence. Writers dangle participles because writers do not define the agent and have nothing to which they can attach the participle.

A *gerund* is a verb form that, through custom and usage, has come to function as a noun—a word like *hunting, fishing,* and *swimming* that can serve as a subject or an object. Many gerunds are acceptable in both written and spoken discourse, but if you refer to our subject specificity scale (p. 4), you will see that gerunds are "off the chart." By making what is essentially a verb a sentence subject, writers who use gerunds remove agents from sentences. Particularly when joined with expletives, gerunds are a clear sign of agentless prose. Consider the seemingly innocent sentence "Bowling is fun." The gerund gives the statement incontestable and absolute authority. But suppose you hate bowling, suppose your associations with the sport are all negative: the smell of stale beer and old cigars, the sound of hundreds of crashing pins, the sight of people in various states of frustration. You do not think that "bowling is fun," and you immediately recognize that the sentence should be "I like to bowl." By specifying the agent in the sentence, you eliminate the overstatement and distortion the gerund creates.

Gerunds, like Latinate diction, weaken subject specificity. But, as dangerous as they are, one-word gerunds and abstractions are far better as sentence subjects than lengthy gerund and infinitive phrases. These phrases used as sentence subjects confuse the action and hide the agent. As much as possible, you should use nouns as the subjects of your sentences, for as long as your subject is a noun, it can at least potentially be specific. Gerund and infinitive phrases, however, cannot be specific because they do not define an agent. You may recall the example of the dangling participial phrase we used:

> After considering the appearance, location, size, and facilities of the rooms, Dickenson Hall is not the most desirable place to live.

The introductory participial phrase is incorrect because the writer never specifies any agent for *considering*. A mistake in slightly different form occurs if you make the phrase the sentence subject and create a gerund.

> Considering the appearance, location, size, and facilities of the rooms is important in judging a dormitory.

This sentence is grammatically correct; the phrase no longer dangles. But the sentence is vague and imprecise because it lacks a noun subject and an agent; the reader cannot tell who does either the "considering" or the "judging." *Infinitive phrases,* which use the infinitive of the verb (*to swim, to run, to bowl, to consider*) are subject to the same misuse.

> To consider the appearance, location, size, and facilities of the rooms is important in judging a dormitory.

This sentence, again, is grammatically correct but imprecise. By using the infinitive phrase as sentence subject, the writer eliminates the agent.

Gerunds, participles, and infinitives, of course, are basic parts of our language. You inevitably will use them a great deal. But to use them correctly, you must give them agents. Gerund and infinitive phrases should serve only in subordinate clauses, not as sentence subjects. You should turn to gerunds for sentence subjects only after you have tried alternatives and found no clearer expression.

EXERCISE 9

Identify the subjects of the following sentences. Then determine if the participial phrases dangle. Rewrite the sentences, and correct the dangling participles as well as the evasive gerunds.

1. Along with studying, these lounges provide students with a quiet place to go and relax.
2. Decriminalizing marijuana probably is the only answer to the smuggling problem.
3. When choosing a topic for an expository essay, he wanted me to pick a topic which showed that I cared about writing the paper.
4. After reading the book, she asked us to submit a paper to her with ten current topics on which to write our papers.
5. Looking at the American working class, another fault in the president's energy policy is perceived.
6. Being an accounting major, it helps to get a good job coming from a school with a good reputation.
7. At first I did not think too much of coming to this university since, being from Hawaii, it was quite a distance away.
8. Before graduating from high school, my mother and I took a week off from the daily routine to inspect many different colleges in the Southeast.
9. After looking at several out-of-state universities, the University of Connecticut was my final choice, because it would, in almost all respects, cost less.
10. Knowing that she loved Denver and enjoyed her four years here played a major role in deciding on a college for myself.

Exercise 10

Participial phrases that use the past participle (the *-ed* ending) and infinitive phrases will also dangle if the writer is not certain of the agent. Isolate the infinitives and past participles in these sentences, and then correct those that dangle.

1. To reach my class by 8:00, the bus must be on time.
2. Thwarted in his life's dream, his father's consoling words meant nothing to him.
3. To properly prepare this dish, sauces must be combined before the actual basting.
4. Whether taken seriously or not, people can find relief or escape from their problems in comedy.
5. Properly equipped, the deer will not escape from the hunter.
6. To improve the quality of their ice cream, only natural flavors and natural sweeteners are used.
7. Aided by laws and experts in its efforts to insure public health and safety, epidemics of disease and natural disasters still threaten the United States.
8. To challenge the conclusion of the opposing team, the debate had to be focused on the source for their data.
9. Collected in animal shelters, the cost of maintaining strays is more than most cities can afford.
10. Battered and bruised, the arena resounded with the gallant fighter's name.

Subject specificity is the first requirement of agent prose. By finding specific subjects, you will automatically avoid a wide array of problems. Agreement errors, weak pronoun reference, dangling modifiers—all these mistakes are much less likely if you develop subject specificity and define an agent. Having defined an agent, you need not worry so much about handbook rules; failing to define an agent, you will continue to make errors, no matter how many rules you memorize. If in place of gerund phrases, infinitive phrases, and gerunds you use nouns as sentence subjects, and if those nouns are doers, you will have achieved subject specificity and taken the first, most important step toward writing agent prose.

Words That Describe Actions: the Predicate

Since in the most specific, most precise sentences a subject-agent performs an action, the way you describe the action is crucial. We call the words that describe actions *verbs;* the sentence part that contains the verb we call the *predicate.* The clearest predicates describe one action with one verb; thus one of your goals as a writer should be what we call *predicate condensation*—the reduction of long multiword predicates to one- or two-word verbs. Predicate condensation focuses the reader's attention on one action instead of dividing it among several. At first glance, the following sentence seems blameless.

> The consumer must choose from this array and make a decision on which brand to buy.

The first predicate, *must choose,* is fine—a two-word verb in the present tense. But the second predicate, *make a decision on,* needs to be condensed. The verb *make* actually hides the main action, which is *deciding.* The sentence actually should read:

> The consumer must choose from this array and decide which brand to buy.

At this point the good writer makes one more condensation. Since *to choose* and *to decide* are similar, to use both is redundant. The sentence can read:

> The consumer must choose from this array.

EXERCISE 11

In the following sentences, locate the predicates, and then indicate if they are condensed (C) or uncondensed (U). Try to rewrite those predicates that require condensation.

____ 1. An outstanding objection may be
____ that many people will argue
____ that the carillon bells are totally
____ unnecessary, especially since they
____ will cost the school a quarter of
____ a million dollars.
____ 2. The University of Kentucky has many
____ problems that should have required
____ immediate attention.

____ 3. All students in high school
____ have to make a decision about whether they
____ are going to get a job after graduation
____ or go to college.

____ 4. We, the counseling staff, hope this
____ letter will enable students to be able
____ to pick a college that will suit
____ their wants, needs, and capabilities.

____ 5. Those who are used to living in
____ a southern climate might have
____ difficulty in trying to cope
____ with the bitter and cold winters
____ of the north.

____ 6. By attending a school close to
____ home, there is more of a chance
____ that one will be able to return
____ home for frequent visits.

____ 7. If a student is interested in
____ forestry and resource conservation,
____ for example, then it might be
____ beneficial for him or her to research
____ schools which are famous in
____ that field.

____ 8. The Crown amplifier acquired its
____ high rating because of its
____ durability and sensitivity.

____ 9. I use my word processor more than any
____ other machine in my office; my word
____ processor allows me
____ to finish duties that I necessarily
____ have to attend to.

____ 10. Thus you actually could end up saving
____ about $1000 by breaking your nose.

You should note that predicate condensation often goes hand in hand with subject specificity. In sentence 1, you can substitute *people* for the abstracton *objection* and condense *may be* and *will argue.* The result is eight words shorter and immeasurably clearer.

> Many people may object that the carillon bells are totally unnecessary, especially since they will cost a quarter of a million dollars.

These sentences also illustrate some keys to recognizing uncondensed predicates. In general you have to condense a predicate when it includes an infinitive or a participle as well as a verb.

> might be beneficial for him to research
>
> will be able to return home
>
> could end up saving
>
> might have difficulty in trying to cope

Otherwise such predicates, since they refer to two or three actions, will inevitably confuse your readers. "What is the sentence about? What is its action?" they will ask. Is it about *having, trying,* or *coping;* is it about *ending* or *saving;* is it about *being able* or *returning;* is it about *benefiting* or *researching?* Such uncondensed predicates fragment the action; the great virtue of the condensed, one-verb predicate is that it directs the attention of your readers to one action instead of dividing it among several.

You should realize, however, that one-verb predicates are not necessarily one-word predicates. Several verb tenses add auxiliary verbs to the main verb and thus use more than one word. In the future tense, the auxiliary is *will* or *shall.*

> I shall fly to Montana.
>
> They will vote on the bill next month.
>
> Our new baby will arrive in July.

In the present and past perfect tenses, the auxiliary is *have, has,* or *had.*

> I have run every night for the past three weeks.
>
> He has been home for a month.
>
> I had run every night for three weeks.
>
> He had been home for a month.

Past, present, and future progressive tenses combine some form of the verb *to be* with the present participle.

> He was working harder than ever.
>
> They are reinvesting all their capital.
>
> The contestants will be arriving soon.

Verbs in the conditional use *would, could,* or *should.*

> If he could, he would swim the channel.
>
> Should you run into any problems, please notify me at once.
>
> The president would lower the prime rate, if it were in his power.

The number of words in a predicate, then, is not always a clear sign that it needs condensation. But four- or five-word predicates are usually a sign that you should rewrite, particularly if they include participles or infinitives.

EXERCISE 12

In the following sentences, locate the predicates, then rewrite those that need condensation. Be on the lookout for auxiliaries.

1. Students will find it difficult to achieve high grades in a subject they find boring.
2. Early in their lives, people must make a choice about their professions.
3. George Perles should be able to accomplish a winning season for the Spartans.
4. By Friday we should have been able to collect enough cans to take to the recycling center.
5. She looked in the paper every day to try to find a used car.
6. He was spending all his time working hard to prepare the meals.
7. They may be able to fix the boat in three hours.
8. The university has a basic duty to perform of educating all qualified citizens.
9. The government makes a financial judgment to determine who is eligible for food stamps.
10. In baseball the pitcher has the responsibility of covering first base on balls hit to the right side of the infield.

You can combine progressive and perfect tenses, but in many instances a long multiword predicate results—a predicate that you can condense. Consider the following sentences:

He has been struggling with the problem for months. (present perfect progressive)

She had been learning Spanish ever since she visited Puerto Rico. (past perfect progressive)

They will have been working for seven hours. (future perfect progressive)

You can greatly improve these sentences by putting the verbs in simpler tenses that condense the predicate. In the first sentence, you can substitute the present perfect tense for the present perfect progressive.

He has struggled with the problem for months.

In the second, you can use the simple past tense.

She learned Spanish after she visited Puerto Rico.

And in the third, you can substitute the simple future tense for the future perfect progressive.

They will work for seven hours.

In some rare cases, you may have to combine the perfect and progressive tenses to emphasize that an action is continuing in time. If the idea of continuity is basic to the sentence, simplification of the verb tense may be inappropriate. Consider the sentence "He has been meditating for over three days." You could change it to "He has meditated for over three days," but if you wish to emphasize that his meditation is continuing right up to the present moment, you should keep the present perfect progressive tense. However, situations that call for a perfect progressive tense are rare; usually the perfect or progressive tense alone will do.

EXERCISE 13

In the following sentences, simplify the verb tenses and condense the predicates. Note any sentences that you feel are changed in meaning by the substitution.

1. At this point in the program, Casals had been playing for three hours.
2. We have been looking for a house for six months but still have not found one.
3. Palmer's arm was tired because he had been pitching for nine innings.
4. At this stage in their trip, they will have been traveling for over three months.
5. Muhammad Ali has been fighting for over twenty years, but his face is still unmarked.

Eliminating the Agent: the Passive Voice

Use the active voice.
William Strunk, Jr.

Never use the passive voice where you can use the active.
George Orwell

Passive verbs are also compound verbs. They combine some tense of the verb *to be* with a past participle. Passive verbs *may* look like verbs in the present or progressive tense, but the distinction between passive and active verbs is totally separate from the question of verb tense.

> He *was captured* by three courageous citizens. (passive verb, past tense)
>
> Three courageous citizens *had captured* him. (active verb, past perfect tense)
>
> Three courageous citizens *were capturing* him when the police arrived. (active verb, past progressive tense)

When we refer to a verb as passive, we refer to its *voice* rather than its tense. Voice is crucial because it indicates whether the subject *performs* or *receives* the action the verb describes. A transitive verb—a verb that takes a direct object—will be either active or passive. When the subject of the verb is the agent for the action the verb describes, the verb is active. When the subject of the verb is not an agent, but rather is acted upon, the verb is passive.

In the best of all possible worlds, differences between sentences written in the active and passive voice would be merely matters of emphasis; for example, the passive sentence "I was cheated by him" and the active sentence "He cheated me" have the same meaning. However, the passive sentence uses two additional words and is therefore less direct. Also the passive voice easily leads to obscurity and vagueness if writers and speakers fail to provide an agent for the verb. To use our simple example once more, to say, "I was cheated," is not to say, "He cheated me." Without the agent, *by him,* the passive voice merely expresses a feeling of ill-use without helping us understand how or why the ill-use came about. Along with Latinate diction, the passive voice stands as the greatest threat to agent prose. It allows writers to create sentences that are grammatically correct but that hide agents. The passive voice is very popular with students who do not understand a topic on which they must write, and who want to fill paper without saying anything, because it avoids the tough questions of responsibility and cause.

The agentless passive voice sabotages straight talk and clear thinking. It produces sentences in which the responsibility for decisions and actions vanishes with the agent. The reader who can identify a writer with a high quotient of passive verbs may be dealing with a person who waxes eloquent about problems but is unwilling to talk about who created them. When you find numerous passives in your work, you should take them as a sign that you need to rethink your topic (define an agent) and then revise your sentences.

In its basic form, the passive voice is easy to recognize. It combines some tense of the verb *to be* with a past participle. Most past participles end in *-ed,* although as the following list indicates, exceptions to this rule abound.

IRREGULAR PAST PARTICIPLES

Infinitive	**Past Participle**
to become	become
to begin	begun
to bite	bitten
to blow	blown
to break	broken
to bring	brought
to catch	caught
to choose	chosen
to do	done
to draw	drawn
to drink	drunk
to drive	driven
to eat	eaten
to fight	fought
to fly	flown
to forgive	forgiven
to freeze	frozen
to give	given
to grow	grown
to know	known
to make	made
to ride	ridden
to ring	rung

Infinitive	Past Participle
to shake	shaken
to sing	sung
to sink	sunk
to speak	spoken
to spin	spun
to steal	stolen
to swear	sworn
to swing	swung
to take	taken
to tear	torn
to wear	worn
to write	written

Exercise 14

In the following sentences, locate each predicate, define its tense, and decide if it is passive.

1. He had helped their volleyball team win the league championship.
2. They were saved by the courage and intelligence of one woman.
3. Political candidates have promised everything and delivered nothing.
4. He was speaking eloquently when the fire alarm rang.
5. The grass had been cut the day before, but he was going to cut it again.
6. He would have helped us, but his schedule was already set, and he was going out of town.
7. The college has negotiated a new salary schedule, but it is not guaranteeing that it will be implemented.
8. Her batting slump has depressed her, and she is taking extra batting practice.
9. The students are angered by their inability to graduate.
10. Since the strike has dragged on, many workers are applying for food stamps.

When you use a passive verb, a preposition, frequently *by* or *in,* will follow the past participle and introduce an agent.

subject	**verb**		**preposition**	**agent**
I	was	bitten	by	the dog.
	↓	↓		
	past tense of *to be*	**past participle**		

The following examples show the passive voice in a variety of tenses and show how it often obscures the truth.

> The garage must be cleaned. (present tense)

The obvious unanswered question is who is going to do the dirty work, or even more problematic, who *should* do the dirty work.

> Walt Garrison was tackled. (past tense)

The truth that goes unspoken here is that Ken Houston made a game-saving tackle.

> The Watergate had been broken into. (past perfect tense)

Yes, but who did the breaking in, and who paid the (in this sentence anyway) nonexistent criminals?

We chose the last example by design. To understand how passive verbs lead to bad (agentless) prose, you could look at Richard Nixon's various Watergate justifications. In general these speeches are so full of passive constructions that you might begin to wonder if a real agent for the crime ever lived. Besides noting how many passive verbs Mr. Nixon used, you can also see that he (or his speech writer) has an undeniable genius for using them to smooth over potential rough spots. Thus in the fifteenth paragraph of his 29 April 1974 Address to the Nation, the speech in which he announced the release of transcripts of his taped conversations, Mr. Nixon used the agentless passive voice to avoid the crucial issue of who was responsible for selecting and editing the tapes that the transcripts included:

> In these transcripts, portions not relevant to my knowledge or actions with regard to Watergate are not included, but everything that is relevant is included.

The passive verbs *are included* and *is included* neatly hide the fact that Mr. Nixon was attempting to establish standards of admissibility for his own trial. Even at that moment, he was not including the transcript of the tape that later would drive him from office.

Mr. Nixon's speeches, however, were not a new or great breakthrough in vague, agentless prose. They rather perfected uses of the passive voice that have long been popular with students and bureaucrats who want to avoid responsibility for questionable actions or unfortunate events. Consider again your response when you broke your first window. Even before you tried to hide the agent with vague pronoun reference (''They broke it''), you probably turned to the passive voice. You did not say to your mother and father, "I broke the window," but rather announced

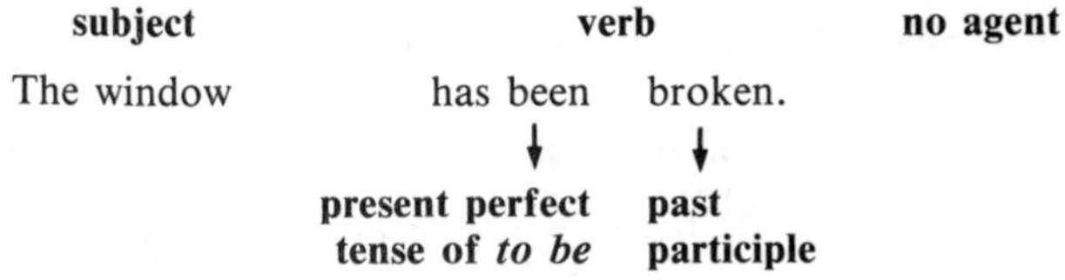

While it may have delayed a spanking, the last sentence is not as clear as the first; it obscures the question of responsibility and hides important information.

As you grew older, your use of passive verbs probably became more sophisticated. During adolescence, as you attempted to avoid unpleasant chores, you perhaps created sentences like these:

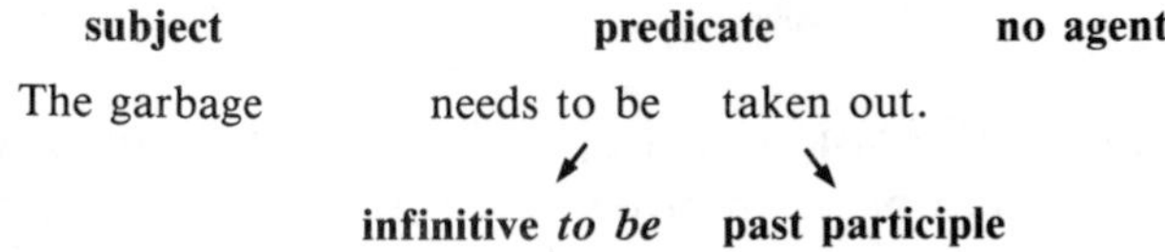

The example leads to the question "Who will do the taking?"

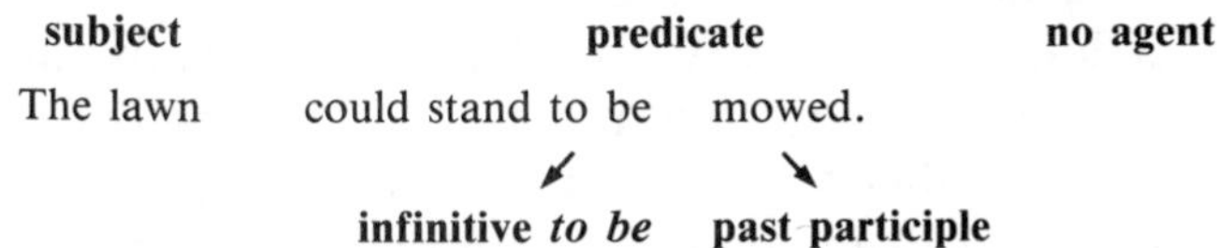

Yes, but who will do the mowing?

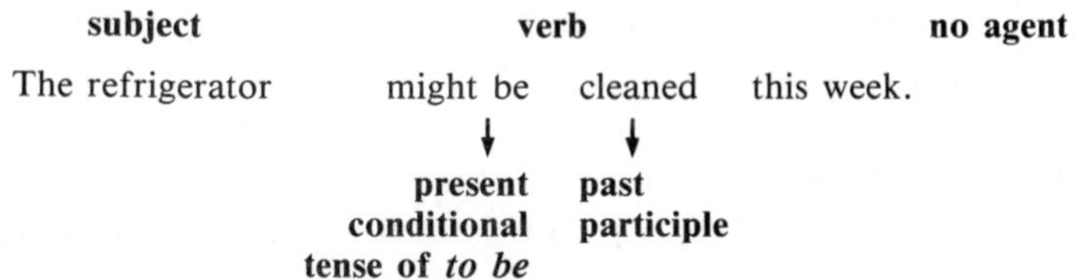

Yes, but who will do the cleaning?

Even if you have started a family of your own, you still have many opportunities to use passive verbs. Only the most dedicated of parents, upon noticing a powerful and distressing odor coming from their child, will use the active voice.

subject-agent	**verb**	**object**
I	will change	Sam's diapers.

Rather, the temptation always is to turn to the passive voice.

subject	**predicate**		**no agent**
Sam's diapers	need to be	changed.	
	↙	↘	
	infinitive *to be*	**past participle**	

Translation to spouse: Why don't you change Sam's diapers?

This basic shift away from clear personal responsibility, away from an agent, can occur in a multitude of forms.

Sam should be dressed.
bathed
fed
burped
comforted
rocked

Of course, the small evasions of responsibility that the passive voice allows people may not be ruinous in the home (although passive verbs probably have been the source of more than one domestic fight). But outside the home, in the office or in the political arena, passive verbs are dangerous. Consider then-candidate Jimmy Carter's claim: "Unnecessary pork-barrel projects by the Army Corps of Engineers must be terminated." This sentence sounds good but says nothing. Candidates who make such promises will have a hard time delivering on them, for the promise never defines an agent for change—never defines which members of Congress will have to give up their pet projects.

If passive verbs are a political menace, they are even more dangerous in the classroom, particularly when you are uncertain about what you want to say. Consider this example—the introductory paragraph of an essay about the Florida Board of Education's Functional Literacy Test for high school juniors. The passive verbs are underscored.

> Many recent high school graduates <u>were required</u> to take the Functional Literacy Test (FLT). The test <u>was designed</u> as a means of testing certain basic skills a student should have mastered by graduation. While most people will agree that some standards for graduation <u>should be established</u>, many people argue against the validity of the present test, claiming it is unfair because of ethnic discrimination, education opportunities, and ambiguous questioning.

This paragraph begins a typical *D* paper, and you should understand what is wrong with it. Its main problem is vagueness—a failure to define with any specificity either the agent responsible for the test, or the reason for the test. Rather than think about these problems, the author turned to a series of passive verbs. She filled her page with words, yet said nothing. The passive verbs made the paper easy for her to write, but they also made her work worthless. She says nothing of importance about recent attempts to test the basic skills of high school students because she says nothing about the reasons for those attempts. Her passive verbs both illustrate and promote her lack of ideas. You should recognize that when agentless passive verbs dominate your writing you face an analogous situation. You should either rethink your topic and rewrite your paper or prepare yourself for the inevitable "*D*—vague, lacks specifics."

In the active voice, and with specific subjects, the paragraph might look something like this:

> The Florida Board of Education has recently required graduating high school seniors to take a Functional Literacy Test (FLT). The board's goal is to insure that all high school students have mastered certain basic skills by the time they graduate. While many agree that the board should maintain standards for graduation, some argue that the present test is invalid, claiming, most particularly, that it discriminates against blacks. The board's chairman, Ralph Turlington, denies that the FLT is discriminatory in either its intent or effect. But does statistical evidence support his claims?

If the passive voice contributes so greatly to obscurity, why then is it a part of our language? Do situations exist in which it is appropriate, even necessary? Obviously, when you cannot locate an agent for the action you are describing, the passive voice is appropriate. The sentence "I was cheated" is fine, as long as you have no idea who cheated you. But you must bear in mind that few of us will submit to being cheated anonymously. Most of us will investigate our loss and try to find out who has victimized us. Similarly, you must view your passive constructions with great suspicion. You must take them as a signal to ask if you are failing to be specific, failing to identify an agent, and failing ultimately to define your topic.

Passive verbs may also be appropriate if you want to protect yourself from an angry response. Medical school deans who find themselves in the position of rejecting thousands of applicants may blanch at the thought of telling them:

subject-agent	**verb**	**object**
I	am rejecting **present progressive**	your application.

Instead they will write:

subject	**verb**	**no agent**
Your application	has been rejected. **present perfect tense** **passive voice**	

Only the angriest employers will write:

subject-agent	**verb**	**object**
I	am firing **present progressive**	you.

Instead they will write:

subject	**verb**		**object**
A decision	has been made	to terminate	your employment.
	present perfect **passive voice**	**infinitive**	

Although we can recognize and tolerate the small evasions of unpleasantness that the passive voice permits, we must not forget that this evasion is really a type of dishonesty—the dishonesty we can see so clearly in Richard Nixon's manipulation of passive verbs.

Passive verbs are also appropriate if you believe that human behavior is the result of neuroses or the product of an environment over which the individual can exert little control. Then you quite properly can describe people as always acted upon, never active. In this context agent prose, the kind of prose we would have you write, becomes irrelevant, but so too do the notions of human freedom and dignity.

The choice between the active and the passive voice is not merely a technical matter; it is fraught with all manner of metaphysical considerations. The traditional notion that good prose is clear, direct, and active may ultimately be of little value to you if our age grows ever more deterministic. If personal responsibility continues to erode, however, this discussion will still stand you in good stead. To make your writing conform to the new dehumanized metaphysics, you need only reverse all that we have said about defining an agent: avoid subject specificity; turn to

Exercise 15

Identify the passive verbs in the following sentences, then make the sentences active. In the sentences that are agentless, try to invent an appropriate agent. Note the instances in which passive sentences use expletives and fail to have either subject specificity or predicate condensation.

1. I was pleased by the wide variety of courses offered in many different fields.
2. If these people have their way, we may all be doomed.
3. The cigarette tax will be increased to discourage use.
4. New energy measures should be enacted now to assure the nation of not having another winter without sufficient heating oil supplies.
5. Computerization means greater standardization in the workplace, but this should be considered an advantage.
6. It is generally accepted that a good writing course should improve the organization, sentence structure, and grammar of the student's writing.
7. This is done by taking a stand, and then bringing it under inspection.
8. Halfway through the semester, she canceled classes and told us to see her if help was needed.
9. When he graded papers, they usually were not returned until the next paper was due.
10. In other classes, in which students memorize textbooks and reproduce them on exams, the material is easily forgotten after the class ends.
11. This fact, of cohabitation being nowhere closer to being married than going steady, has been established.
12. In America the topic of euthanasia is traditionally avoided in public discussions because death is such a taboo subject in the country.
13. When the rare opportunity to shoot one is presented, the hunter must be properly equipped.
14. If contestants are judged by the celebrities to have any talent at all, they are awarded points from one to ten (ten being the perfect score).
15. It is now clearly established that a woman who wants to give her child every opportunity to develop properly should abstain from smoking during pregnancy.

expletives, gerunds, and infinitives for sentence subjects; use long Latinate words; be sure to write in the passive voice. Or, if you wish to retain your independence, your individuality, your dignity, you may choose to stay in the active voice. In either case you should grasp the connection between agentless passive verbs, agentless prose, and an agentless life. You should be able to distinguish between passive and active verbs and understand why the former are so totally alien to agent prose.

Exercise 16

Read the following editorial with care. Locate the passive verbs, and then decide which ones you would change and which ones you would keep for emphasis.

TAXING TRAUMA
Sun Editorials

Rooted in Shakespeare is the folk wisdom about acting in haste and repenting at leisure.

No better example is found than the nuclear accident at Three Mile Island in Pennsylvania. And, in a fashion, it can be blamed on federal tax policy which fired up the nuke's management, Metropolitan Edison Co.

The troublesome nuclear reactor is called Unit 2. It was fired up for testing on March 28, 1978. But a few weeks later, on April 23, it was shut down for 20 weeks so the main steam relief valves could be replaced. On November 3, a worker erroneously closed valves and the reactor shut down. On November 7, malfunctioning pumps forced another shutdown. On December 16, Unit 2 closed down for five days for replacement of a major pump.

In mid-December, the Nuclear Regulatory Commission gave the all-clear for Unit 2 to start the commercial production of power. In doing so it ignored one of its inspector's complaints about the lack of test data. One item on his list was a major valve which later contributed to the crisis at Unit 2. It didn't close when it was supposed to.

So Unit 2 went on the line at 11 P.M. last December 30, virtually on the eve of the new year 1979. The timing was not accidental.

By cranking up in the waning hours of 1978, Metropolitan Edison was seizing a whole year's benefit from U.S. tax law. The company was able to claim a $12 million investment tax credit and a $20 million depreciation allowance.

Unit 2 continued to have troubles. For two weeks in February, it operated at reduced power while a pump and valve were repaired. On March 6, the turbines kicked out and the reactor shut down, but the company hastened to get Unit 2 operating again the next day.

Then on March 28, a year to the day that it was first fired up, Unit 2 popped its lid—releasing radiation over the countryside. The fault seems to have been human error in which valves were closed for days when they should have been open, a valve which did not close automatically when it should have, and malfunctioning gauges. This was enough to make a mess of things when the other machinery functioned normally.

The whole thing has been shrugged off as a close call, with the radiation exposure compared to dental X-rays. Nuclear critics say this is a vile comparison.

A lot depends on what type of radioactive chemicals were released in the gases, and the on-site instruments were not sophisticated enough to tell. Some may decay into deadly elements, like strontium 90.

Anyway, the dental X-ray analogy is a weak one because an X-ray exposes a couple of inches of a hardy part of the body for a fraction of a second. The Three Mile Island exposure was over the whole body for a longer length of time. But the most deadly factor is inhalation, which increased the dosage by 130 times. Those points, which seem rather salient, are developed by radiological physics professor Ernest Sternglass of the University of Pittsburgh School of Medicine.

Metropolitan Edison, of course, is saying it will go bankrupt if the cleanup cost of Unit 2 is not passed on to its customers. No doubt it would, and no doubt the customers will pay.

There must be a better way for utilities to skip out on federal taxes. (Adapted from *The Gainesville Sun*)

Weak Predicates: the Imprecise *to Be* and *to Do*

If you look back at Exercises 1–4, you can observe an interesting and important fact. Unspecific subjects, particularly subjects that use participial or infinitive phrases, tend to take some form of *to be* or *to do* for their predicates.

> Being aware of the problem is important.
>
> Another example of this procedure is the rapid advance of technology.
>
> Improvement in individual cases does nothing for the original problem.
>
> Expanding the students' vocabularies does wonders for their writing.

Of course such subjects can (and sometimes do) take almost any verb as a predicate. But time and again, *is, was, will be, does, did,* or *will do* accompany them. The reason for this is not hard to find. The unspecific subject is not an agent; it usually cannot do anything. Thus the unspecific subject will sound ludicrous with a verb that describes a specific activity. Consider this somewhat extreme case:

> Technology swims along, hitting people where it hurts, throwing them out of work.

The verbs and participles here—*swimming, hitting, throwing*—are jarring because they call attention to the abstractness of *technology.* But if some form of *to be* or *to do* accompanies *technology,* the abstractness is less apparent, less obvious. This is because *to be* and *to do,* although verbs, are such general, multipurpose, and common words that they do not denote any clear, precise action. Authors who want to avoid subject specificity or are simply careless will use *to be* and *to do* very frequently.

> Technology is the great enemy of the poor, causing unemployment and social dislocation.
>
> Plagiarizing in the classroom does have serious consequences.

This usage sounds fine, but the smooth sound hides a lack of substance. How can technology, an abstraction, be anyone's enemy? People and corporations (agents) who apply and profit from developments in engineering and science may be the enemies of the poor, but technology is an abstraction, an idea lacking physical substance. Similarly, while people may plagiarize, *plagiarizing* itself cannot perform an action.

Questions about technology and plagiarism aside, a prevalence of *to be* and *to do* verb forms in your writing is one sign that you have not defined an agent. You are probably using *is, was, does,* or *did* to hide unspecific subjects. Consider this principle a corollary, then, to subject specificity: use verbs that are not only in the active voice but also are active—that is, describe a specific event. If possible, you want to use verbs like *to run, to fight, to die* rather than the catch-all verbs *to be* and *to do.*

EXERCISE 17

In the following sentences, find the subject and the predicate. Try to eliminate all *to be* and *to do* verb forms by developing subject specificity. Note that several other common verbs—particularly *to make* and *to help*—also accompany vague subjects.

1. To follow up on the original visit is crucial.
2. Working on the quarter system does both professors and students a great disservice.
3. To work long hours at a regular job is difficult for students.
4. The rapid pace of technology helps create alienation.
5. Hitting the opposing player solidly with both arms around him makes for good tackling.
6. Still another example of this lowering of academic standards is grade inflation.
7. Complicating the whole issue is the question of the Palestinians.
8. This unfortunate incident at the fraternity houses does the university's reputation little good.
9. To study all night and still fail the test is discouraging.
10. The growth of fast-food franchises is one of the most noticeable events of the 60s and 70s.

Describing the Agent and the Action: the Complement

Keep related words together.
William Strunk, Jr.

Few sentences have only a subject and a predicate, and these are usually found only in first-grade readers.

Alice plays.

Jerry reads.

Spot chews.

The most basic addition to this simple sentence is an *object*—a person or thing who receives the action of the sentence.

Alice plays ball.

Jerry reads the book.

Spot chews the bone.

As much as possible, you want objects to be specific—to conform to the same standards you set for your subjects.

Objects can be *direct* or *indirect,* depending on their relation to the predicate. In the sentence "Alice threw the ball to Jerry" Jerry receives the action, but not as directly as the ball does. Thus *ball* is the direct object; *Jerry* is the indirect object.

Sentences begin to get complicated when writers complement (or modify) subjects, predicates, and objects—that is, give additional information about them. The point of William Strunk's rule is simple: you should place the complement (or modifier) as close as possible to the word it modifies. You will spare your reader the trouble and confusion of trying to figure out where the complement belongs. Adjectives and adverbs are the two most basic complements, and if you use them properly, you can hope to use their counterparts properly: adjective and adverb phrases and clauses.

Adjectives

Adjectives complement nouns. They are words that tell us something about a person, place, or thing, rather than about an action. All colors are adjectives, as are all words that describe sizes, shapes, textures, smells, tastes, sounds, appearances, and judgments. Here are some typical uses of adjectives.

> Sara has a green shirt.
>
> Sara has a little cold.
>
> Sara has a square room.
>
> Sara's diaper has a foul odor.
>
> Sara has smooth skin.
>
> Sara is a happy baby.

In general the link between adjective and noun is so basic and strong that you will probably have little trouble keeping them together.

ADVERBS

Adverbs present more of a problem. Their principal role is to complement predicates, although they also can complement adjectives and other adverbs. When they complement a predicate, they tell us something about an action: how it took place, when it took place. Most adverbs end in the letters *-ly,* but several important ones—*now, then, afterwards, before, yesterday*—do not. Here are some typical uses of adverbs.

> Felipe ran quickly up the stairs.
>
> Andrea arrived yesterday.
>
> Horribly burned, her skin showed how long she had been in the sun. (Note that here the adverb *horribly* modifies the adjective *burned.*)
>
> The army marched relentlessly.
>
> Now, the students yawned even more intensely.
>
> Remarkably quickly, the old man ran up the stairs. (Note that here the adverb *remarkably* modifies the adverb *quickly.*)

As a clear writer, you should place your adjectives close to the nouns they modify, your adverbs close to the verbs, adjectives, or adverbs they modify. In the case of adverbs, particularly when you use them to introduce a sentence, you may not choose to place them right next to the verb (see the sentence above about the old man), but you should make sure the adverb is closer to the verb it modifies than to any other verb. Its relation to that verb must be clear.

Exercise 18

In the following sentences, locate the adjectives and adverbs, and relocate any that are misplaced.

1. Green and quickly, she put on her shirt.
2. Tirelessly, he stopped only to eat after he walked all day long.
3. Unjust, unfair, cruel, the students should fight against this rule before time runs out, now.
4. The dog attacked the jogger as she ran by viciously.
5. The farmer talked about her goats and how they ran away humorously.
6. Big and red, the gardener bragged about his tomatoes.
7. Unbelievably, I saw her leap high into the air.

Nonspecific Adverbs

If you remember that adverbs should modify only verbs, adjectives, or other adverbs, you can avoid an error so popular in American speech that many today no longer criticize it—the misuse of the adverb *hopefully* and its counterparts *surely, clearly,* and *truly.* In conversation we typically use *hopefully* as a synonym for *I hope.*

> Hopefully, the rain will stop.
>
> Hopefully, the Packers will beat the Vikings this weekend.
>
> Hopefully, peace in the Mid-East is at hand.

By using *hopefully* in this way, we distort it, for *hopefully* is actually an adverb that means *with hope. Hopefully* should describe an agent who does something with hope and not serve as shorthand for *I hope.* When it replaces the agent, *hopefully* permits all sorts of dishonesty; it gives an impression of universal assent to views that may be contestable. A farmer, for example, may not share a tourist's hope that rain will stop; a Viking fan will not hope for a Packer win; a member of the PLO may not hope for peace as the Israelis define it. To use *hopefully* correctly, then, you must write agent prose; you must, as in the following sentence, include an agent that hopes: "Ten-point underdogs, the young Packer team entered the stadium hopefully."

The adverbs *surely, clearly,* and *truly* are misused in much the same way as *hopefully* is. They should mean *with sureness, with clarity, with truth.* Yet most Americans use them as vague catch phrases whose meaning is never clear.

> Surely, that is the correct answer. (But who is sure here?)
>
> Clearly, the problem is one that requires immediate attention. (But to whom is this clear?)
>
> The Patriots truly are a young and improving team. (But who has discovered this truth?)

All these sentences distort adverbs because they lack a true agent. Except for the third, they use unspecific, abstract noun subjects. The way to avoid this problem is to use adverbs like these to modify verbs (actions) that specific subjects (agents) perform. Note that in all the following sentences the adverbs are correct.

> He spoke clearly and confidently.
>
> She grasped the club surely, with all the skill of a veteran player.
>
> I truly felt that these were great writers.

Clauses and Phrases

Adjective and adverb clauses and phrases have the same functions as adjectives and adverbs but provide more information and require more words. They are also easier to misplace. Before you study these complements, you first must understand what we mean by the words *clause* and *phrase.* Both words refer to basic word groups from which we build sentences. The clause contains a noun and a verb; the phrase contains one or neither. Two types of clauses exist: independent and dependent. The *independent clause* contains both a subject and a verb and makes a complete statement; it could in fact be a sentence. The *dependent clause* contains both a subject and a verb, but also contains a subordinating conjunction or expression that prevents it from making a complete statement. Dependent clauses, the class that includes adjective and adverb clauses, must complement an independent clause—must tell us something about an agent or an action. Consider the following examples.

> The vampire sharpened his fangs (independent clause)
> in the evening (phrase)
> because he was attending a dinner party. (dependent clause)

You can see the independent clause names an action, *sharpened,* and indicates a doer or agent, *the vampire.* It makes a complete statement. The phrase gives additional information about when the action took place, but it must be attached to the independent clause; it cannot stand alone as a sentence. The same holds true for the dependent clause since it also lacks a complete thought, even though it has a subject (agent), *he,* and a verb (action), *was attending.* The word *because* makes this clause dependent; it cannot stand alone.

Adjective and *adverb clauses,* then, are groups of related words that contain both a subject and a predicate and modify, respectively, a noun and a verb. But like adverbs, adverb clauses and phrases can also modify adverbs or adjectives. *Adjective* and *adverb phrases* are groups of related words that do not contain both a subject and a predicate, but still complement, respectively, a noun and a verb. But how exactly can you identify adjective and adverb phrases and clauses? What signals tell you that you should place a group of words close to a noun or to a verb? William Strunk's rule is admirable, but how exactly do you put it into practice?

Adjective and Adverb Clauses

To identify adjective and adverb clauses, you must recognize the *subordinator*—the word (like *because* in our vampire example) that makes the clause dependent. A great help to you in this regard is the distinction between subordinators that introduce adjective clauses and subordinators that introduce adverb clauses. With a few exceptions, adjective clauses are introduced by *relative pronouns: that, what, which, who, whoever, whom, whomever, whose.* Adverb clauses, on the other hand, are introduced by *subordinating conjunctions,* or by *subordinating phrases,* which are expressions built around subordinating conjunctions. Subordinating conjunctions include words like *after, although, as, because, before, during, if, once, since, that, though, till, unless, until, when, whenever, where, wherever, while.* Subordinating phrases include *as if, as soon as, as though, even though, in order that, in that, no matter how, so that.* If you are writing agent prose, you should be sure relative pronouns modify the agent; you should be sure subordinating conjunctions and expressions modify the action.

Adjective and Adverb Phrases

You may have more difficulty distinguishing adjective and adverb phrases because the same words can introduce both. Both *prepositional* and *infinitive* phrases can serve as complements and both can complement subjects and predicates. We already have discussed infinitives—verbals like *to be, to do,* and *to see.* Prepositions are small words that precede and prepare us for a noun or a pronoun. Some of the most common prepositions are *across, after, as, at, because, of, before, behind, between, by, for, from, in, in front of, in regard to, like, near, on, over, through, to, together with, under, until, up, with.*

To appreciate problems you may face when you use prepositional and infinitive phrases as complements, consider the prepositional phrase *of many things.* In the sentence

> She spoke of many things,

of many things is an adverb phrase, telling us how she spoke. But in the sentence

> The appearance of many things can be deceiving,

of many things is an adjective phrase, complementing the noun *appearance.*

Infinitive phrases also can serve double duty. In the sentence "He went to night school to build for the future" the phrase introduced by the infinitive *to build* is adverbial; it tells us about the action "he" performed. But in the sentence

> A plan to build for the future is always important,

the same infinitive phrase is adjectival; it complements the noun *plan.* While you can easily recognize prepositional and infinitive phrases, you will determine whether they are adjective or adverb phrases only by analyzing their function. Do they complement the agent or the action? This must be the most important question.

EXERCISE 19

In the following sentences, underline the adjective and adverb phrases and clauses. Then indicate if the complements are placed correctly (C) or incorrectly (I).

____ 1. In 1974 we moved from North Dakota to California.
____ 2. Even though Ruth has the better statistics, Jackson is
____ more dynamic.
____ 3. Before she left, she looked at me with anger and disdain.
____ 4. The Century Tower has sat silently waiting for chimes to
____ ring out from its belfry since 1953.

____ 5. My brother has run a sub-four-minute mile who is a great
____ athlete.
____ 6. When the rain began to fall in the middle of the sixth
____ inning, the umbrella that they brought proved
____ indispensable.
____ 7. Although sororities may offer many advantages, the
____ student who chooses to join one
____ should do so with care.
____ 8. If the United States had continued its policy of
____ détente with Russia, we could have looked forward with
____ hope to an easing of world tension.
____ 9. Jazz excites young and old, rich and poor, black and
____ white with its improvisational techniques.
____ 10. When movies give us characters with ideals and emotions
____ rather than scenes of violence and debased sexuality, then
____ I will go to them once more.

Adjective phrases and clauses, like adjectives, can modify objects as well as subjects. In sentence 10, *with ideals and emotions* modifies the object *characters* and *of violence and debased sexuality* modifies the object *scenes.* Adverb phrases and clauses, like adverbs, can modify verbs in dependent as well as independent clauses. In sentence 6, the adverb phrase *in the middle of the sixth inning* modifies the verb *began to fall.*

If you grasp the basic principles of agent prose, you will deal with complements more effectively. You will understand that complements come in only two basic forms: those that tell you something about the agent and those that tell you something about the action the agent performs. If you keep your information about the agent close to the agent, if you keep your information about the action close to the action, then you will meet Strunk's standard.

EXERCISE 20

In the following paragraph, underline the complements. Then define their functions (are they adjectives or adverbs?), and decide if they are placed properly. Rewrite all incorrect sentences.

> After the first week of college, the average freshman, who may be homesick, confused, and overworked, usually feels very unhappy. With papers to write, with friends to make, with new situations to face, the tasks pile up, and the freshman is overburdened. One freshman at the University of Michigan has

a solution for this problem who has found it. Brilliant and original, the university could profit from this idea greatly. Hopefully, before they start classes, the proposal is for a week-long orientation program that would help students adjust to college life. They would be able to straighten out their rooms, make new friends, overcome their first bout with homesickness, and then start their schoolwork first. Throughout this week, students would meet their professors, but the meetings would not cause tension in a nonclassroom situation. Surely this plan is one that university administrators will consider seriously, for it could improve the freshman program at the university greatly.

Sentence Variety and Sentence Structure

No long complex sentence will hold up without parallel construction.
Sheridan Baker

In general you do not want all your sentences to be alike. A succession of simple sentences will bore your readers; a succession of compound or complex sentences may confuse or tire them. (If you need help with the terms *simple, compound,* and *complex,* refer to the appendix.) Your writing should offer your readers a variety of sentences.

As you develop sentence variety, you should remember, however, that the heart of the sentence is the independent clause and that complements must have a clear relation to the independent clause. If you open your sentence with the independent clause—a sentence structure we will call loose—then the main part of the sentence (your main idea) has come first. The reader's attention will wander if you pile up complements after this independent clause. The relation of the complements to the main part of the sentence will become increasingly tenuous. In this sentence, the main clause "I ate the pizza" is followed by several complements, each of which is introduced by an italicized word.

> I ate the pizza *which* my sister baked *after* I got home from work *where* I had a tough day.

Nothing is wrong with either the main clause or the complements taken by themselves. But the sentence structure is ludicrous. Usually you can add no more than two complements to an introductory independent clause. As you write, look for simple sentences that you have overextended and made loose. Shorten them, and start new sentences.

One way to increase the number of complements you can add to a sentence is to lead up to the main clause by placing it at the end of the sentence. This kind of simple or complex sentence is often called the *periodic sentence*. Periodic sentences are not a cure-all for confusing complements, but they do give you some flexibility.

> When I got home from work after a tough day in the store, I ate pizza that my sister baked.

Here the periodic sentence allows you to get most of your complements into the sentence without confusing the reader.

Should you want to begin with your main clause but still add multiple complements—that is, should you want to write a long loose sentence—you must, as Baker points out, use *parallel structure*. You must balance your phrases and clauses. To write a particularly long sentence you may need to combine periodic and parallel structure. Consider this famous example from Abraham Lincoln—one of our most eloquent presidents. We have underscored the independent clause on which Lincoln centered the sentence.

> With malice toward none; with charity for all; with firmness in the right as God gives us to see the right; let us strive on to finish the work we are in, to bind up the nation's wounds; to care for him who shall have borne the battle, and for his widow, and his orphan—to do all which may achieve and cherish a just, and a lasting peace, among ourselves, and with all nations.

Lincoln's long sentence is easy to follow and powerfully clear. This is because he balances prepositional phrases (*With malice, with charity, with firmness*) and infinitive phrases (*to finish, to bind up, to care for, to do*) and places one of the parallel structures before his independent clause, "let us strive on," and one after it. Parallel structure, which he develops by carefully balancing phrases, allows Lincoln to add seven complements to this independent clause. Consider how the sentence would have suffered if Lincoln had started with the main clause.

> Let us strive on to finish the work we are in with malice toward none, with charity for all, with firmness in the right as God

> gives us to see the right to bind up the nation's wounds, to care for him who shall have borne the battle, and for his widow and his orphan—to do all which may achieve and cherish a just, and a lasting peace, among ourselves, and with all nations.

As you revise your work, then, look for the independent clause and choose a sentence pattern that is appropriate to the location of the clause and the number of complements. Use loose structure for strong, direct, simple statements but do not overextend sentences that open with a main clause. Use periodic structure to set off multiple complements and lead your reader to a conclusion. But recognize that a long sentence, a sentence with more than four complements, almost inevitably requires some balancing of phrases and clauses.

EXERCISE 21

Rewrite the following paragraph by revising those sentences that use an inappropriate structure.

> My brother Stan seemed to me a giant while we were children growing up during the depression in a home darkened by our mother's unemployment and our father's early death. Stan could throw a ball harder and farther than anyone in the neighborhood full of good athletes like the Diaz twins, Duke Szymanski, and Robert Jefferson. He could run fast. He could find good fishing holes. He could do his paper route in less than an hour. He could sing too. He always smiled. He was a great guy. Stan always had to budget his time between the church choir, going out to play whatever sport was in season, and to help with my homework. He enlisted in the Marine Corps in January 1942, a month after the Japanese attack on Pearl Harbor which President Roosevelt said before the Congress would always live in infamy. On March 10, 1943, during the assault on Saipan, as he was running across a stretch of beach, under enemy fire from machine guns, Stan was killed. When I heard the news of his death, I felt sadness and hurt so intense that I still cannot explain or deal with them.

The basic parts of the sentence, then, are the subject, the predicate, and the complement. If, by defining an agent, you develop subject specificity and predicate condensation, you should be able to place your complements correctly. Your thoughts will be clear; your sentences will be well written. But while subject-predicate-complement is the basic sentence form, you can put subjects, predicates, and complements together in several different patterns. In fact, one of your goals as a writer should be what composition teachers call *sentence variety.* To include multiple complements, a loose sentence will have to lead into a parallel structure.

> I ate the pizza which was hot and tasty, chewy and fresh, spicy and aromatic, homebaked and good.

As we go on in the next chapter to discuss paragraph organization, we will frequently mention sentence variety. At this point you should be able to identify loose, periodic, and parallel sentences and to judge when each is appropriate.

II Developing Ideas: the Agent and the Paragraph

In the first chapter, we stressed the importance of defining an agent in every sentence by advising you to use specific subjects, to condense your predicates, and to write in the active voice when possible. We showed how mastering these techniques of agent prose can help you write efficiently, clearly, and directly. But how can specifying an agent help you create better paragraphs and better essays? These are questions the next two chapters address.

The American philosopher Kenneth Burke has argued that no agent stands alone. Once you clearly establish the identity of your *agents,* they naturally suggest questions on which you can base an essay. These questions can concern the agents' *acts,* the *means* by which they act, the *scene* (or background) for their acts, and their *purposes* (or motives). In his book *A Grammar of Motives,* Burke calls these five features of agency (agent, act, means, scene, purpose) a *pentad.* As you write paragraphs, you may not develop all the features of the pentad, but you must develop at least some of them. When you do, you will begin to see ways to develop your topic and probe whatever issues you may be raising.

The following sentence from a student paper has a clear agent.

> As they start their college careers, students usually share complicated, time-consuming, frustrating, and yet exciting experiences.

Because she has cited definite agents (students), the writer can now get to questions about the agents' act or scene or means or purpose. Let's quickly suggest some possibilities: her *agents* are the students; their *act* involves starting a college career; their *means* are the as yet unspecified "time-consuming, frustrating, and yet exciting experiences"; their *purpose* would seem to be higher education; the *scene,* if developed, would probably be a college campus. Now the writer must make an important choice—which part(s) of the pentad will she focus on and develop? Does she want to write about the actual physical *scene* at her university? Does she want to analyze her *motive* (purpose) for being there or simply describe in more detail the *actions* of her first days at college? Does she want to write about the changes in herself as *agent?* All these essay topics are possible, but a likely topic seems to be the new procedures, ideas, and responsibilities she encountered. In other words, the *means* of her orientation to college seem to offer a good possibility for development; she naturally will want to describe more specifically those "time-consuming, frustrating, and yet exciting experiences."

> As they start their college careers, students usually share complicated, time-consuming, frustrating, and yet exciting experiences. I spent my first day at Cal State San Luis Obispo waiting three hours in a registration line (only to discover that I did not have the required signatures), struggling to locate both the bookstore and the texts I needed, and, in general, feeling homesick. When the roommate a computer had selected for me wouldn't let me into our room, I thought of returning to Fresno.

Note that in these sentences the student not only has described in concrete terms the means of her orientation (registration procedures, computer hassles), she has also defined her *agent* further (going from *students* to *I*) and established a fairly specific *scene* (Cal State San Luis Obispo). Now she can go on to explain from her own observations the excitement of beginning college.

> As they start their college careers, students usually share complicated, time-consuming, frustrating, and yet exciting experiences. I spent my first day at Cal State San Luis Obispo waiting three hours in a registration line (only to discover that I did not have the required signatures), struggling to locate both the bookstore and the texts I needed, and, in general, feeling homesick. When the roommate a computer had selected for me wouldn't let me into our room, I thought of returning to Fresno. But despite these problems, I began to enjoy my new life. Once I found my classes, they were challenging; once I met other students, I began to attend dances, football games, and parties.

> I believe that if freshmen can withstand the hassles that go with beginning college, they can start to fit into campus life.

As parts of the pentad, agents and acts inevitably suggest scenes or motives or means. When you write agent prose, your problem becomes not finding something to say, but choosing the aspect (or aspects) of the pentad you will pursue. Burke points out that no single term in the pentad can exist in isolation; by defining agents, you tie into an almost infinite source of questions, commentary, and analysis.

The San Luis Obispo student could get specific because she composed her initial sentence according to the standards of agent prose and then used the questions raised by several features of the pentad—*agent, scene,* and most important, *means*—to help develop her ideas. If your sentences meet the standards of agent prose, they should lead you to discover features of the pentad and enable you to generate content—to come up with something to say. By clearly focusing on one of the features of agency, you can investigate its relationship to the other features and make your writing assignments more than meaningless exercises in paper filling.

Linking Features of Agency: the Topic Sentence

You should be aware that essays can vary quite widely depending on the feature of the pentad to which they give greatest emphasis. The San Luis Obispo student emphasizes *means* and thus commits herself to talking about registration procedures. But, depending on her data and interests, she might have chosen the *scene* and committed herself to detailing the physical features of the campus (dormitory and building locations, architecture, natural setting) and how they affected her. Or she might have focused on her *motive* and committed herself to detailing why exactly she came to college (were her interests social, academic, or both?). Or she could have chosen the *act* itself and committed herself to a more detailed narrative of her experiences with the registration line and with her roommate. Or she might have developed the *agent* in her paragraph and committed herself to further description of her personal adjustment and growth. As the agent in the writing process itself, this student had to figure out which direction to take.

The requirements of agent prose become particularly important when you write the topic sentence of your paragraph. The topic sentence defines the main idea of the paragraph and indicates how you will develop it. This is vital since a paragraph consists of a group of *related sentences,* that is, sentences that explain and support *one central topic*. Frequently the topic sentence is the first sentence in the paragraph, although, as we will explain later, it need not be. For years composition teachers have urged students to pay particular attention to their topic sentences and make them as precise, detailed, and clear as possible. But exactly how students were to reach this goal remained something of a mystery. With the principles of agent prose and the five features of agency in mind, you can see that a good topic sentence will have certain predictable characteristics. It will have a specific sentence subject (preferably an agent) and a succinct verb (preferably one describing the action that the agent performs). In other words, the topic sentence should define at least one feature of agency and raise questions about its relation to the other features; it will in some way link agent with act or scene or means or motive.

When you write agent prose, you use the active voice whenever possible; therefore the *agent* typically will be the initial feature of agency you define and the act the agent performs will be the next. In the topic sentence you might also determine the *means* by which the agent performed the act, the *scene* of the act, or the *motive* for the act. Your own frame of reference and purpose will determine which of these links you want your topic sentence to highlight. Also your previous teachers may have pointed out that good writers often make their topic sentences double as transition sentences; writers use topic sentences to link a paragraph to the one that comes before it. Usually then, an effective topic sentence begins with some sort of reference, ideally a subtle one, to a previous idea. Such transitions might at first seem complicated and unattainable. But you will find that they come quite naturally in practice, as long as you define agents and then link up features of agency.

The following topic sentence comes from a student essay about television advertising. The student was trying to analyze a persuasive advertising technique and then give an example of a specific commercial that employs that technique. The topic sentence was supposed to introduce an example commercial and the subsequent sentences were supposed to describe the commercial and how it used the technique.

> The new health craze is another aspect that advertisements play on.

This topic sentence is vague and abstract—it does not meet the standards of agent prose. *The health craze* is not a specific sentence subject, one that we can picture. The writer adds confusion by equating this vague subject with an abstraction—*aspect*. We necessarily ask, "Aspect of what?" Then the student, further obscuring the point, indicates that "advertisements play on" this aspect. Obviously the most important feature of agency here is *means*—advertisements *use* the health craze as a means of selling their products. But the topic sentence needs to explain this *means* more clearly and to connect it with other features of agency—*agent* and *purpose*—to clarify the central idea of the paragraph. Here is how the student eventually rewrote the sentence:

> Advertisers promoting Tab appeal to all health-conscious Americans by showing slim, energetic people exercising while drinking it.

This topic sentence provides clear agents (*advertisers*) and defines them specifically. We are not talking about just any advertisers, but about those promoting Tab. These agents perform a clear action; they "appeal to all health-conscious Americans." And the means by which they appeal to health-conscious Americans are clearly described—"by showing slim, energetic people exercising while drinking" Tab. This revised topic sentence meets the standards of agent prose: its subject is specific, its verb precise, its language concrete. These virtues, however, would not necessarily make it a good topic sentence. To be that, is has to meet the other requirements we have described, and it does. It clearly states the central idea, or topic, of the paragraph by linking agent and action with a third feature of agency—*means*—which the rest of the paragraph will describe and explain.

The ways in which this sentence might meet the final requirement of a topic sentence—that it make a transition—are numerous and will depend on the writer's purposes. Transition here could be subtle. Perhaps in the previous paragraph the student had discussed advertisers promoting Quaker Oats. In that case the student could link the paragraphs by beginning this one with a similar phrasing—*advertisers promoting Tab*. But if the student felt that the link between paragraphs needed to be more obvious, she might have written:

> Like the advertisers promoting Quaker Oats, those promoting Tab appeal to health-conscious Americans. But instead of connecting their product with a concerned mother and her warm kitchen, they show slim, energetic people exercising while drinking Tab.

As you see, this added transition sentence links the two paragraphs so that the reader will not wonder what Tab has to do with Quaker Oats or what either has to do with the health-consciousness of Americans. The paragraph now has two sentences that perform a transition and state its topic.

Since effective topic sentences are so important, let us go through a different example.

> My first example is about the Wella Balsam Shampoo commercial with Jaclyn Smith.

Again, this sentence does not meet the standards of agent prose. The sentence subject is abstract, vague. Because of this, the wording is illogical. The abstract subject, as is typical, takes the weak verb *is* and promotes the puzzling diction. Readers must ask, ''Can an example be 'about' something?'' Obviously this student, like the one who wrote the paragraph on the Tab advertisement, needs to focus more on means—Jaclyn Smith—and on how the Wella Balsam advertisers achieve their purpose (motive) through her. As this topic sentence stands, it mentions two features of agency. The commercial is the act; Jaclyn Smith is the means. But the sentence lacks an agent (advertisers) and fails to achieve a crucial connection between means and motive. That connection, once made, can give focus and meaning to the paragraph.

Again, transition here could be subtle. Perhaps in the previous paragraph the student had discussed advertisers who use another celebrity, for example, Cheryl Tiegs. In that case the student could link the paragraphs by using similar phrasing—*by hiring Jaclyn Smith* would parallel *by hiring Cheryl Tiegs*. But if the student felt that the link between paragraphs had to be more obvious, he might have written:

> Like their counterparts at Cover Girl, Wella Balsam's advertisers, by having Jaclyn Smith promote their product, subtly imply that by using this product women will look like the beautiful model.

EXERCISE 1

Look closely at the following topic sentences. Do they define and link features of agency? If not, can you make them stronger?

1. Exxon, yet another company claiming to have found the answer to the question of how to save gas, has run proof-by-comparison advertisements pitting its own Uniflo Motor Oil against other popular motor oils.
2. Plain folks come in all sizes and ages, short and tall, young and old.
3. When famous model Cheryl Tiegs became the focus of attention, *Time* magazine used her beauty to entice customers.
4. Muhammad Ali is considered one of the best boxers in history, and people believe what he says.
5. A pipe adds the finishing touch to any man's appearance and makes him look distinguished.
6. One of the most entertaining yet ineffective commercials is the Acme Used Car ad with its zany announcer.
7. Cereal companies totally dedicate Saturday morning ads to convincing children that cereals make them strong.
8. Another commercial is Meow Mix.
9. A commercial using sex to sell its product is the one for Close-up toothpaste.
10. Old Spice seems to get every sailor gorgeous women in every port.

Here, then, is a definition of the topic sentence that recapitulates principles with which you should now feel familiar and comfortable. *Effective topic sentences meet the standards of agent prose, focus on a feature or features of the pentad, and provide some form of transition, some reference to the idea of the preceding paragraph.* This last characteristic is particularly crucial because you seldom write isolated paragraphs; you typically put paragraphs together to form essays. When we consider the essay in this way—as a group of related paragraphs all developing the same central idea, or thesis—we can appreciate even more the importance of transition. Topic sentences must link the different steps in the writer's thought process represented by the individual paragraphs in the essay. If topic sentences do not double as transition sentences, the reader cannot read the essay as a coherent whole.

In his essay "Who Killed King Kong?" X.J. Kennedy masterfully uses his topic sentences to establish a logical thought progression from paragraph to paragraph. Kennedy wants to ask and answer a central question: "Why does the American public refuse to let King Kong rest in peace?" ("Why is King Kong so enduringly popular?") To prepare his readers for this question, he uses his opening three paragraphs (introduction) to establish the film as a classic, one that succeeding generations see again and again. In his body paragraphs, he proposes possible explanations for the film's hold on us, and then in his conclusion he restates the question and provides one final explanation. To show how topic sentences can also make transitions, we have underlined the topic sentences Kennedy uses and indicated the transitional devices in boldfaced type.

X. J. KENNEDY
Who Killed King Kong?

The ordeal and spectacular **death** of King Kong, the giant ape, undoubtedly have been witnessed by more Americans than have ever seen a performance of *Hamlet, Iphigenia at Aulis,* or even *Tobacco Road*. Since RKO-Radio Pictures first released *King Kong,* a quarter-century has gone by; yet year after year, from prints that grow more rain-beaten, from sound tracks that grow more tinny, ticket-buyers by thousands still pursue Kong's luckless fight against the forces of technology, tabloid journalism, and the DAR. They see him chloroformed to sleep, see him whisked from his jungle isle to New York and placed on show, see him burst his chains to roam the city (lugging a frightened blonde), at last to plunge from the spire of the Empire State Building, machine-gunned by model airplanes.

Though Kong may die, one begins to think his legend **unkillable.** No clearer proof of his hold upon the popular imagination may be seen than what emerged one catastrophic week in March 1955, when New York WOR-TV programmed *Kong* for seven evenings in a row (a total of sixteen showings). Many a rival network vice-president must have scowled when surveys showed that *Kong*—the 1933 B-picture—had lured away fat segments of the viewing populace from such powerful competitors as Ed Sullivan, Groucho Marx and Bishop Sheen.

But even television has failed to run *King Kong* into **oblivion**. Coffee-in-the-lobby cinemas still show the old hunk of hokum, with the apology that in its use of composite shots and animated models the film remains technically interesting. And no other monster in movie history has won so devoted a popular audience.

None of the plodding mummies, the stultified draculas, the white-coated Lugosis with their shiny pinball-machine laboratories, none of the invisible stranglers, berserk robots, or menaces from Mars has ever enjoyed so many resurrections.

Why does the American public refuse to let King Kong **rest in peace?** It is true, I'll admit, that *Kong* outdid every monster movie before or since in sheer carnage. Producers Cooper and Schoedsack crammed into it dinosaurs, headhunters, riots, aerial battles, bullets, bombs, bloodletting. Heroine Fay Wray, whose function is mainly to scream, shuts her mouth for hardly one uninterrupted minute from first reel to last. It is also true that *Kong* is larded with good healthy sadism, for those whose joy it is to see the frantic girl dangled from cliffs and harried by pterodactyls. But it seems to me that the abiding appeal of the giant ape rests on other foundations.

Kong has, **first of all,** the attraction of being manlike. His simian nature gives him one huge advantage over giant ants and walking vegetables in that an audience may conceivably identify with him. Kong's appeal has the quality that established the Tarzan series as American myth—for what man doesn't secretly image himself a huge hairy howler against whom no other monster has a chance? If Tarzan recalls the ape in us, then Kong may well appeal to that great-granddaddy primordial brute from whose tribe we have all deteriorated.

Intentionally or not, the producers of *King Kong* encourage **this identification** by etching the character of Kong with keen sympathy. For the ape is a figure in a tradition familiar to moviegoers: the tradition of the pitiable monster. We think of Lon Chaney in the role of Quasimodo, of Karloff in the original *Frankenstein.* As we watch the Frankenstein monster's fumbling and disastrous attempts to befriend a flower-picking child, our sympathies are enlisted with the monster in his impenetrable loneliness. And so with Kong. As he roars in his chains, while barkers sell tickets to boobs who gape at him, we perhaps feel something more deep than pathos. We begin to sense something of the problem that engaged Eugene O'Neill in *The Hairy Ape:* the dilemma of a displaced animal spirit forced to live in a jungle built by machines.

King Kong, it is true, had **special relevance** in 1933. Landscapes of the depression are glimpsed early in the film when an impresario, seeking some desperate pretty girl to play the lead in a jungle movie, visits souplines and a Woman's Home Mission. In Fay Wray—who's been caught snitching an apple from a fruitstand—his search is ended. When he gives her a big feed and a movie contract, the girl is magic-carpeted out of the world of the National Recovery Act. And when, in the film's climax,

Kong smashes that very Third Avenue landscape in which Fay had wandered hungry, audiences of 1933 may well have felt a personal satisfaction.

What is curious is that audiences of 1960 **remain** hooked. For in the heart of urban man, one suspects, lurks the impulse to fling a bomb. Though machines speed him to the scene of his daily grind, though IBM comptometers ("freeing the human mind from drudgery") enable him to drudge more efficiently once he arrives, there comes a moment when he wishes to turn upon his machines and kick hell out of them. He wants to hurl his combination radio-alarmclock out the bedroom window and listen to its smash. What subway commuter wouldn't love—just for once—to see the downtown express smack head-on into the uptown local? Such a wish is gratified in that memorable scene in *Kong* that opens with a wide-angle shot: interior of a railway car on the Third Avenue El. Straphangers are nodding, the literate refold their newspapers. Unknown to them, Kong has torn away a section of trestle toward which the train now speeds. The motorman spies Kong up ahead, jams on the brakes. Passengers hurtle together like so many peas in a pail. In a window of the car appear Kong's bloodshot eyes. Women shriek. Kong picks up the railway car as if it were a rat, flips it to the street and ties knots in it, or something. To any commuter the scene must appear one of the most satisfactory pieces of celluloid ever exposed.

Yet however violent his acts, Kong remains a gentleman. Remarkable is his sense of chivalry. Whenever a fresh boa constrictor threatens Fay, Kong first sees that the lady is safely parked, then manfully thrashes her attacker. (And she, the ingrate, runs away every time his back is turned.) Atop the Empire State Building, ignoring his pursuers, Kong places Fay on a ledge as tenderly as if she were a dozen eggs. He fondles her, then turns to face the Army Air Force. And Kong is perhaps the most disinterested lover since Cyrano: his attentions to the lady are utterly without hope of reward. After all, between a five-foot blonde and a fifty-foot ape, love can hardly be more than an intellectual flirtation. In his simian way King Kong is the hopelessly yearning lover of Petrarchan convention. His forced exit from his jungle, in chains, results directly from his single-minded pursuit of Fay. He smashes a Broadway theater when the notion enters his dull brain that the flashbulbs of photographers somehow endanger the lady. His perilous shinnying up a skyscraper to pluck Fay from her boudoir is an act of the kindliest of hearts. He's impossible to discourage even though the love of his life can't lay eyes on him without shrieking murder.

The tragedy of King Kong **then,** is to be the beast who at the end of the fable fails to turn into the handsome prince. This is the conviction that the scriptwriters would leave with us in the film's closing line. As Kong's corpse lies blocking traffic in the street, the enterpreneur who brought Kong to New York turns to the assembled reporters and proclaims: "That's your story, boys—it was Beauty killed the Beast!" But greater forces than those of the screaming Lady have combined to lay Kong low, if you ask me. Kong lives for a time as one of those persecuted near-animal souls bewildered in the middle of an industrial order, whose simple desires are thwarted at every turn. He climbs the Empire State Building because in all New York it's the closest thing he can find to the clifftop of his jungle isle. He dies, a pitiful dolt, and the army brass and publicity-men cackle over him. His death is the only possible outcome to as neat a tragic dilemma as you can ask for. The machine-guns do him in, while the manicured human hero (a nice clean Dartmouth boy) carries away Kong's sweetheart to the altar. O, the misery of it all. There's far more truth about upper-middle-class American life in *King Kong* than in the last seven dozen novels of John P. Marquand.

A Negro friend from Atlanta tells me that in movie houses in colored neighborhoods throughout the South, *Kong* does **a constant business.** They show the thing in Atlanta at least every year, presumably to the same audiences. Perhaps this popularity may simply be due to the fact that *Kong* is one of the most watchable movies ever constructed, but I wonder whether Negro audiences may not find some archetypical appeal in this serio-comic tale of a huge black powerful free spirit whom all the hardworking white policemen are out to kill.

Every day in the week on a screen somewhere in the world, King Kong relives his agony. Again and again he expires on the Empire State Building, as audiences of the devout assist his sacrifice. We watch him die, and by extension kill the ape within our bones, but these little deaths of ours occur in prosaic surroundings. We do not die on a tower, New York before our feet, nor do we give our lives to smash a few flying machines. It is not for us to bring to a momentary standstill the civilization in which we move. King Kong does this for us. And so we kill him again and again, in much-spliced celluloid, while the ape in us expires from day to day, obscure, in desperation.

Assertions and Supports: Deductive, Inductive, and Combination Paragraphs

Deductive Paragraphs

Except for his concluding paragraph, all of Kennedy's paragraphs begin with their topic sentences, and most of the paragraphs you write will follow this form. The technical term for this paragraph structure is *deductive*. You make your general statement first in your topic sentence and then support and explain it with "particulars." These particulars can be examples, statistics, comparisons, quotes from experts, or simply details and facts that refer to the topic idea. Let's look again at Kennedy's second paragraph.

> Though Kong may die, one begins to think his legend unkillable. No clearer proof of his hold upon the popular imagination may be seen than what emerged one catastrophic week in March 1955, when New York WOR-TV programmed *Kong* for seven evenings in a row (a total of sixteen showings). Many a rival network vice-president must have scowled when surveys showed that *Kong*—the 1933 B-picture—had lured away fat segments of the viewing populace from such powerful competitors as Ed Sullivan, Groucho Marx and Bishop Sheen.

Note that the topic sentence states a general idea—Kong's legend seems unkillable. The particulars that follow—in this case, statistics concerning *Kong*'s ratings during a 1955 television showing—support this claim.

Inductive Paragraphs

While deductive structure is the most typical, paragraph forms can vary. Another common form, called *inductive,* places the topic sentence at the close of the paragraph. In this position the topic sentence serves as a summary or general statement that draws a conclusion based on the specific details which precede it. Usually, inductive paragraphs serve as *introductions and conclusions.* Because *introductory paragraphs* must provide background information and details that orient the reader, they naturally fall into the inductive form. In the following example, a student begins her introduction with particulars—statistics on handgun production and related crimes. Only after she provides these details does she state the idea that she will develop in subsequent paragraphs. The underlined topic sentence draws a general conclusion from her details and gives order to the paragraph.

> Over 25,000 Americans die each year because of shooting accidents, suicides, or murders caused by handguns, mainly because so many Americans possess handguns. In 1973 handguns were used to commit 53 percent of the 19,510 reported murders and two-thirds of the reported robberies and assaults. The annual output of handguns has increased from 568,000 in 1968 to 2.5 million in 1974. Gun manufacturers produce more guns each year, and the number of American gun-related deaths increases right along with the output of firearms. We cannot allow this trend to continue in our civilized society. The United States must create a new, nationwide system to eliminate the buying and selling of handguns.

Let's think of this paragraph in terms of agent prose as well as structure. The opening statistics actually describe a *scene*—a lawless America where handguns figure in many violent crimes. This depiction of the scene leads to a call for action since we must ask, "If the situation is so bad, what can we do to change it?" Thus a definition of one feature of agency, *scene*, inevitably leads us to a related feature, *act*.

> The United States must create a new, nationwide system to eliminate the buying and selling of handguns.

Inevitably, we must also ask about the other features of agency: Who will implement this system (agents)? How will the system work (means)? Why have people not controlled gun production and distribution before this (motive)? These questions, which arise quite naturally from the strong topic sentence, will show the student how to proceed, how to develop the central idea of the essay which involves an *act*.

This next paragraph, even though it begins by mentioning *agents* and questioning *motive*, concentrates on only one feature of agency, *act*. It is an inductive paragraph because its final sentence sets the focus for the rest of the essay—the problems associated with the name Jeannette (consequences of the *act*). The other features of agency are subordinate to the *act*. Study this introduction:

> I don't think my parents fully considered the consequences when they gave me a name like Jeannette. Now I don't think I have an ugly name. In fact, many people have told me that

> I have a pretty name, one that fits my personality and is pleasant to say and hear. But none of these people have had to live with "Jeannette" and all of the problems that go along with the name.

This paragraph is much more informal, its topic much more personal, than the gun-control paragraph. For this reason, the student uses the first person and contractions. Because she deals with only a small part of her experience—her problems with her name—the central idea, which the topic sentence states, is straightforward and uncomplicated. She focuses on only one feature of agency—the consequences of her parents' act of naming her Jeannette. The topic sentence shows that the student is not interested in developing any feature of agency but *act*. The inductive paragraph structure indicates that we are not to know anything about her parents themselves, their *motive* for naming her Jeannette, the *scene* where they named her, or their *means* for arriving at that name. We are to know only about their *act* and the problems it has caused their daughter. And, in fact, in the body paragraphs of the rest of her essay the student adheres to this focus on *act*. She discusses the tendency of people to misspell and mispronounce her name and laments the mutilation that her name undergoes on all computer print-outs. She also explains her own feeling of isolation since she has never met any other "Jeannette." She ends her essay by calling for another *act* on all our parts—to consider well the consequences when we name our children.

Both of these inductive introductions—the one that brings up all the features of agency and the other that focuses on only one—are successful because the students cite particulars and logically move us on to the topic sentence. The inductive form can also appear in *concluding paragraphs*. X.J. Kennedy, for example, begins his conclusion by describing once more the *act*—audiences witnessing the destruction of the big ape. In his third sentence, he shifts from the *act* ("we watch him die") to our *motive* for the act ("and by extension kill the ape within our bones"). Then the rest of the paragraph further defines the motive, describing the catharsis *Kong* evokes in urban dwellers.

> Every day in the week on a screen somewhere in the world, King Kong relives his agony. Again and again he expires on the Empire State Building, as audiences of the devout assist his sacrifice. We watch him die, and by extension kill the ape within our bones, but these little deaths of ours occur in prosaic surroundings. We do not die on a tower, New York before our feet, nor do we give our lives to smash a few flying

> machines. It is not for us to bring to a momentary standstill the civilization in which we move. King Kong does this for us. And so we kill him again and again, in much-spliced celluoid, while the ape in us expires from day to day, obscure, in desperation.

Note that the final sentence, the topic sentence of the paragraph, pulls together all of the particulars, culminating the discussion of *motive* in the concluding paragraph as well as in the essay as a whole.

Combination Paragraphs

One other paragraph form that we should mention calls for two topic sentences—one minor, one major—and so combines the inductive and deductive structures. The *minor topic sentence* states the idea for the paragraph; the *major topic sentence* states an idea that reaches beyond the immediate concerns of the individual paragraph. Study the following paragraph which uses the combination (or combined) structure to introduce an essay.

> To mark its debut last week, the "Good Night" talk show set out to present television's first live coverage of a death-row electrocution. The choked-up host conducted a phone interview with the doomed inmate. The soon-to-be-widowed wife was lining up book, movie, and T-shirt deals. And three viewers got to play key roles on "Electrocution Night '84." All had won an essay contest titled, "I would like to throw the switch because . . ." Television achieved either a new comedic high or a new nadir of bad taste.

As you see, the paragraph begins with a topic sentence that tells us what the writer will discuss—the debut of the "Good Night" show. This minor topic sentence focuses on the *act*. The subsequent sentences define the act, or presentation, which consisted of an interview with the inmate, his wife's wheeling and dealing, and the Electrocution Night essay contest. Based on these particulars the major topic sentence makes a general statement about the show: "Television achieved either a new comedic high or a new nadir of bad taste." The topic sentence goes beyond the immediate topic of the paragraph to introduce the central idea of the essay; it calls for a judgment concerning the *act*. In the rest of the essay, the writer made a judgment and supported his choice, asking questions about the *agent* (Who produced the show?), the *scene* (How does this show fit into the television medium?), the *means* (How does the producer hope to be comical?), and the *motive* (What reason does the producer have for bringing this odd show to the public?). By answering these questions, set in motion by the major topic sentence, the author elaborated and supported an informed judgment.

EXERCISE 2

Choose two of the following lists of particulars. First, formulate topic sentences that will organize them. Then develop three paragraphs—inductive, deductive, and a combination—from each list by varying the placement of the topic sentences.

1. A stay in the hospital
   —Nurses waking patients at 3 A.M. to give sleeping pills
   —three-hour waits for X-rays
   —Multiple blood tests
   —Frequent visits by interns who ask millions of questions; infrequent visits from the doctor who could give real information
   —Roommate with a family of forty, all of whom visit at every opportunity
   —Custodians who think they are opera stars and sing arias as they mop
2. A Sunday afternoon at an NFL football game
   —Parking six miles from stadium in a swamp
   —Waiting 45 minutes in a concession line for a quart of warm beer costing $3
   —Sitting next to a fan who thinks that if he does not shower for a week before the game, his team will win
   —Listening to the same fan repeat a limited number of obscenities as his team loses
   —Witnessing first-hand the onslaught of a cold front with preliminary thunder showers
   —Trying with 70,000 other people to squeeze through one of three exits
   —Paying $15 to see the home team lose 50–10
3. First night after cashing first paycheck
   —Feeling of elation
   —Fine dining
   —Attending a concert
   —Looking at new cars which now seem affordable
   —Visions of grandeur while driving through the wealthiest part of town
   —Plans for taking over the company

4. The ravages of inflation
   —Paying 40¢ for a candy bar that you remember buying for 15¢ as a child
   —Paying $5.00 to see a movie
   —Watching the price of gasoline become a three-digit number
   —Finding out that your new summer wardrobe will be a T-shirt
   —Watching a lifetime .250 hitter sign a baseball contract for $400,000 a year
   —Finding out that your heating bill is higher than your rent

---

Making the Paragraph Complete: Paragraph Development

In your reading, you will notice that writers use many paragraph forms; one American scholar has counted over twenty. The three forms that we have discussed are the most common and the most obvious. Remember that paragraph form is usually determined by the nature and placement of the topic sentence. But no matter what form your paragraphs take, they should meet certain standards. Composition teachers continually ask that paragraphs be well-developed and unified. But what do these terms really mean? How can agent prose help you develop and unify paragraphs?

Let's return to the topic sentence. A clear, precise topic sentence should locate the idea that you want to support and explain, that is, *develop*. Only when you locate the idea can you begin to find things to say about it—to select relevant data from your store of information. By the same token, if your topic sentence is strong, you will also avoid problems with the second obsession of composition teachers—unity. Every sentence in an effective paragraph should refer to and help define the feature or features of agency focused on by the topic sentence. If you lose this focus, you destroy paragraph unity and almost always confuse your reader. A strong topic sentence that effectively states the central idea of the paragraph will help you keep to the point; a weak topic sentence makes digression almost inevitable.

Let's further discuss how the topic sentence affects development. Compare the following body paragraphs from two different essays on the film *Star Wars.*

> 1. *Star Wars* provides terrific special effects. All sorts of monsters and robots are in the film. A scene in a space-age bar is really wonderful.
>
> 2. *Star Wars* gives us special effects never before attempted or considered possible. R2-D2 projects Princess Leia's form on the floor of her spaceship with a spectacular 3-D effect. No less spectacular is a scene in which R2-D2 and his friend Chewbacca play a space-age form of chess, using projected 3-D forms in place of the usual pieces. Rather than a bishop capturing a knight, a dinosaur devours a small blue-eyed monster. Monsters are common in *Star Wars* and thanks to Rick Baker, makeup expert for the 1976 remake of *King Kong,* audiences are treated to a time-honored John Wayne barroom scene complete with a brawl involving a freak from every galaxy. The special effects are remarkable and a definite force behind the movie's appeal.

The two essays from which these paragraphs come examine the reasons for the film's success, and both paragraphs explore one *means* by which *Star Wars* fascinated the public—its special effects. The topic sentence in paragraph 2 gives a bit more detail than the topic sentence in paragraph 1, but they are basically similar. The paragraphs themselves are quite different, however, because one defines the *means* through examples while the other does not. From the first paragraph, we get no clear idea of the special effects that *Star Wars* offers. Words such as *terrific, all sorts,* and *really wonderful* do not provide mental images for the reader; they are too vague and merely appreciative. The second paragraph cites key scenes and techniques in some detail and defines the *means* more thoroughly. It gives readers a clear idea of exactly *why* the film's special effects were unusual. It ends with a summary statement that again places the focus on *means*—the special effects are "a definite force behind the movie's appeal."

As the first paragraph on *Star Wars* reveals, one sign that a paragraph lacks development—other than a weak topic sentence—is brevity. In expository prose, paragraphs that are one, two, or even three sentences long will almost always be inadequate. They cry out for additional details, illustrations, analogues—for *particulars* that will define a feature of agency. In the following paragraph on "Barney Miller" and "M*A*S*H," the length warns us of its inadequacies, as does the writer's weak topic sentence and agentless prose.

> The most striking similarity of the two shows is the characterization. Both shows make good use of a vast array of characters. And if their interplay is not watched closely, the humor is likely to be missed.

Note the long noun phrase that stands in the subject place in the topic sentence—*the most striking similarity of the two shows*—and the weak passive verbs in the third sentence—*is not watched closely* and *is likely to be missed*. The illogical phrasing *similarity of* and the trite *vast array* also do little to clarify the writer's meaning or develop her ideas.

The focus of the paragraph is on *means*—the characterization of the two shows—but the topic sentence fails to show us how the student will define *means*. Because she fails to make her topic sentence specific, the student also fails, in the subsequent sentences, to tell us anything about the means—to name the characters and describe them. How would we go about writing a paragraph that develops the means? First of all, we would have to think about and specify that "vast array of characters." Who are they? Even an occasional viewer of "M*A*S*H" knows Hawkeye, BJ, Colonel Potter, Klinger, Hot Lips, Father Mulcahy, and Major Winchester, just as an occasional viewer of "Barney Miller" knows Captain Miller, Detectives Dietrich, Harris, Wojo, and Officer Leavitt. Having defined the characters (means) more precisely, we might want to link them to another feature of agency. In this case the *scenes*—the army base in "M*A*S*H," the squad room in "Barney Miller"—loom most important since they, in many ways, shape the characters.

Once we think about the topic in this way, we can begin to see the kind of topic sentence we want to formulate. It will focus on the characters, give us specific information about them, and place them in their scenes.

> In both "M*A*S*H" and "Barney Miller," groups of likable but very different characters find themselves in odd, trying situations; the characters' conflicts and misunderstandings make otherwise grim scenes—a surgery ward, a police station—humorous.

This infinitely more effective topic sentence links, through its compound structure, *means* with *scene* and suggests ways to develop its idea in subsequent sentences. We first have to identify and describe the characters; then we might further define them by placing them in their scenes.

> In both ''M*A*S*H'' and ''Barney Miller,'' groups of likable but very different characters find themselves in odd, often trying situations; the characters' conflicts and misunderstandings make otherwise grim scenes—a surgery ward, a police station—humorous. ''M*A*S*H'' gives us the irreverent Hawkeye and BJ, the saintly Father Mulcahy, the snobbish Major Winchester, the passionate but professional Hot Lips, the ''military'' but humane Colonel Potter, and the downright wacky Max Klinger. Turned loose in a Korean War military hospital, surrounded by dead and wounded soldiers, these characters work at cross purposes even as they seek the same goal—to save lives. And their peculiar ways of staying sane—Hawkeye's wisecracks, BJ's devotion to his family, Hot Lips' affairs, Potter's painting, Klinger's wardrobe—make us laugh. ''Barney Miller'' gives us the fatherly but harried Captain Miller, the intellectual Dietrich, the strong and simple Wojo, the witty detective Harris, and the pushy but nice would-be detective, Officer Leavitt. Barney and his men seemingly have to deal with every strange person in New York City, and they too share a goal—justice and order. Their devices for staying sane—Harris's wit and style, Dietrich's esoteric knowledge, Wojo's commitment to his job, Leavitt's ambition, Miller's patience—also create humorous conflicts. In a squad room full of such diverse personalities even a homicidal maniac can become amusing, just as even major surgery becomes almost lighthearted as Hawkeye, BJ, Winchester, and Potter exchange insults and witticisms.

This revised paragraph is also impressive because of the other possibilities for development it creates. In comparing the characters and scenes of ''M*A*S*H'' and ''Barney Miller,'' the paragraph also suggests comparisons of other techniques the shows share or comparisons of the agents (the writers and producers who use the techniques) and their motives (laughs, popularity). Therefore, by developing this one paragraph, the student might improve her whole essay.

The unrevised paragraph on ''M*A*S*H'' and ''Barney Miller'' and the first *Star Wars* paragraph appear undeveloped even at first glance because they are short. But without a strong topic sentence, even long paragraphs of more than five sentences can often be undeveloped. This happens because an imprecise topic sentence frequently encourages writers to use agentless prose—to write much while saying little. Look at this example paragraph which, though eight sentences long, is undeveloped. Locate the breakdowns in agent prose.

> (1) For a student just out of high school, his knowledge of life is at a minimum. (2) Yet many of these "social know-nothings" have had as many of life's experiences as a Ph.D. graduate. (3) A certain glow surrounds the first quarter freshmen, the way they hold their head, and strut to class is telling us all they have made it. (4) Freshmen feel they have licked the world already when their foot is only through the door. (5) This same air surrounds the graduating senior. (6) The "I'm done, you're not" feeling exudes from this person to others, but he too is just entering a bigger world than he left. (7) In both cases the signs are much more prominent if they were in cheerleading, sports, student government or otherwise active in school. (8) Many times "cocky" is an understatement of their activities.

We can see that the student fails to set up a topic idea even though he writes eight complete sentences. He begins with a confusing observation about students just out of high school; he ends with a description of college seniors. Without a topic sentence to orient us, we do not know how these groups are related. The agentless, awkward, illogical sentences that the paragraph comprises do little to aid our understanding of his purpose. The abstract sentence subjects (*his knowledge of life* in sentence 1, *a certain glow* in sentence 3, *this same air* in sentence 5, *the "I'm done, you're not" feeling* in sentence 6, *the signs* in sentence 7, and *cocky* in sentence 8) do not define agents or any other features of agency. In addition, the trite phrases—*knowledge of life, life's experiences, licked the world, foot only through the door,* and *they have made it*—mean little. They stand in the place of concrete examples, explanations, and details that would develop the paragraph.

The student also has problems with vague pronouns, problems that reveal how agentless prose helped him avoid specific questions about agency. To whom do the pronouns *they* in sentences 3 and 7 and *their* in sentence 8 refer? Readers would have to search for logical antecedents. When the student says in sentence 7 that "the signs are much more prominent," readers must ask, "What signs?" and, "More prominent than what?" Rather than define some link between agent, act, scene, motive, and means, this student leaves the work to the reader.

If this student had determined his agents, thought about their relation to the other features of agency, and then decided on a focus for his comparison, he could have easily formulated a topic sentence to guide him and his readers. To rescue this paragraph, he would have to rethink his idea and, after providing a topic sentence, rework the paragraph using specific sentence subjects, active verbs, and evocative diction. He would have to develop his topic by defining agents and linking them to features of agency. Look at this successfully revised paragraph and try to see how agent prose aids its development.

> While freshmen just entering college and seniors just graduating might seem to have little in common, they actually share a certain sense of exhilaration and confidence. Entering freshmen have just completed high school where they were seniors themselves. They feel mature and experienced, ready to meet the social and academic challenges of college. Many of them were athletes, cheerleaders, band members, and student government representatives in high school, and they plan to continue these activities as college students. All of them passed the

---

Exercise 3

The following paragraphs all have problems with development, principally because they are too short. Choose two and rewrite them. Be sure to provide a strong topic sentence, if one is lacking, and to add details and illustrations that will help to develop the topic.

1. The impression I get from beer commercials is that each brand of beer appeals to a different group of people. Some commercials appeal to everyday working people; others to more wealthy people. Producers of these commercials try to make them so vague, people can identify with them.
2. Many students find owning a car more of a pain than a pleasure. When I came to college for the summer quarter, I was told that my car had to be parked a half a mile away because the places behind the dorm were strictly for juniors and seniors.
3. The quality of television situation comedies has certainly decreased in recent years. This can be seen if one compares any new situation comedy with an old classic.
4. Applying for jobs can be a tedious process. From the looks through the want ads, to the many interviews, to the waiting to hear, it is all exhausting. I wish it were over.
5. Our city needs many new bike paths to insure bicycle riders' safety. The present conditions for riders are deplorable. Many could be hurt.

---

required courses for their high school diplomas, and most feel sure that they can do this in college also. College seniors feel the same way when contemplating their move into the job market. Having dealt with temperamental professors, deciphered calculus texts, survived lecture classes with 500 other students, and coexisted with all kinds of weird roommates, most of them are sure that the outside world can present no obstacles that they can't surmount. Therefore, the students arriving at college have much the same outlook as those who are leaving it.

EXERCISE 4

Here are two paragraphs that, although long, are also undeveloped. Their agentless prose allows the writers to proceed without ever defining a topic. First look for sentences that are repetitive, agentless, and vague. Then see if you can rewrite the paragraphs by (1) developing a topic sentence that defines and links features of agency, (2) adding logical particulars, and (3) writing agent prose. The paragraphs serve as introductions, so you may want to use either combined or inductive form. For a model, look at the revision made by the student who wrote the paragraphs on college freshmen and seniors (p. 70).

1. In the mid-70s a new breed of music listeners and active participants embarked on an upward journey on the ladder of success. A whole different aspect of the musical field had been set loose. Disco was the latest in contemporary music movements. This particular art form, however, had risen up at the cost of the uniqueness and availability of the art form known as rock and roll. The effect of the disco movement was felt by rock and roll artists and their fans alike. The essence of personal style and imagination was abandoned. The effects of this invasion are still being felt by millions of people today.

2. The Olympic games have evolved through many years of great talent and ambition in the wide world of sports. These games hold the largest and heaviest type of competition between people of all nations. It is each nation's dedication to work and strive to be the best they can. Competing for those three glorious medals, the sportsmanship, the teamwork, the thrill of victory, and the agony of defeat are tremendous aspects pertaining to the Olympic games. Occasionally, many political grievances spring to the surface, causing tension as the Olympic games begin.

Problems with paragraph development inevitably lead to problems with unity, particularly in long paragraphs. Here's why. If you are unable to develop an idea, yet wish to write a long paragraph, one that *appears* developed, the temptation grows to throw in extraneous material. You will pile undeveloped point on undeveloped point, as in the unrevised paragraph on college freshmen and seniors. In the revision, however, the topic sentence draws our attention to an *act*—the sharing of a sense of exhilaration and confidence. With this center established, the student unified the rest of the essay by developing only one point—*how* freshmen and seniors (agents) share this feeling. Note that this clear focus manifests itself in the specific sentence subjects he provides—*entering freshmen, they, many of them, all of them, college seniors, most of them,* and *the students.* Note also that by developing subject specificity, he avoids the reference problems that plagued his first paragraph; the reader has a clear sense of the antecedents for *they* and *them.*

Giving the Paragraph Focus: Paragraph Unity

Besides development, composition teachers look for unity in paragraphs; they hope to find each sentence linked to those around it. A paragraph can lack unity because not all the sentences develop the idea of the topic sentence *and* because the sentences do not work like links in a chain. Consider the following paragraph:

> Students frequently do poorly on essay exams because they do not follow sound procedures before they begin to write. Many do not read the question carefully to determine exactly what it asks them to do. They should search for the key term that will direct them; for example, *compare, contrast, evaluate, summarize,* and *discuss* each instruct students to answer the question in a special way. Teachers give essay exams to test the full extent of their students' knowledge. Some students prefer essay tests because they are not tricky. Multiple choice tests often are, and many students end up guessing. They cannot guess on essay exams though, and that is another reason teachers like to give them.

The writer strays from the topic sentence in which he links *agent* (students) with *act* (doing poorly on essay exams). At first the writer focuses clearly on *act,* but midway through the paragraph, he changes both agent and focus; he begins to discuss teachers (a new agent) and their *motives* for giving essay exams. Then once again he shifts his focus back to students and *their* motives for preferring essay exams. These shifts violate paragraph unity and certainly confuse readers. They also break the chain of logical reasoning that the sentences in a paragraph must form. After the writer says in the third sentence that students must look for the "key term" that gives directions, he must begin his next sentence by referring to this idea. He might say, for example, "After studying the key term and understanding what it asks them to do, students should . . ." Instead, the writer talks about teachers and breaks the chain of ideas.

The student who wrote the paragraph on essay exams does provide a strong topic sentence, but then strays from it. Some writers do not develop a strong topic sentence at all, making paragraph unity impossible to achieve. The following inductive paragraph illustrates this problem.

> Being on the quarter system is a part of life at Kalamazoo College. Ten weeks does not allow for the first week to be for counseling, book shopping, or drop-adding; instead, all three of these plus attending classes must be tackled the first week. Students are hurt by the tension brought on by trying to fit all of their administrative duties in as well as attending classes and receiving assignments into the first week. For instance, I can remember arriving at the English department at 6:00 A.M. to add Argumentative and Persuasive Writing, only to find the line of students already wrapped around the building. I stood in that line for three hours, wasn't able to get the class, and missed two of my other classes that day. I am sure I am not the only one who has experienced drop-add problems.

This paragraph serves as an introduction to an essay comparing the quarter system to the semester system. While the paragraph includes some good, specific examples, it lacks a closing topic sentence and loses effect. The opening statement is general—the college is on the quarter system. But this statement does not link features of agency; it does not set the focus for the rest of the sentences, which describe troubles students have during the first week of the quarter when they must fulfill administrative duties as well as go to classes. The student ends the paragraph by describing her own problems with dropping and adding classes. She never relates these problems to the quarter system, and she never even mentions the semester system. Since the writer never develops a strong topic sentence, the paragraph lacks unity. It fails to introduce a comparison of the two systems, which in terms of the pentad would be the *means* by which universities organize their courses.

Unlike the paragraph on the quarter and semester systems, this next paragraph at least tries to *develop* a topic sentence, though it too fails.

> Oddly enough, it seems that luck was a major part of Clark Gable's success. Gable's first movie triumph was his performance in *It Happened One Night* which not only brought him an Academy Award, but also established him as the most popular movie actor in the world. After indeed lucking into that first box-office hit, Gable continued his streak in movie after movie. When it was time to cast Rhett Butler in *Gone With the Wind,* luck took a back seat to Gable, for he was established as an actor and the public gave a unanimous yell for Gable. No one else but Clark Gable would suit the public, and besides, only Gable had the guts and finesse to capture the dashing Rhett Butler. Maybe if someone else had played Rhett Butler the movie would still have been a success, but how can a string of successful movies make one man a legend?

The student loosely links *agent* (Gable), *act* (a successful career), and *means* (luck). His focus seems to be on *means,* the part luck played in Gable's success. He never explains the lucky circumstances to which he says Gable owed his popularity. Rather he talks about Gable's performance in *It Happened One Night* and his role as Rhett Butler, ending the paragraph with a seemingly unrelated question. While the student mentions *luck* twice, he never shows how luck was a *means* bringing about Gable's success. Therefore, his paragraph lacks unity—it does not define the feature of agency (means) that the topic sentence mentions.

Had the student written agent prose, his topic sentence might have contributed to rather than detracted from paragraph unity. The expletive *it* stands in the subject slot, encouraging him to use a weak form of *to be* as a predicate. His wording is imprecise—"luck was a major part of Clark Gable's success." If he had chosen an agent as a sentence subject—for example Clark Gable—he could have made his topic sentence more specific. Also, if he had narrowed his focus to *means,* perhaps to Gable's first lucky break, he could have defined this feature of agency much more thoroughly. He would not have succumbed to sweeping, unconnected, general statements about Gable's overall success. He might have written:

> Clark Gable owed his early success to the lucky circumstances that got him his role in *It Happened One Night*.

This more specific topic sentence would also help the student unify his paragraph by forcing him to describe these lucky circumstances. The topic sentence would force him to maintain his narrowed focus on *means*. The rewritten, unified paragraph with its limited focus might look like this:

> Clark Gable owed his early success to the lucky circumstances that got him his role in *It Happened One Night*. At the time that Frank Capra, the director, was casting the picture, Gable was out of favor with the MGM bosses. He had balked at the banal, limited roles they gave him and began to drink because he was depressed. As a result, he had received bad publicity and damaged the star image that the MGM public relations people were building for him. To discipline their star, MGM executives ordered him to accept the lead in Capra's film, which they considered unimportant. Gable reluctantly took the lead and consequently won the best actor Oscar in 1935. The unimportant *It Happened One Night* also brought Oscars to Claudette Colbert (best actress) and Capra (best director) and was named best picture of the year by the academy. Gable inadvertently took the one role that could give the greatest boost to his fledgling career.

Because the topic sentence links *luck* with the one *act* it was responsible for—Gable's getting the role in *It Happened One Night*—we have no trouble unifying the paragraph by keeping to the narrowed focus.

We return to our opening question: How can agent prose help you write better paragraphs? If your topic sentences use agent prose, link features of agency, and focus on one of those features, they should lead to a paragraph that is developed and unified. Your paragraph will be developed because it will thoroughly define a feature of agency by using as many concrete details, examples, and explanations as possible. Your paragraph will be unified because it will subordinate all its information to that one feature of agency and never stray from it.

Exercise 5

Look at the following paragraph. In every sentence, the writer uses the words *gun* or *handgun* and has seemingly achieved unity. But she hasn't. Write a short critique of this inductive paragraph in which you analyze why it does not lead to a topic sentence, or, in other words, why it lacks unity.

A criminal makes a deliberate choice of a gun over another weapon. Guns are quick and easy to use. In a fit of anger, which is when most murders are committed, guns are often too easily accessible. Guns are deadly accurate; the fatality rate of knife wounds is about one-fifth that of gun wounds. There are approximately 35 million handguns in private ownership in this country and because handguns are available people use them. Unless new regulations to reduce this huge number of handguns available are put into effect, the United States can expect the upward trend of gun-caused accidents, suicides, assaults, and murders to lead eventually to the point where the United States will become a lawless society.

Exercise 6

Study the following two paragraphs, both of which lack unity. First determine at which point the writers stray from the focus provided by the topic sentence. Then rewrite the paragraphs, omitting irrelevant particulars and adding relevant ones when necessary.

1. The foreign study program at Ohio University provides an inexpensive way for a student to visit Europe. The program's costs are no more than the regular costs students incur each quarter when they pay for tuition, housing, meals, and medical insurance. Plus, a short break of one week is given to the students at the end of the quarter for traveling. Parents need not worry because a group of licensed faculty supervise the students. These teachers are in total control of the students' academic and social activities. The whole quarter can be so much fun for students who see new sights and meet many new friends.

2. Hollywood producers seem to think that the American public prefers a steady diet of cheap horror movies. Following the success in the late seventies of *Halloween* and *Alien,* both well made, we have been bombarded with shoddy imitations such as *Maniac, My Bloody Valentine, Alligator, Bloody Beach,* and *Prom Night.* What ever happened to the great horror films of yesteryear? *Psycho* was a classic: Who can forget the shower scene in which Tony Perkins, dressed as an old woman, stabs Janet Leigh to death while Hitchcock focuses on her surprised, dying eyes? The latest horror flick shows people whose heads

explode and whose eyes turn white and atrophy. Surely we deserve better.

EXERCISE 7

Look at the following sets of introductory and first body paragraphs. All these paragraphs suffer from agentless prose which leads to problems with unity and development. Choose one of the topics and write your own introductory and first body paragraphs on it. Try first to give agents to all the sentences in the original paragraphs. See if this helps you define your topic with precision and helps you discover how to develop it.

Set 1: High School Graduation

A senior's year is filled with anticipation for the great day called graduation day. Although it is a sad occasion, it will always be remembered as a time of joy. Some graduates are busy saying good-bye to their fellow classmates. Others are planning and looking forward to the most memorable event that is about to occur, which is graduation weekend. That special weekend will never be forgotten.

The last night of my graduation weekend was the best. My friends and I had steak and potato dinners. We have a friend who had access to twelve steaks from The Red Lobster, his place of employment. He cooked the plump and juicy steaks outside on the grill. We also baked potatoes and had salad which made the dinner even more delicious.

Set 2: Bicycles on Campus

Many college students use bicycles as a means of transportation around the college campus. Using a bicycle is faster than driving an automobile. Students rush every day to make class on time. There are many good uses for a bicycle on a college campus; however, bicycles can also be a danger.

One example of a danger involves pedestrians. Pedestrians tend to walk in front of bicycles as they are coming down the street. The pedestrian is walking on the sidewalk and may decide to cross the street. The bicyclist, going at a much faster pace, does not realize the pedestrian has decided to cross the street. The pedestrian does not look, and the bicyclist, going faster than necessary, cannot stop. As a result the bicyclist and the pedestrian collide.

Making the Paragraph Readable: Sentence Variety

Development and unity are great virtues in any paragraph. But the best paragraphs have one other important characteristic—sentence variety. In your writing, you should use all the sentence forms—loose, parallel, and periodic—rather than rely on just one. In this way you can keep your prose from becoming monotonous and your readers from becoming bored. Therefore, after you have written your paragraphs according to the principles of agent prose, you should go over them at least once to check for sentence variety. Make sure that they read well, that you don't have a simpleminded "Run, Spot, run, see Jane jump" progression of short, loose sentences. Make sure that you don't have too many complicated periodic or parallel sentences that can make your prose tiresome and impenetrable. Look, for example, at this paragraph from Martin Luther King's "Letter from Birmingham Jail" in which he achieves sentence variety.

> Oppressed people cannot remain oppressed forever (*loose*). The yearning for freedom eventually manifests itself, and that is what has happened to the American Negro (*loose*). Something within has reminded him of his birthright of freedom, and something without has reminded him that it can be gained (*parallel*). Consciously or unconsciously, he has been caught up by the Zeitgeist, and with his black brothers of Africa and his brown and yellow brothers of Asia, South America, and the Caribbean, the United States Negro is moving with a sense of great urgency toward the promised land of racial justice (*parallel*). If one recognizes this vital urge that has engulfed the Negro community, one should readily understand why public demonstrations are taking place (*periodic*). The Negro has many pent-up resentments and latent frustrations, and he must release them (*loose*). So let him march; let him make prayer pilgrimages to the city hall; let him go on freedom rides—and try to understand why he must do so (*parallel*). If his repressed emotions are not released in non-violent ways, they will seek expression through violence; this is not a threat but a fact of history (*periodic*). So I have not said to my people, "Get rid of your discontent"(*loose*). Rather, I have tried to say that this normal and healthy discontent can be channeled into the creative outlet of non-violent direct action (*loose*). And now this approach is being termed extremist (*loose*). (*Why We Can't Wait,* New York: Harper and Row, 1963)

A paragraph that lacks sentence variety makes us notice the way it is written. Because its sentence progression is choppy, singsong, or repetitive, we are conscious of poor writing, even if the paragraph is grammatically correct, unified, and developed. Study for example the following paragraph on roller-skating:

> (1) Roller-skating is relaxing, yet challenging. (2) Roller skaters claim that skating eliminates depression and anxiety. (3) Skaters also can release their tensions in the free movements of roller-skating. (4) By increasing their speed, skaters can get out their frustrations. (5) Through freedom and speed regulation, skaters can express their emotions. (6) Skating is a relaxing sport. (7) Skating can also be challenging as well as relaxing. (8) Skaters find a challenge in learning new tricks and disco steps. (9) Skaters need coordination and practice to learn new skating moves. (10) Disco has been an important influence on skating: many new skating moves are the result of adding the disco beat to roller-skating.

Without doubt, the paragraph is boring. In consists of a succession of loose sentences broken only by two periodic sentences midway through it (sentences 4 and 5). Note the repetitive sentence subjects—*roller-skating, roller skaters, skaters* (five times), *skating,* and *disco*—and short sentence length; seven of the sentences are between eight and eleven words long. This repetitive structure makes the paragraph tiresome to read. But the problems with this collection of loose sentences go beyond their repetitive sound. Loose sentences do not allow you to subordinate one idea to another or to establish causal relations. A series of loose sentences can only describe an event, not interpret or analyze it. If the writer had reread this paragraph and noted the predominance of loose sentences, she could have recombined her phrases and clauses with sentence variety as her goal. She might have used pronouns to eliminate those repetitive sentence subjects. But above all, she could have set about defining major features of roller-skating to which she could then subordinate details. Look at this rewrite:

> Roller-skating is relaxing yet challenging. It is relaxing because the demanding movements it requires help skaters release tension. As a result, they can eliminate the depression and anxiety these tensions cause. Skaters can also express their emotions by regulating their speed. If they feel energetic, they can skate rapidly, using all their muscles; if they feel content, they can move slowly and freely. But skating can be challenging as well as relaxing. For example, disco dancing has greatly

> influenced skating, introducing many new moves. To learn these moves and perform them to the disco beat, skaters have to work long hours on their coordination and timing. They indeed face a challenge.

Clearly, this rewrite reads much more smoothly; its sentences do not call attention to themselves. The most important thing to note is how the rewritten paragraph subordinates descriptions of roller-skating to a discussion of its benefits—mental health and relaxation. The sentences flow into one another because the student used transitions (*because, as a result, also, as well as, for example*), pronouns, and repetition of key words (*relaxing, challenging*). She also varied sentence form and length to eliminate the "singsong" structure.

EXERCISE 8

Look at the following paragraphs, and indicate which sentences are loose, which periodic, which parallel. Then rewrite the paragraphs to increase their sentence variety. Why do you think the first paragraph is so boring? As a model for your work, look at the revisions made by the student on her paragraph on roller skating.

1. Some students participate in intramurals through the dormitory league. This league is divided into three parts—men's, women's and co-rec teams. The dorm league is composed of teams whose students live in individual dorms on campus. Any student living in a dorm can enter a team in the league. Usually, students living on a single floor can sign up for a sport. Any person living on the floor may participate, including resident assistants. Sometimes not enough students are interested in their respective divisions. For co-rec teams men's floors will generally enter a team with students from its floor and students from its sister floor. Some dormitory floors have both men and women in separate wings; therefore these floors contain both male and female students for all three divisions in the league. For team names most floors enter their dorm name along with some sort of nickname. For instance, third-floor Simpson enters a team under the name of Simpson Strikers and first-floor Graham uses Graham Crackers.

2. During the seventies "The Midnight Special" was a contemporary musical television show late on Saturday nights. The majority of the viewers were older teenagers and younger adults. The show was built upon a rock and roll format. The bands consisted of both well-known groups and new groups obtaining

exposure to the greater rock audiences. The Doobie Brothers were new material on the show in 1973. As the show got older, the groups got better. The material that was labeled new usually obtained public acknowledgement in a year or two. This format lasted until early 1978. Disco format replaced rock in as little as a week. The concert-style seating was replaced by a large dance floor. All of the lights were rearranged. Wolfman Jack, who appeared in the rock and roll film *American Graffiti,* now sat high above the dance floor in a disk jockey's booth. The effect of this takeover was expressed in my school. My friends were all amazed and disappointed. Rock and roll Saturday nights were dead.

EXERCISE 9

In this exercise we ask you again to write agent prose as a means of effectively revising your work. The three sets of introductions and first body paragraphs that follow all deal with interesting topics. All provide evocative details and stay on topic, but they fail because the writers' agentless prose makes the paragraphs unreadable. Related problems with choppy sentence progression, lack of transitions, and lack of sentence variety also mar the work. Analyze these paragraphs, pinpointing weak sentence subjects, passive or wordy verbs, obscure or awkward diction. Also note places where you can combine sentences for a smoother flow. Then rewrite the paragraphs.

Set 1: Advertising, an important factor in the economy, is an industry that will always possess the nation's attention. Advertisement firms are constantly creating new ideas and gimmicks to sell to the public. One of the most widespread uses of advertising is seen in magazine articles. Magazines tend to be the encyclopedias of good taste and dress for most Americans today. As a result, magazines are a tool that many profiteers choose to display their products. In order to sell more products, dealers will use sensuality as a popular device. Such articles as Hanes, Jovan, and Breck shampoo all show that the uses of sexual overtones in advertising are prevalent in today's America.

Sexual overtones play a large part in the selling of Hanes pantyhose. The Hanes gimmick line—"Gentlemen prefer Hanes"—is supposed to lead a woman to unconsciously believe she needs this product to be desired. The type of desirability that is advertised is often very unrealistic. How many women stand in a train station, wear five-hundred-dollar outfits, and hike their skirts up to their thighs while men look on? Not too many. This is the kind of image that the Hanes advertisement firms try to portray. This picture of the "perfect" woman is described as being perfect only because she is wearing their product. American women, through social pressures and competition, are expected to believe that they can be flawless with this product.

Set 2: Television is detrimental to the minds that watch it. Television programs are not as wholesome and educational as they used to be. The quality of television has declined to the point that viewers are subjected to programs that contain too much sex. Sex plays a definite role in many programs today. Producers and directors have discovered many methods to use the human body to attract attention. Many types of shows use sex as an attraction. Police drama, soap operas, and comedy use sex as a feature of their shows.

The police drama, "Charlie's Angels," uses sex as a main feature of the show. Three young, beautiful actresses are utilized to capture the audience's attention. The three actresses play private investigators employed by a man named Charlie Townsend. They are sent on undercover assignments. The assignments usually require them to wear bikinis or tight-fitting dresses. The detectives supposedly rely on their abilities as policewomen, but in reality they use their sex appeal to catch the criminal. The detectives use their beauty to entice the criminal, who is usually a male, to give himself up. This obvious use of sex to grab the attention of the viewer is degrading.

Set 3: Rock and roll music has created more social and moral change than any other type of music. Since rock and roll has traditionally attracted teenagers, they are more open-minded to accept the basic lyrics of rock. This willingness to accept the music as a way of life has resulted in a complete change of ideals from twenty years ago. The three main categories of change are in the dress style, the "sex, drugs, and rock and roll" motto, and the increase in violent lyrics and reactions to those lyrics.

Within the past twenty years, the fashion-conscious rockers have changed their taste in clothing, accessories, and hairstyles. For example, during the Beatles' era, long hair, jeans, T-shirts, and flip-flops became the accepted way to dress. However, this lasted only a decade, as disco made its debut. No longer was sloppiness the main diet in fashion. It was replaced by rayon dresses, nylons, heels, loads of makeup, intricate hairstyles with hair spray, three-piece suits, silk shirts, leather

Guccis, and of course, gold jewelry. Soon to follow the glamour of the discotheque, a raw cult evolved labeled "punk rock." The "punks" brought in layered hair, strange hair colors, and odd accessories. Much of the dress reflected the Beatles' era. They wore the infamous safety pins, badges, faded jeans, T-shirts, leather jackets with zippers, and sneakers. The female punk brought heavy eye makeup back into circulation. "New wave" was a mixture of the disco and punk looks combined, therefore it was a more cultured fad. Many clothing articles were common in both sects—such as spandex pants, heels, leather jackets, T-shirts, and badges.

Paragraph Content

In the previous section we have discussed the *structure* of paragraphs; we have noted that most of the paragraphs you write will take one of three forms—inductive, deductive, or a combination. And we have described and discussed isolated paragraphs that—because of the nature and placement of their topic sentences—demonstrate these forms. But we can also talk about paragraphs in terms of their content. If you make a statement which you support with examples or if your whole paragraph develops one example, you have an *illustration* paragraph. If you discuss the similarities and/or differences between two items, you have a *comparison* paragraph. If you examine the effects of a particular cause or the cause of particular effects, you have an *analysis* paragraph. And if you place your subject into a specific class, you have either a *definition* or a *classification* paragraph. These paragraphs can take any of the three *forms* (inductive, deductive, or combination) that we have discussed; all paragraphs, of course, require unity and development.

In Chapter III, we will discuss five models for short essays—illustration, comparison, analysis, classification, and definition; the essay models are named for the content which preponderates in them. For example, when you write the short comparison essay, you will probably use only comparison paragraphs; when you write the short illustration essay, your body paragraphs will develop examples that prove your point. Beginning with illustration, let's look specifically at four paragraphs. (We will treat definition and classification paragraphs together, since both require placing an object in its class.)

Illustration

Illustration simply means supporting through examples. To understand how an illustration paragraph works, we must first briefly consider the kind of essay in which it will appear. To follow the illustration essay model, we suggest that you make a general statement, or thesis, in your introduction and support it with at least three specific examples. The thesis states the central idea of the essay; each body paragraph develops one of the examples. For an illustration essay on Gerald Ford's 1976 presidential campaign, a student wrote the following thesis statement for her introduction.

> Unfortunately, the Gerald Ford campaign in 1976 showed that presidential campaigns remain inefficient, despite the huge sums of money that candidates spend.

To support her general statement, the student cites and develops, in three body paragraphs, three examples of the inefficiency she witnessed as a campaign worker for Ford. Here is the first.

> The Reagan-Connally speeches are a good example of the inefficient foul-ups that plagued the Ford campaign. Ronald Reagan was not making many television advertisements for President Ford, and the speech he was to make in San Francisco would be aired over many stations throughout the western states and was thought to be quite important for Ford's reelection. All speeches were prepared at campaign headquarters in Washington, D.C., and wired over the telephone to the person giving the speech. The worker assigned to wire Reagan's speech sent it by mistake to John Connally in Austin, Texas, and he sent the Connally speech to Reagan. Reagan noticed the error halfway through the speech when he began talking about aid to cattle ranchers. John Connally told his fellow Texans that Ford would take whatever measures were necessary to insure the protection of their property through federal aid after any earthquakes.

Note that the student uses her topic sentence to focus on the *act* that illustrates campaign inefficiency. She links the topic sentence with the thesis by repeating the key word—*inefficient*. The rest of the sentences in the paragraph further define the *act*. This illustration paragraph is *deductive*—the topic sentence begins the paragraph and is followed by particulars. You can, however, use any of the three paragraph forms—inductive, deductive, or combination—in illustration paragraphs.

This illustration paragraph occurs in an illustration essay, but you can use illustration paragraphs in any essay you write. For example, the student who wrote the following illustration paragraph used it as an introduction to an essay calling for improvements in nursing home care. He describes an *act*—the neglect and death of an elderly patient—that illustrates his point. He uses the *inductive* form; the topic sentence, which serves as the thesis of the essay, draws a conclusion about the *scenes*—nursing homes—based on his description of the *act*.

> On June 19, 1976, an eighty-two-year-old man was found dead on the floor of his nursing home bedroom. A coroner's examination revealed that the man had suffered a fatal heart attack. The coroner also found filth and bacterial infection on a huge boil on the man's left thigh, evidence that the man had not been bathed or examined in several weeks. Further investigation showed that the man had not been checked on by his assigned nurse in over four days and had not been examined by a physician in five weeks. This shocking case history represents the nearly five thousand reports every year of mistreated or neglected residents in privately operated nursing homes. An extensive study by the national consumer organization Right to Quality shows that nursing homes provide inadequate care and unsanitary conditions.

Of course, illustration paragraphs can discuss several examples rather than just one. Look at the following paragraph from George Orwell's "Politics and the English Language."

> In our time, political speech and writing are largely the defence of the indefensible. . . . Thus political language has to consist largely of euphemism, question-begging and sheer cloudy vagueness. Defenceless villages are bombarded from the air, the inhabitants driven out into the countryside, the cattle machine-gunned, the huts set on fire with incendiary bullets: this is called *pacification*. Millions of peasants are robbed of their farms and sent trudging along the roads with no more than they can carry: this is called *transfer of population* or *rectification of frontiers*. People are imprisoned for years without trial, or shot in the back of the neck or sent to die of scurvy in Arctic lumber camps: this is called *elimination of unreliable elements*. Such phraseology is needed if one wants to name things without calling up mental pictures of them. Consider for instance some comfortable English professor defending Russian totalitarianism. He cannot say

outright, "I believe in killing off your opponents when you can get good results by doing so". Probably, therefore, he will say something like this:

> While freely conceding that the Soviet régime exhibits certain features which the humanitarian may be inclined to deplore, we must, I think, agree that a certain curtailment of the right to political opposition is an unavoidable concomitant of transitional periods, and that the rigours which the Russian people have been called upon to undergo have been amply justified in the sphere of concrete achievement.

Orwell chose to open with his topic sentence (deductive form) and use a series of examples to develop and support it. In the topic sentence, he links *scene* (our time) and *acts* (speech and writing). His *agents*—politicians—are implied. He focuses on *acts,* defining them in general terms—they are "the defence of the indefensible." He illustrates this with selections from actual political speeches and writings. Orwell ends the paragraph with a striking summarizing example; the typical academic justification for brutality totally obscures harsh realities through abstract, Latinate diction.

As Orwell points out, you are the agent in the writing process—it's up to you to create clear prose that means something. When writing illustration paragraphs, you must decide whether to focus on one example (as in the nursing home paragraph) or to use several examples (as Orwell does). You must also decide whether to use inductive, deductive, or combined form. You must judge which paragraph form will be most appropriate in relation to both the essay as a whole and the part the paragraph plays in it. Do you want to state your generalization first or lead up to it? Do you want to orient your readers with a minor topic sentence, give examples, and then draw a conclusion in your major topic sentence? If the student who wrote the nursing home paper had decided to set a scene for his readers first, he might have used a minor topic sentence and therefore a *combined* rather than an inductive form. He might have written:

> Investigators of privately operated nursing homes have uncovered many grim realities over the past few years. On June 19, 1976, an eighty-two-year-old man was found dead on the floor of his nursing home bedroom. A coroner's examination revealed that the man had suffered a fatal heart attack. The coroner also found filth and bacterial infection on a huge boil on the man's left thigh, evidence that the man had not been bathed or examined in several weeks. Further investigation showed that the man had not been checked on by his assigned

> nurse in over four days and had not been examined by a physician in five weeks. This shocking case history represents the nearly five thousand reports every year of mistreated or neglected residents in privately operated nursing homes. An extensive study by the national consumer organization Right to Quality shows that most nursing homes provide inadequate care and unsanitary conditions.

Here the minor topic sentence introduces us to the *scene* and leads us into the example as knowing readers.

Examples provide powerful particulars when you want to develop and support the idea in your topic sentence. Examples force you to be concrete, to create mental pictures. The student's description of the huge, dirty boil on the elderly man's leg certainly does more to convince us of the neglect he received than either an abstract account, words like *real bad* or *terrible,* or unevocative statistics about the general state of nursing home patients. Therefore, the illustration paragraph is valuable and you will use it often in all kinds of essays.

Comparison

The comparison paragraph also will prove very useful to you; like illustration paragraphs, they are a versatile tool. You will use comparison paragraphs in many longer essays as well as in the short comparison essay that we will talk about in the next chapter. When you write a comparison paragraph, your content obviously consists of either similarities or differences between two features of agency—two *agents,* two *scenes,* two *acts,* two *motives,* or two *means.*

Again, you have many variations to choose from. In deductive paragraphs you can state the basic comparison in your topic sentence, probably by linking features of agency and focusing on similarities or differences between them. Then you can devote half of your paragraph to defining one feature and the other half to defining the comparable one. Composition teachers call this the *divided pattern.* This pattern appears in the following paragraph which is part of an essay that compares the way two different professors teach the same kind of accounting course. The student begins with her topic sentence, which links *agents* (Professors A and B) with their *acts* (presenting material). Her focus is on their *acts* and the differences between them.

> In addition, Professor A and Professor B present material differently. As a student, I did not enjoy Professor A's class because he was a poor lecturer. He spoke in a monotone which did

nothing to help the somewhat boring lecture material. In presenting the material, he tried to cover everything in the text during class. Consequently, he did only half a job on everything, rather than an in-depth job on one particularly difficult area. I learned more from the text than I did from his lectures. Professor B, whose booming voice is quite the opposite of Professor A's monotone, covered in class only the areas in the text that were vague or extremely difficult. Therefore, he used class time much more efficiently than Professor A. I left his class understanding everything that he covered. I did not have to go home and sort through the text to make sense of the lecture as I did after Professor A's discussions.

This student could also have chosen to write this deductive comparison paragraph in what is called the *alternating pattern*. That is, she could have immediately countered her points about Professor A with contrasting points about Professor B. Keeping the same topic sentence, she would have alternated between the two throughout the paragraph.

In addition, Professor A and Professor B present material differently. As a student, I did not enjoy Professor A's class because he was a poor lecturer. He spoke in a monotone which did nothing to help the somewhat boring lecture material. Professor B's booming voice was quite the opposite of Professor A's monotone. Because Professor B seemed enthusiastic and interested in the material, he kept his students alert. Professor A tried to cover everything in the text during class. Consequently, he did only half a job on everything, rather than an in-depth job on one particular area. Professor B covered in class only the areas in the text that were vague or extremely difficult; therefore, he used class time much more efficiently than Professor A. After Professor A's class, I had to go home and sort through the text to make sense of his lectures, while Professor B's lectures helped me make sense of the text.

For another paragraph in the same essay, this student chose to place her topic sentence last (inductive form) but still used the *divided* pattern. She uses the paragraph to define her *agents* (Professors A and B) and describes their contrasting appearances and ways of approaching instruction—*acts*.

Professor A, who taught me the first course, could not relate well to his students, perhaps because he was in his fifties. I found identifying with him difficult. Because he dressed in light, solid-colored cotton shirts and knit slacks, Professor A looked more like a businessman than a college instructor. He

> arrived early for class, and before the bell rang, he closed the door and immediately began lecturing. Professor B, who is teaching me the second course now, always wears faded Levi's, a T-shirt, and tennis shoes. Because he is young and dresses so informally, he could easily be mistaken for a student. Like many students, Professor B has the unbusinesslike habit of being two to ten minutes late every day. Because of the casual atmosphere in his class, Professor B can relate well to his students. Professor A's coolness and distance did not foster learning, while Professor B's informality did.

If the student had used the *alternating* pattern, she would simply have needed to rearrange her points, giving information about Professor B's age as soon as she gave it about Professor A's and doing the same for their clothing and promptness. The alternating pattern is particularly appropriate if you have clear areas of contrast. But if the differences or similarities between the two features of agency are not clear-cut, not easy to break down into clear points of comparison, then you might prefer the divided pattern. The following paragraph discusses changes that a fan has perceived in the game of baseball.

> When we were children and my cousin and I worshipped the Chicago White Sox, the game of baseball was quite different from the game we know today. Our heroes—Minnie Minoso, Luis Aparicio, Nellie Fox, Jim Landis—played for years with the Sox. They *were* the Sox, in fact. We knew at the start of each season what we could expect from them; our dreams were attached to well-loved, familiar faces. Today we are no longer Sox fans or fans of any other particular team for that matter. Over the years we watched sadly while the Sox disposed of key players because of bizarre trades or contract disputes. We could no longer develop affection for specific players—the revolving door policy had them coming and going too quickly—or identify with a stable team. We think the sad changes in the Sox reflect sweeping changes in the game itself. Free agency, arbitration, and perpetual trading have destroyed the souls of many more teams than the Sox.

Obviously, this student's thoughts about baseball then and now would be difficult to break down into clear points of contrast. He is talking about feelings and attitudes. The *divided* pattern allows him to trace changes in the "essence" of the game. Note that the student uses the *combined* form here. He begins with a minor topic sentence that identifies the *agents* (him and his cousin) and their *act* (worshipping the White Sox). He focuses on the basic contrast—baseball then and now (a *scene* that changes). He concludes the paragraph with the major topic sentence, which sums up the essence of the change. Since this paragraph serves as an introduction, the topic sentence leads to natural transitions by suggesting topics for subsequent body paragraphs—*free agency, arbitration,* and *perpetual trading.*

A student writing a comparison of *Jaws* and *The Exorcist* uses the *combined* form with the *alternating* pattern in his first paragraph. His thesis states that the two films, although they seem completely different, actually share similar situations, characters, and resolutions. In his first body paragraph, he focuses on the similar situations with which both films deal.

> In both *Jaws* and *The Exorcist,* an evil force preys upon innocent people. In *Jaws* the evil force is a great white shark that snacks on bathers at a seaside resort. In *The Exorcist* the evil force is Satan himself; he decides to possess a young girl and forces her into all kinds of unnatural and grotesque actions. Despite the dissimilarities—one an actual animal and the other a supernatural being lacking any stable physical form—both the shark and the devil represent forces that people cannot control; these forces terrify us. Both the shark and the devil strike unexpectedly and choose their particular victims for no apparent reason. Although aware of the presence of these forces, people cannot predict attacks or defend themselves from them. The young girl in *The Exorcist* can no more understand what has happened than the quickly disappearing victims in *Jaws,* and this incomprehensibility is the source of the terror that both movies evoke.

Using the alternating pattern, the student focuses on the comparable elements in the *acts* the films portray—both show evil forces preying on innocents. He frequently talks about both films in the same sentence. His minor topic sentence identifies the films and the acts they depict. His closing major topic sentence draws a conclusion about the reason these acts are terrifying.

Analysis

In analysis paragraphs you will most frequently examine the relationship between causes and effects. In a deductive analysis paragraph, your topic sentence will identify a central cause whose effects the rest of the paragraph describes; or it will identify a central effect whose causes the rest of the paragraph explores. In an inductive analysis paragraph—one which concludes with a topic sentence—your topic sentence will describe an effect to which the causes identified earlier in the paragraph have led; or it will describe a cause to which the effects identified earlier in the paragraph are owing. If this seems confusing, you need only remember that in deductive paragraphs the conclusion comes *first* with supporting details following, whether the conclusion is a *cause* or an *effect.* In inductive paragraphs, the details *lead up to* a conclusion.

In terms of the pentad, an effect will most likely be a *scene* or an *act;* a cause most likely will be an *act* or an *agent*. An analysis that tries to discover causes is basically concerned with *motive* and *means*. The following examples should clarify these descriptions. Note that the two paragraphs, which treat the same topic in slightly different ways, focus on an effect—the *act* of Jim Cox and his crew stopping work to watch "Guiding Light." The cause (*motive*) is a feeling of relaxation and relief about their own troubles, which seem minor in comparison to those of the show's heroine. The first paragraph is *deductive,* beginning with the end effect and moving through a discussion of the causes; the second paragraph is *inductive,* beginning with the causes and moving to an effect.

> 1. At three o'clock every afternoon, all work stops at Jim Cox's busy garage as Jim and the other mechanics pause to watch "Guiding Light." Jim instituted the break over a year ago when he discovered that after watching the show, his mechanics were relaxed, happy, and ready to work. Since "Guiding Light" recounts an almost endless litany of suffering and woe, one might wonder how it achieves this effect. Consider, for example, the life of Rita Bauer, the show's heroine. She has been on trial for murder, had an affair with the villainous Roger, been raped by Roger, fallen in love with Ed, married Ed, had an affair with Greg, gotten pregnant, wondered who the father was, moved out on Ed, considered an abortion, been kidnapped by Roger, and lost her baby. Jim Cox and his crew feel that problems with exhaust manifolds, clogged carburetors, and engine timing pale in comparison with Rita's. As they watch her, they feel a sense of relief about their own troubles and are invigorated.
>
> 2. Each day on "Guiding Light" something new happens to Rita Bauer. Rita has been on trial for murder, had an affair with the villainous Roger, been raped by Roger, fallen in love with Ed, married Ed, had an affair with Greg, gotten pregnant, wondered who the father was, moved out on Ed, considered an abortion, been kidnapped by Roger, and lost her baby. Throughout all this, Rita has conferred extensively with a sex therapist but still cannot seem to find the secret to

happiness and fulfillment. Her perpetual problems interest viewers all over the country. But perhaps her most unusual group of fans work at Jim Cox's busy garage. Jim and his mechanics pause every day at three o'clock to watch "Guiding Light." Jim finds that Rita's travails make problems with exhaust manifolds, clogged carburetors, and engine timing pale in comparison. After watching the show, he and his men are relaxed, happy, and ready to work. Since Jim instituted the "Rita Bauer break," productivity is up.

The next two paragraphs focus on a cause for the success of *Star Wars*—George Lucas's demand for excellence at all levels of production (*act*). The effects of his demand for excellence were unusual technical tricks, creative makeup, a compelling musical score, and expert editing. The first paragraph is *deductive;* its topic sentence states the cause, linking *agent* (Lucas) to *act* (the demand for excellence). The subsequent sentences in the paragraph explain the effects of this cause by defining Lucas's coagents and their contributing acts. The second paragraph is *inductive;* it first describes the effects and then concludes with the topic sentence that sums up the cause.

1. *Star Wars'* mastermind George Lucas demanded excellence from every one of his production heads, supervising each of them and synthesizing their efforts. John Dykstra responded to Lucas's challenge by creating special effects that won an Academy Award. Dykstra's robots, laser-shooting spaceships, air-cushioned car, space-age chess game with projected images, and looming Death Star amazed audiences. Makeup man Stuart Freeborn's striking monsters—Chewbacca and the flashing-eyed ghouls who kidnap C-3P0 and R2-D2, for example—also met Lucas's standards and complemented Dykstra's technical miracles. John Williams worked with Lucas to provide an Oscar-winning musical score, which never allowed audiences to relax. It recreated in sound the mood of the movie's visual images. Lucas expertly synthesized the work of these and other production heads; he used fast-paced, slick editing to blend characterization, action, technical effects, and music into an entertaining whole.

2. John Dykstra's special effects for the movie *Star Wars* set new standards for technical wizardry in film; his robots, laser-shooting spaceships, air-cushioned car, space-age chess game with projected images, and looming Death Star amazed audiences who had never seen the future in quite this way before. For his innovations Dykstra won an Academy Award. Equally exciting

> was the work of makeup man Stuart Freeborn. His striking monsters—Chewbacca and the flashing-eyed ghouls who kidnap C-3P0 and R2-D2, for example—complement Dykstra's technical miracles. John Williams's Oscar-winning score upheld the standards of achievement set by Dykstra and Freeborn. Williams recreated in sound the mood of the movie's visual images and never allowed audiences to relax. The mastermind behind all these virtuoso performances, director George Lucas, demanded excellence from each of his production heads, supervised their efforts, and then through expert editing synthesized them to create an entertaining film.

Note that although the student used the same facts when he transformed his deductive paragraph into an inductive one, he had to change the transitions and sentence lengths to meet the demands of the inductive form. Remember that the inductive form requires you to capture your reader's attention with interesting particulars; you must then provide strong links between sentences so that your readers move easily from particular to particular. Only if your readers can follow your thought progression will they understand your concluding topic sentence, your central point. In the second paragraph, the student writer had to present the effects in a detailed, interesting way so that his readers would progress through them to discover their underlying cause—Lucas's *act* of demanding excellence from his production heads and himself.

The deductive form presents a different challenge. It forces you to make your topic sentence specific and interesting so that readers will want to explore the supporting particulars. (Only dedicated composition teachers read on when faced with vague, unfocused topic sentences.) In the first paragraph, the student writer had to focus on an *agent* (Lucas) and his *acts* (demanding excellence and supervising and synthesizing the efforts of his production heads). Had the student written a wordy, passive, abstract topic sentence like the following, he never would have inspired readers to explore the effect of Lucas's demands.

> *Star Wars* was worked on by a number of capable people and particularly by George Lucas who did a really great job overall.

Introduced by a weak topic sentence like this one, the entire deductive paragraph would have failed.

The analysis paragraph also allows you to use the combined form. If, for example, you are emphasizing cause, you might use the minor topic sentence to state a cause either partially or in very general terms. You then might describe its effects, building toward your closing major topic sentence which would describe the cause completely and specifically. X.J. Kennedy writes a causal analysis paragraph in *combined* form in his essay "Who Killed King Kong?"

> Kong has, first of all, the attraction of being manlike. His simian nature gives him one huge advantage over giant ants and walking vegetables in that an audience may conceivably identify with him. Kong's appeal has the quality that established the Tarzan series as American myth—for what man doesn't secretly image himself a huge hairy howler against whom no other monster has a chance? If Tarzan recalls the ape in us, then Kong may well appeal to that great-granddaddy primordial brute from whose tribe we have all deteriorated.

Note that Kennedy uses his minor topic sentence to state an obvious *cause* for our fascination with the film—Kong is manlike. The next two sentences explore the effects of his similarity to people—we can identify with him, and we long to be like him. Kennedy uses his major topic sentence to elaborate a far more subtle cause than the first—Kong appeals to the "primordial brute" in all of us. As we said earlier, an analysis that tries to discover *causes* (as does Kennedy's) is inherently concerned with *motive*. In this particular paragraph, Kennedy examines one *motive* we might have for watching the film.

You can also use the combined form with analysis paragraphs if you use the minor topic sentence to ask a question about the cause or effect. You can then answer this question in subsequent sentences and sum up your conclusion in the major topic sentence. Look at the following example from Betty Rollin's "Motherhood: Who Needs It?"

> If motherhood isn't instinctive, when and why, then, was the Motherhood Myth born? Until recently, the entire question of maternal motivation was academic. Sex, like it or not, meant babies. Not that there haven't been a lot of interesting contraceptive tries. But until the creation of the diaphragm in the 1880's, the birth of babies was largely unavoidable. And, generally speaking, nobody seemed to mind. For one thing, people tend to be sort of good sports about what seems inevitable. For another, in the past, the population needed beefing up. Mortality rates were high, and agricultural cultures, particularly, have always needed children to help out. So because it "just happened" and because it was needed, motherhood was assumed to be innate. (*Look,* September 22, 1970)

Rollin asks a question in her minor topic sentence, a question about *cause*—Why was the Motherhood Myth born? In her subsequent sentences, she considers causes: Before birth control people accepted babies as inevitable. In past times and cultures babies beefed up the population and provided help for parents. Then Rollin uses the major topic sentence to summarize the causes she has uncovered and unify the paragraph. In terms of the features of agency, Rollin is questioning *acts* to establish the *means* by which society established the Motherhood Myth. She is also subtly questioning *motives*.

DEFINITION

One last type of paragraph we want to isolate is the definition paragraph. You will use this type of paragraph in classification and definition essays; both require you to place your subject in a specific class and to explain its specific characteristics in relation to other members of its class. When you emphasize the class and its subclasses, you will probably use the classification model. When you emphasize a specific term and wish to define it by placing it in its class, you will probably use the definition model. Even though your emphasis will differ in the two essay models, you can use the same type of paragraph in both—the definition paragraph.

When writing a definition paragraph, you will probably use your topic sentence to place the subject in its class and to focus on some particular characteristics that you will describe in the rest of your paragraph. For example, if you were defining the term *psychosis,* you would first determine the class to which it belongs (probably personality disorders) and then select the specific characteristics that distinguish psychosis from all other members of its class (for example, the fact that psychosis involves an individual's loss of contact with reality). From this focus provided by the topic sentence, you could go on to develop your paragraph, describing in detail the symptoms of this particular personality disorder.

> Psychosis is a personality disorder characterized by the individual's loss of contact with reality. Psychotics become so overburdened with daily conflicts and anxiety that they give up the struggle to cope with everyday life. As a result, they may lapse into a fantasy world or respond to events in the real world with exaggerated emotions. For example, they may imagine voices talking to them in abusive language, or they may respond to constructive criticism with violence. Because

> they have lost touch with reality, many psychotic individuals require hospitalization and/or protective care.

This definition paragraph is in *deductive* form. The topic sentence states the term's class and particular characteristics, and the rest of the sentences develop and support this general definition. However, you can also use the *inductive* form for definition paragraphs; you begin your paragraph by describing the particular characteristics of your term and move toward a final definition in the concluding topic sentence.

> Some people become so overburdened with daily conflicts and anxiety that they give up the struggle to cope with everyday life. As a result, they may lapse into a fantasy world or respond to events in the real world with exaggerated emotions. For example they may imagine voices talking to them in abusive language, or they may respond to constructive criticism with violence. Because they have lost touch with reality, many of these individuals require hospitalization and/or protective care and are labeled psychotic. Psychosis is a personality disorder characterized by the individual's loss of contact with reality.

In the case of definition paragraphs, you must decide, on the basis of your evidence and your audience, whether to proceed inductively or deductively. Are you confident enough in your generalization to open with it (the deductive approach)? If you want to lead your reader to a conclusion with convincing particulars, are you confident enough in the unity and development of your illustrations to leave your generalization for your last sentence (the inductive approach)? If neither the deductive nor inductive form is suitable, an alternative open to you is the *combined* form. You can begin your definition paragraph with a minor topic sentence that introduces the term, follow this with particulars, and then conclude with your major topic sentence in which you place the term in its class and sum up its main characteristics. Your minor topic sentence for the psychosis paragraph might look like this:

> Our society uses the term *psychosis* to describe a specific set of problems.

The combined form lets you orient your readers by stating the term first. Then you can lead your readers through particular characteristics of the term to the concluding definition sentence: "Psychosis is a personality disorder characterized by the individual's loss of contact with reality."

In the next chapter, we will ask you to combine paragraphs by following illustration, comparison, analysis, classification, and definition essay models. You will work to write agent prose, to link features of agency, and to insure that your paragraphs are unified and developed. You will also edit your work with sentence variety in mind. You will, in other words, face the same challenges that we presented to you in isolated paragraphs, only now you will be joining related paragraphs in sequences that the different essay models suggest. Having developed the ability to write good paragraphs, you now stand ready to write good essays. But first, work on one more set of exercises.

EXERCISE 10: Illustration

A. Look at the first paragraph on nursing homes (p. 85) in which the student uses a single illustration to call our attention to a problem and then suggests that the problem is widespread. Using this paragraph as a model, write a paragraph in which you, by means of a provocative illustration, call attention to a problem that you feel some organization or person must remedy. Concentrate on making a transition from your description of the specific case to your claim that the problem is pervasive. Study the last two sentences in the first nursing home paragraph as an example of this kind of transition. As in the first and second nursing home paragraphs (pp. 85–86), write your first paragraph in inductive form and then convert it to combined form.

B. Look at the following list of thesis sentences and choose one which you will then support in a well-developed and unified illustration paragraph. If you want to use only one example in your paragraph, follow the model provided by the paragraph on the 1976 Ford presidential campaign (p. 84). If you want to use several examples, follow the model provided by Orwell (pp. 85–86). Since this paragraph will be a body paragraph, you will probably want to make it deductive, although you could use combined or inductive form too.

1. Baseball players earn entirely too much money.
2. Teaching assistants make better instructors than regular faculty.
3. Disney World is a great tourist attraction because of the variety of activities it offers.

Exercise 11: Comparison

Choose any two competing products, and write a comparison paragraph on their relative merits. Use the divided pattern for your first paragraph; then convert to the alternating pattern. Use as a guide the paragraphs on Professors A and B (pp. 87–88).

Exercise 12: Analysis

A. Choose any currently popular phenomenon, fad, product, or sport. Then write a paragraph in which you analyze the causes of its popularity, moving from most to least obvious. Although you can choose any form you like, the combined form will serve you well in this case. Your first sentence (minor topic sentence) can mention the popularity (the effect). Then after discussing causes, in your major topic sentence you can state the most subtle, important cause.

B. Take a problem in your life—for example, parking hassles, inconvenient bank hours, an inconsiderate roommate or spouse. Then write a paragraph in which you describe its effects. The deductive form is useful in this kind of paragraph. State the cause (the problem) in your topic sentence, and then give particulars about the effects.

Exercise 13: Definition

Choose a term which you, because of your particular expertise in a field, understand, but which others might not—for example, *curve ball, dwell timing, sauté, mulch.* Write a paragraph in which you define this term by placing it in its class and describing its particular characteristics. You might use the first paragraph on psychosis (p. 95) as a model.

III Combining Paragraphs: Essay Organization

Agent prose forces you to say something specific and therefore forces you to think, to trace causes, and to define terms. By reducing the opportunities for vagueness and imprecision, the principles that we have discussed in earlier chapters require you to be an active statement maker who chooses specific subjects and verbs and tests topic sentences for clarity and precision. In this chapter we will discuss ways you can take the meaningful statements that agent prose generates and make them the basis for a complete, well-organized essay.

Finding Something to Say: Brainstorming As a Strategy of Invention

You should always write for one purpose—to make a meaningful statement to a particular audience. When you make a statement, you take on the responsibility of explaining and supporting it to your audience's satisfaction. In a composition class, the statement you make is frequently prompted by an imposed assignment, and the audience is designated by your instructor. This situation may seem artificial to you now, but it is not unlike actual situations you will encounter as you pursue a career. If you eventually go into business, law, accounting, medicine, scientific research, engineering, social work, teaching, or any similar profession, you will often find that you have to write reports, briefs, or articles as part of your work. In such instances your topic and audience are defined by the situation. For example, lawyers will write briefs on particular cases to appeal to certain courts; research scientists will write reports on their findings for other scientists. Therefore, the training you receive now in composition class can prepare you to fulfill demanding writing requirements in your chosen field.

Also, your writing course can help you with a more immediate concern—performing well in other college classes. In any class, instructors may ask you to demonstrate your understanding of course material by having you write papers on assigned topics or answer specific examination questions. In a history class, you may be asked to compare and contrast Hitler's and Napoleon's defeats in Russia or to analyze the causes of America's isolationist stance before the bombing of Pearl Harbor. In a marketing course, you may be asked to explain how you would promote a new product. In biology you may be asked to define the terms *meiosis* and *mitosis* and differentiate between the two. All of these assignments will require you to make definite statements and then explain and support these statements in an orderly essay. Defining and organizing ideas are the very skills you should master in a composition class.

If a particular assignment designates the topic, your initial task is to find out what you have to say about that topic, or what kind of statement you can make. We suggest that you *brainstorm,* that is, that you jot down everything you know about the particular topic. The pentad can be an invaluable tool at this point because it gives you a way to organize your brainstorming and prevent it from becoming totally random and unproductive. The pentad provides the key questions you must ask in probing your topic: Who is (are) the *agent(s)?* What is the nature of the *act?* What *means* does the agent use? What *motive(s)* does the agent have? At what *scene* does the act take place? Suppose that your history professor does, indeed, ask you to compare Hitler's and Napoleon's invasions of Russia. You should start by filling in as many details about the acts as you know.

Hitler's Invasion	Napoleon's Invasion
ACTS	
—began 1942	—began 1812
—three-pronged attack on Stalingrad, Moscow, and the Ukraine	—a single mass movement of troops on Moscow

—occupied large sections of Russia while Russians retreated	—occupied large sections of Russia
—did not take Moscow or Stalingrad	—took a burning Moscow
—overextended supply lines	—overextended supply lines
—men starved and froze	—men starved and froze
—army lost	—army lost
—Russians counterattacked and took Germany	—Russians counterattacked and drove the French out of Russia

After writing down these details concerning the two *acts,* you should further explore your topic by asking questions about scene, means, purpose, and agents.

Hitler's Invasion	Napoleon's Invasion
SCENE OF INVASION	
—vast, open countryside of Russia	—vast, open countryside of Russia
—brutal winter weather with little shelter	—brutal winter weather with little shelter
—hostile people who destroyed supplies	—hostile people who destroyed supplies
MEANS OF INVASION	
—tanks, aircraft, trucks, automatic weapons, artillery	—horses, rifles, artillery
—mass executions of population	—attempt to win over the population
—lengthy seige	—short seige of Moscow then takeover of empty city
AGENTS OF INVASION	
—Hitler, a totalitarian and unorthodox leader with charismatic hold over troops	—Napoleon, a totalitarian and unorthodox leader with charismatic hold over troops
—Hitler stayed away from action, sent orders from Berlin, interfered with generals	—Napoleon was with the troops although he abandoned them
MOTIVES FOR INVASION	
—the domination of Europe	—the domination of Europe

—Russia a persistent enemy of Germany

—Russia an intriguing land of great wealth

Once you explore your topic with the help of the pentad, you should consider your specific assignment again. Since your instructor asked you to *compare* the invasions, you should study your list and isolate similarities that might prove significant.

—Hitler and Napoleon had similar motives
—they made similar mistakes
—they faced similar situations in a cold, hostile Russia
—both their invasions were crushed

By isolating these key similarities, you can arrive at a clear focus and a *central statement.* As a topic sentence establishes the focus for a paragraph, so the central statement introduces an observation or idea that the essay as a whole will develop.

> While Hitler and Napoleon invaded Russia in different centuries and with very different war machines, their motives, mistakes, and ultimate defeats were surprisingly similar.

Your list also provides you with the details you can use to explain and support this central statement, and the statement itself gives you a sequence for your discussion. Note that in every step of the brainstorming process leading up to your formulation of a statement, you are taking intellectual action. Just as writing agent prose challenges you to be specific and think your ideas through, brainstorming based on the pentad forces you to rigorously consider what you know and what you will need to know to write successfully on a topic.

Frequently, class assignments provide you with nebulous topics, ones that do not narrow down your search for a statement in the way that the Napoleon-Hitler topic does. With this type of broad topic, we suggest that you bring yourself into the writing process by considering whether you have any personal experience on which you can focus. For example, your composition instructor might ask you to write an essay on popular American films. You could first limit the topic to your own experiences by asking yourself what popular movies you have seen. If you have seen quite a few, you might ask yourself which ones you particularly liked or disliked, since those are the ones about which you will have definite opinions. But suppose you are not a frequent moviegoer and the last two movies you saw were *Jaws* and *The Exorcist,* both of which you enjoyed. You might decide to make a statement about both films, or you might decide to focus on one film and your reaction to it. If, for instance, you choose to examine your reactions to *Jaws,* you might begin brainstorming by thinking about the climactic *acts* the movie presents and the *means* used by the producers to make those acts suspenseful.

Jaws

—suspense, never know when shark will strike
—shark eats people, violent death
—music effective
—victims are unsuspecting, innocent
—characters appealing
—shark attacks suddenly, no warning
—shows complacency of people
—victims cannot defend themselves
—human society vs. nature conflict
—shark mysterious force of nature, perpetual-motion machine
—shark seems evil, preys on innocent victims
—shark represents forces we cannot control or understand
—whole film reminds us of our vulnerability, fragility

By studying this list, you can see that your thoughts about *means* highlight the portions of the film that were horrifying. If you condense the list and pick out the most important highlights, you can sharpen the focus. You may, for example, want to focus more precisely on just how the movie creates strong emotions—fear and horror—in its audiences. Your narrowed-down list might look like this:

—suspense, never know when shark will strike
—shark attacks suddenly, no warning
—victims unsuspecting, innocent
—shark mysterious force, represents forces we cannot control or understand
—whole film reminds us of our vulnerability

After studying this narrowed-down list, you may decide to focus on the one means that you judge is mainly responsible for the horror the film evokes. From the list the most striking and pervasive element seems to be that the film reminds audiences of their own vulnerability before the forces of nature. The central act the film portrays—the appearance of an awesome, elusive shark gobbling bathers at random—certainly evokes feelings of human helplessness. If you make this point the focus of your paper, you need to reexamine your list for details you can use to explain and support this focus. You can easily find such support in the victims' impotence, the swiftness of the shark's unexpected attacks, and the uncontrollable brutality of these attacks. Your central statement might look like this:

> *Jaws* horrifies its audiences because it reminds them of their own vulnerability. The sudden appearances and disappearances of the shark, the helplessness of its victims, and the brutal power of the fish all represent human inability to foresee and control the capricious forces of the natural world.

This statement clearly sets out the essay's central idea and also lets the reader know how you will explain and support this idea in the body of the paper. Although it is based on personal experience, the statement goes beyond that experience by offering general truths that the audience can accept or reject. The statement does not consist of a purely personal reaction: "That fish in *Jaws* scared the hell out of me." Instead it expands personal experience to include general experience.

Therefore, whenever you face a specific or a general topic and need to come up with a central statement, you must examine your knowledge and experience. Such an examination will almost always allow you to find out what you have to say and to formulate a personal statement. Then you can go beyond that personal statement to a generalization. Note the following outline of this process.

STEP I. Topic

STEP II. Your knowledge or your particular experience: brainstorm and make list applying the pentad

STEP III. Central points of list: isolate the points on your list that will prove relevant to one or two parts of the pentad

STEP IV. Personal statement: formulate statement from a reorganized list of points

STEP V. Choice of support: examine list for details to help you support your statement

STEP VI. Attempt to generalize personal statement: do additional research

The key to brainstorming, then, is to use the pentad to stretch and broaden your personal experience and make it more universally relevant. In this process you may discover that your personal experience, while an important starting point, cannot furnish an entire essay. Therefore, you may see the need for additional research. But surprisingly often, intense, effective brainstorming will save you trips to the library.

Despite our emphasis on the universal in writing, we are not saying that essays built on your personal feelings or observations are worthless. On certain occasions the first-person "I" essay is appropriate, and you are right to limit your supports to your own experiences. For example, if you were asked to compose an essay on a trip you have taken, you might decide to write about your spring-break visits to Jacksonville Beach, St. Augustine Beach, and Cocoa Beach in Florida. For a first-person essay based on your own experiences, your central statement might sum up your reactions to the *scenes* you encountered on your trip and describe your *motives* for each reaction; you would then set up a sequence of points for your body paragraphs.

> I traveled to three Florida beaches—Jacksonville Beach, St. Augustine Beach, and Cocoa Beach—over my spring break. I enjoyed visiting all of them, but for different reasons. I liked Jacksonville Beach for its beauty, St. Augustine Beach for its entertaining nightlife, and Cocoa Beach for its low-cost motels.

This statement introduces a paper that will tell more about your stays at each beach, and it will indeed be a paper limited to personal experience. But consider how rarely you are asked to write such an essay in college classes. Your economics professor will not ask you to list your feelings about the gross national product or deficit spending. Your history professor will not ask you to write an essay on Napoleon and Hitler based on your personal experience. Think of the bizarre statements you would be forced to come up with.

> I just do not like deficit spending; it gives me an uneasy feeling.
>
> I thought Napoleon was a grim fellow until I met Adolf.

On the job you likewise cannot expect to write personal, first-person essays. Your law partners would look askance on briefs that merely documented your "impressions" of a case, or your "reactions" to your client. You could not expect job security if you wrote a report about "why I liked San Francisco" after representing your company at a meeting there.

Obviously, your college and professional work will require general statements that are based on your own knowledge and experience but which then go beyond these. Your teachers and future colleagues will expect your writing to give them information beyond the realm of your emotions or personal observations. Therefore, you cannot stop short in your brainstorming process. You must begin your search for a central statement by finding out what you know, but you will then have to examine your data, isolate the points that seem significant, determine if you need to do additional research, and finally decide on the statement. Note how the Florida beach essay can change once you go beyond your personal impressions and brainstorm the topic. You now are trying to make your experience of interest to college students in general.

STEP I. Topic—trip to three beaches

STEP II. List—personal experiences with emphasis on scenes and acts
—sunbathing
—swimming
—night spots and partying and drinking
—college crowd from northern schools
—crowds from Florida schools
—inexpensive lodgings
—variety of people to meet

STEP III. Central Points with particular reference to motives
—sun
—swimming
—lodging
—nightlife

STEP IV. Personal Statement
When I went to Florida for spring break, I was looking for bright sun, good swimming, cheap lodgings, and wild nightlife.

STEP V. Experiences at Jacksonville, St. Augustine, and Cocoa beaches

STEP VI. Here you must make a choice—
Can your experience alone, without further research, support a central statement? In this case it probably can, and your central statement will be something like this:

Every year students from all over the country spend their spring vacations at Florida beaches. Some have good times, some have great times. The difference in quality often depends on the beach they choose. What should students look for in a beach? Bright sunshine, good swimming, cheap lodgings, and wild nightlife insure great times.

This central statement springs from your personal observations, but it is not limited to them. It goes beyond your immediate experience and gives a general conclusion about the motives of vacationing students—motives that will interest a broad audience. It is the kind of statement you will need to make for your college and professional writing. Once you have made this kind of statement, you still face the challenge of organizing an essay around it. That challenge is the topic of the next section.

EXERCISE 1

Take the following general topic assignments and practice the brainstorming techniques that we have explored in this unit. Your goal is to arrive at a central statement that gives the central idea for your essay, indicates the supports you will use, and sets the sequence in which they will come.

1. Nuclear-free zones
2. Compare Reggie Jackson and Babe Ruth
3. Academic majors
4. Define the term *superstar*
5. Study methods
6. Distinguish terrorism from legitimate political protest
7. Hamlet's indecision
8. Explain how to recognize pornography

Finding a Way to Say It: Organizing the Essay by Prewriting

After you have brainstormed your topic, isolated the significant details on your brainstorming list, and formulated a central statement from them, you have to plan the organization of your essay before you begin to write. Your statement should give the central idea for your paper, indicate the main supports you will use to explain your idea, and set up a sequence for these supports. If the statement you formulate does all of these tasks, the organization of your paper will logically follow. Note that a central statement should be compact, but is not necessarily limited to just one sentence. You may need to use several sentences to convey your central idea, supports, and sequence. We can take our central statement about *Jaws* as an example.

> *Jaws* horrifies its audiences because it reminds them of their own vulnerability. The sudden appearances and disappearances of the shark, the helplessness of its victims, and the brutal power of the fish all represent human inability to foresee and control the capricious forces of the natural world.

This example shows how a well-formulated central statement logically leads to good essay organization. The statement itself sets up the content and sequence of the body paragraphs. Our discussion of the central idea divides into three parts—the shark's sudden appearances and disappearances, the victims' helplessness, and the fish's power. We can deal sequentially with each part in the three body paragraphs. Working from the central statement, we can make the following preliminary outline for a five-paragraph essay.

I. Introduction and Central Statement
II. Shark's sudden appearances and disappearances
III. Victims' helplessness
IV. Fish's power
V. Conclusion

(all are *means* by which the film frightens us)

From this outline, we can go on to fill in the topic sentences for each paragraph and consider strategies for the introduction and conclusion before beginning to write the essay. Let's work first on the introductory strategy.

To determine how to introduce an essay, you should study the central statement to find out what kind of background information you will have to give your audience to prepare them for this statement. If we look at the central statement on *Jaws,* we see that it deals with the reason *Jaws* horrifies its audiences—it reminds them of their own vulnerability. To prepare the audience for this statement, we should probably give background information concerning the film's theme, its box-office success, and its special ability to frighten audiences. This could lead us quite smoothly to the point of the paper—examining the means by which *Jaws* so effectively scares its viewers. If you think out the steps you will need to prepare your audience for the central statement, your introduction will come to you quite easily. Here is a sample introduction based on the reasoning process we just went through.

> In 1975 the film *Jaws* was released and immediately began its assault on all previous box-office attendance records.

> Taking its theme from a best-selling novel, *Jaws* presents a unique villain—a great white shark that tirelessly feeds upon unsuspecting bathers at an island resort. Eventually, three exceptional men risk their lives to hunt and kill the shark. But this is no ordinary fish story, since the shark ultimately hunts the men with purpose and malevolence. This summary should help explain *Jaws'* reputation as a film that scares people—in fact, scares them right out of the water. But while there are many scary movies, few have had the impact of *Jaws.* The film is particularly horrifying because it reminds its audiences of their own vulnerability. The sudden appearances and disappearances of the shark, the helplessness of its victims, and the brutal power of the fish all represent human inability to predict and control nature.

After writing the introduction, you might try to formulate the topic sentences for your body paragraphs before you begin to write the whole essay. If your central statement establishes a sequence, you should have no difficulty creating topic sentences. Consider these sample topic sentences for the *Jaws* essay.

I. Statement at conclusion of Introduction: The sudden appearances and disappearances of the shark, the helplessness of its victims, and the brutal power of the fish all represent human inability to predict and control nature.

II. Topic Sentence 1: Throughout *Jaws,* the shark bursts from the sea without warning, chews apart its victims, and disappears, leaving onlookers staring in disbelief at a calm ocean.

III. Topic Sentence 2: Along with the startling abruptness of the shark's attacks, the victims' pitiful helplessness horrifies the audiences.

IV. Topic Sentence 3: The brutal power of the fish awes the public as well.

Once you decide on your central statement, introduction, and topic sentences, you need only consider a concluding strategy before you begin filling out the essay with examples and details. To decide on a concluding strategy, you might study your introductory ideas and in some way refer back to them or carry them one step further. If your introduction and conclusion are connected, your paper will be well unified and will offer a full-circled presentation to your readers. If you begin your paper with a quotation, refer back to that quotation in your conclusion. If you begin with an example or with startling statistics or facts, mention the example, statistics, or facts once again in the conclusion.

In the case of the sample *Jaws* essay, we began by giving essential background information on the film's success and on its reputation as a scary movie. Therefore, we can use our conclusion to link these two things—the film's success and its ability to frighten—in a causal relationship. We can perhaps speculate that *Jaws* is so amazingly popular because it is so peculiarly frightening. Though this strategy is sketchy, at least we have a sense of the point we will be driving at when we fill out the body paragraphs for the paper. Consider this sample conclusion for the *Jaws* essay.

> In advertising the film, the *Jaws* publicity corps made much of the fact that their incredible fish caused many people to avoid the beaches during the summer of the film's release. Yet the movie's impact is not remarkable considering the basic message of the film. *Jaws* reminds audiences that forces are "out there"—forces they may not be aware of and that they cannot control. But the "there" of this film is an altogether familiar place—a summer beach that audiences probably associate with pleasant and secure times. This agile, brutal shark hunts and kills people who are enjoying the same activites—swimming, fishing, boating, splashing in the water on a raft—that members of the audience themselves have probably enjoyed. And so *Jaws* tells its viewers what they know but might not often think about—that no one is ever completely secure in a universe that takes no special notice of human well-being and that seems at times openly hostile.

The prewriting process we are discussing may seem elaborate and time-consuming to you. But it is essential. If you impatiently neglect prewriting your essay, you end up in the unfortunate situation of trying to generate content, organize, and write at the same time. If you try to do all these things at once, you will find that you lose your train of thought, begin to repeat yourself, and write an ineffective essay. Ideally, you should formulate and organize your ideas first and only then give all of your concentration to writing them down in the kind of clear, efficient agent prose we defined in the previous chapters of this book. Without the prewriting process, the result is all too often an essay marred by jumbled, partially developed ideas and wordy, obtuse prose. Look at this sample *Jaws* essay. In the prewriting process, we formulated an introduction, topic sentences for the body paragraphs, and a conclusion. By developing the topic sentences into full paragraphs, we now complete the process for writing a short essay. Note how the three body paragraphs develop uniformity by providing a specific kind of evidence for their topic sentences—evidence about *means*.

In 1975 the film *Jaws* was released and immediately began its assault on all previous box-office attendance records. Taking its theme from a best-selling novel, *Jaws* presents a unique villain—a great white shark that tirelessly feeds upon unsuspecting bathers at an island resort. Eventually, three exceptional men risk their lives to hunt and kill the shark. But this is no ordinary fish story, since the shark ultimately hunts the men with purpose and malevolence. This summary should help explain *Jaws'* reputation as a film that scares people—in fact, scares them right out of the water. But while there are many scary movies, few have had the impact of *Jaws*. The film is particularly horrifying because it reminds its audiences of their own vulnerability. The sudden appearances and disappearances of the shark, the helplessness of its victims, and the brutal power of the fish all represent human inability to predict and control nature.

Throughout *Jaws,* the shark bursts from the sea without warning, chews apart its victims, and disappears, leaving audiences staring in disbelief at a calm ocean. Its first victim, Chrissie, is skinny-dipping in a placid, moonlit ocean. Suddenly the shark attacks, brutally pulling her under. Audiences are left looking again at a calm, moonlit ocean after Chrissie disappears. Later the shark gobbles down a ten-year-old boy as he swims on a raft a few feet away from other bathers. Audiences see just a flash of tremendous teeth and spurting blood before the sea is still again. Only a bloody, torn raft that washes ashore testifies to onlookers that the tragedy occurred. Even when the three men hunt the shark, it is elusive. It springs out of the water at Chief Brodie when he is least expecting it, and it disappears just as quickly. When Hooper, the shark expert, is underwater in his "shark-proof" cage waiting for the creature, it swims up behind him, fades back into the ocean gloom, and then comes at him suddenly from the opposite direction. For all its bulk, the shark is, as Hooper puts it, a "fast fish." It swiftly carries out its terrible purpose and disappears. Early in the film, audiences understand that the shark's movements cannot be predicted or controlled, and this realization adds to their uneasiness.

Along with the startling abruptness of the shark's attacks, the victims' pitiful helplessness horrifies audiences. The creature's nonfrenzied feeding contrasts sharply with its victims' frantic attempts to escape. Although Chrissie tries to swim free and manages to cling momentarily to a bell buoy, her struggles are futile; the shark methodically eats her. Quint, the professional shark hunter, desperately fights to keep from being swallowed, but, nevertheless, slides into the shark's open jaws. Despite the shark cage and a spear gun, Hooper is helpless before the force of the fish. He escapes only because the shark decides to eat the cage instead of him. All of the shark's victims are terribly vulnerable and almost always doomed.

The brutal power of the fish awes the public as well. Throughout the movie, the shark effortlessly bites people into pieces. At one point, it pulls down a fishing pier. At another, it pierces the bottom of a boat and kills a fisherman. But the great chase scene at the close of the film provides the most impressive exhibition of the shark's strength. Quint shoots three floating barrels into the fish—one is enough to keep an ordinary shark on the surface. But the barrels do not keep the shark in *Jaws* afloat; it dives at will, swims under Quint's boat, and pounds it to pieces. When the men attempt to get the crippled boat ashore before it sinks, the shark pursues them, jumps on the boat, sinks it, and attacks all three men. Quint tells Hooper that he has never before hunted such a powerful fish.

In advertising the film, the *Jaws* publicity corps made much of the fact that their incredible fish caused many people to avoid the beaches during the summer of the film's release. Yet the movie's impact is not remarkable considering the basic message of the film. *Jaws* reminds audiences that forces are "out there"—forces they may not be aware of and that they cannot control. But the "there" of this film is an altogether familiar place—a summer beach that audiences probably associate with pleasant and secure times. This agile, brutal shark hunts and kills people who are enjoying the same activities—swimming, fishing, boating, splashing in the water on a raft—that members of the audience themselves have probably enjoyed. And so *Jaws* tells its viewers what they know but might not often think about—that no one is ever completely secure in a universe that takes no special notice of human well-being and that seems at times openly hostile.

You can see from the organization of this essay that the pentad is a great aid to successful brainstorming. Once more, we suggest that you plan your short essay—the standard length is about five paragraphs in most composition classes—so that the introduction provides adequate background information that leads to a central statement. The statement should both establish the central idea of the essay and indicate the sequence of your discussion. The body paragraphs should follow this sequence, and the conclusion should round out the essay by summarizing and referring back to the introduction.

Of course, you will not write short five-paragraph essays interminably. In college and in your future work, the writing you do will frequently be much more involved and lengthy. But you can still use the principles of prewriting that we suggest, though on a broader scale. While you might not be able to sum up your central idea and main supports in one compact statement, you can still formulate key points and plan the ways you will develop them before you write. If you look in the prefaces or introductory sections of nonfiction books, you will find that even before the first chapter begins, writers announce their central ideas and outline the sequence of supports. Look too at the introductory sections of any substantial research paper, report, or essay. You will find that the writers state the main idea of the essay and at least hint at the sequence of their supports before they begin the body of a long paper.

If you use the prewriting procedures we suggest, you will give yourself the same advantages that professional writers give themselves. The process of prewriting enables you to separate content generation and organization from actual sentence and paragraph writing. Prewriting allows you to concentrate first on clear thinking and then on clear writing. But an additional advantage deserves mention. By thinking your essay through and establishing the central statement and sequence of supports in your introduction, you will help your readers considerably. After reading the introduction, they will know the point you are driving at and will know what sequence of ideas to expect as they read on. Thus they will understand more clearly the points you make in your essay and the ways these points connect with the central idea. Good prose defines an agent and is therefore readable and easily understood. Good essay organization means that you, the writer, have found effective ways to share your thoughts with your readers. To be understood, you must set up a clear sequence of thoughts. Your readers should never have to figure out what you are trying to say in your sentences, nor should they have to figure out where they are in your essay. Good prose and clear organization both require you to be an agent in the writing process, an active statement maker. They allow the reader to comprehend rather than decode your essay.

EXERCISE 2

Take one or more of the brainstorming exercises that you completed for Exercise 1 and set up an essay outline. Formulate an introductory strategy, topic sentences, and a concluding strategy. Follow our example in the essay on *Jaws*.

Five Models for Short Essays

COMPARISON

When you make a value judgment or describe the unfamiliar, you almost always use the techniques of *comparison* and *contrast.* If you choose to buy a Nissan Sentra instead of a VW Rabbit because the Nissan is less expensive, roomier, and gets better gas mileage, you have considered both cars in terms of your own needs and have decided on the *better* car for you. If you encounter an unfamiliar game such as lacrosse for the first time, your initial thought will probably be that it is like hockey, soccer, or some other game with which you are familiar. Once these comparisons give you a basic understanding of the game and it is no longer totally strange, you will probably begin to notice the special qualities that distinguish lacrosse from other games. Or if you hear for the first time the term *oligarch* applied to a repressive ruler, you will probably first notice the term's similarity to other terms that refer to absolute leaders—*dictator* and *despot*—terms with which you are more familiar. Then you can differentiate the *oligarch* from these others.

These uses for comparison and contrast are obvious; others are less so. You can use the techniques of comparison and contrast to point out important differences between two people or things that on the surface seem very similar. You can also use these techniques to point out important similarities between two people or things that seem very different.

If you ever took two calculus classes, they probably presented the same type of material with similar class lectures, homework, and exams. But if you enjoyed one and detested the other, there must have been differences underlying their superficial similarities, differences that caused your opposite reactions. Perhaps the teacher in one of the courses showed enthusiasm, made the lecture material interesting, and provided individual help, while the instructor of the other course seemed bored, gave confusing explanations, and remained remote. Or consider two versions of the song "That'll Be the Day," one by Buddy Holly and the other by Linda Ronstadt. Even though these artists are singing the same words to the same basic notes, the songs differ—in musical arrangement, instrumentation, and vocal style, for example. Therefore, things that seem as alike as two classes on the same subject or two versions of the same song can differ significantly; analysis of these differences can provide you with material for an essay.

In the same way, analysis of similarities can lead you to essay topics. People or things that seem very different are often alike in important ways. For instance you might compare the tactics of a populist politician, such as Jimmy Carter, with those of an evil, cunning ruler like the one depicted in Machiavelli's *The Prince.* While the two seem far apart, you might say Carter used many of the practical tactics that Machiavelli advised: Carter practiced fiscal prudence, gave national self-interest priority over moral stands, and broke treaties with weaker nations to form them with stronger ones. As a second example, consider two films—*Jaws* and *The Exorcist*—which seem indisputably different. *Jaws* features a killer shark that feeds on bathers and boaters at an island resort; *The Exorcist* features the devil, who possesses a young girl and drives her to all sorts of shocking behavior. But if you take the one obvious similarity between the two films—box-office success—and go on to search for reasons for the films' popularity, you will find that basic similarities unite the two. Both portray uncontrollable evil forces as they prey upon innocent victims. Both climax when brave men seek out these evil forces, battle them, and bring about a temporary resolution. Once you discover these similarities, you can make a substantive statement about the two films.

Note that in all these instances you make comparisons to reach certain conclusions about your experience. In the transition from thinking to writing, your conclusions become central statements and your comparisons become the supports you develop in your body paragraphs. If you are actually deciding on a car to buy and you have narrowed your choice down to the Sentra and the Rabbit, you will compare the two and then draw a conclusion. You might consider cost, gas mileage, and space and conclude that the Sentra is the better car for you because it costs one thousand dollars less than the Rabbit, gets better gas mileage, and provides more leg and cargo space. During the course of your life, such a thought process is natural and essential whenever you have to choose between things—two cars, two houses, two jobs, two majors. You can take this familiar thought process and use it in your essay writing. Your conclusion—that the Sentra is the better car for you—will become the central statement in your essay. The differences that you noted between the two cars—differences in cost, mileage, and space—will form the supports for your statements.

These supports become the topics for your body paragraphs. The outline for your essay will look something like this.

I. Introduction
Statement: For me, the Nissan Sentra will be a better car than the VW Rabbit because the Sentra is less expensive, gets better gas mileage, and provides more leg and cargo space.

II. Topic Sentence 1: I need a car that I can pay for without overextending my budget, and I can afford a Sentra more than I can afford a Rabbit.

III. Topic Sentence 2: I also need a car that will help me save money on gas, and the Sentra gets better mileage than the Rabbit.

IV. Topic Sentence 3: In addition to a moderate price and good gas mileage, I also need ample cargo and leg room in the car I buy, and for this reason too I prefer the Sentra.

V. Conclusion

This outline flows from your own thinking and certainly provides a clear form for your essay. But whenever you can, you should move out of the first person and practice writing in the third—you should make impersonal statements that will interest a broad audience. By moving out of the first person, you can, for example, expand the scope of an essay on the two college classes or the two songs we mentioned earlier. Instead of saying, "When I took Calculus 102 and Calculus 103 during successive quarters, I noticed many differences between the two teachers even though they were teaching similar courses," you can say, "At the University of Vermont, Calculus 102 is a very different class from Calculus 103 because of the different approaches of the instructors." This third-person statement encourages you to arrive at broad conclusions about the importance of the teacher in *any* class. Your essay will appeal to a general audience since you are talking about more than just your own experience. In the same way, instead of saying, "I noticed that Linda Ronstadt and Buddy Holly sing 'That'll Be the Day' in very different ways," you can say, "Although they are singing the same song, Linda Ronstadt and Buddy Holly produce very different versions of 'That'll Be the Day.' " This third-person statement encourages you to develop general conclusions, perhaps about the differences between the early rock and roll music of Buddy Holly and the country-rock music of Linda

Ronstadt. Since it is based on a general statement, your essay will interest a broad audience.

For the Sentra-Rabbit essay, you can shift from the reasons that the Sentra is better than the Rabbit for you personally to the reasons that the Sentra would be better for the general public. You could perhaps stress that high gasoline prices have created special requirements for cars—requirements that the Sentra fulfills better than the Rabbit. Your revised central statement might be:

> For inflation-poor Americans now buying small cars because of high fuel prices, the Nissan Sentra is a better car than the VW Rabbit. The Sentra not only gets better gas mileage; it is less expensive and has more cargo and passenger space.

Your topic sentences will easily follow this shift into the third person. However, when you change an evaluative statement from first person ("I think") to third person ("The Nissan Sentra is . . ."), you also assume a burden of proof. When you are explaining a personal preference or opinion, you are not arguing; that you think or feel as you do is not debatable. But if you make a third-person statement that the Sentra is more economical than the Rabbit, you must *prove* your claim because it is debatable. Many VW dealers, at the very least, will insist that you back up this assertion. In the next chapter, we deal extensively with argumentative essays. All the essay models in this chapter are expository, but with some alterations they can also be used in argumentation.

Another example that can illustrate the use of generalizing personal experience is the *Jaws-Exorcist* essay topic. After you examine in your essay the similarities between the two films, you can comment on why other films using the plot formula common to *Jaws* and *The Exorcist* appeal to viewers. Therefore, by comparing and contrasting two people, things, events, or ideas, you can discover statements about a variety of topics. These statements almost always start with your own observations or knowledge. But you can expand your limited first-person statements into third-person general statements that will interest a broad audience.

Many times the topic of your comparison and contrast essay will be determined for you. Teachers might ask you to compare Hitler and Napoleon, to explain the differences between a mob and a crowd, to distinguish fission from fusion, to explain the similarities between Beethoven and Brahms, or to examine the differences between a ballad and a rondeau. When you receive assignments like these, you should immediately begin brainstorming to determine what you know about the two items. Then select the similarities or differences you wish to stress, and at this point decide whether you have to do additional research. If not, you can go on to formulate your central statement and indicate the sequence for your supports. Then you can formulate your topic sentences, plan out your introductory and concluding strategies, and begin to write your essay.

If you must hunt for a topic, consider the kinds of central statements that the techniques of comparison and contrast allow you to make—statements that make value judgments, statements that explain the unfamiliar by comparing it to the familiar, statements that point out differences between very similar items, and statements that point out similarities between very different items. Examine your interests and knowledge to see if you can formulate any of these kinds of statements.

For example, if one of your interests is music, you could explain why two recording artists are dissimilar even though they seem to produce similar music, or you could argue that one is superior to the other. You might liken contemporary folk music to the social-statement music of the sixties, or you might explain reggae music by comparing it to more familiar musical forms. If you are interested in running, you might argue that the Nike running shoe is better than the Puma. You could differentiate between jogging and running or compare a marathon to a car race. Almost all subjects that you know about will provide you with material for statements and essays if you understand how to look at these subjects. However, your statements will remain undeveloped unless you assume the role of active statement maker.

As an example, we can again take the *Jaws-Exorcist* essay idea and outline it; then we will talk more about the ways to organize your essay. Suppose your teacher has assigned an essay on contemporary American movies. After considering your experiences, you come up with *Jaws* and *The Exorcist*—two movies that you think you know well enough to talk about. These two films seem very different on the surface, but both of them scared you quite a bit, and both of them were very popular. You suspect that they might have more in common than you originally thought. Therefore, the kind of statement you will probably make is one that reveals similarities between seemingly different items. With this purpose in mind, you should make a brainstorming list with the help of the pentad, which, as we have already discussed in this chapter, is the first step in the writing process. For comparison and contrast, the best way to do this is to consider each item separately, listing all the data you can muster for first one movie and then the other.

Sample Data Listing

Jaws	*The Exorcist*
AGENT OF DISASTER	
—shark	—devil
—natural force	—supernatural force
—malevolent and strong	—malevolent and strong
—seems unconquerable	—seems unconquerable
ACTS CONCERNING AGENT	
—eats innocent bathers	—possesses innocent child
—violent, horrible killings	—violent acts forced on young girl
—destroyed by exceptional men at great personal sacrifice	—exorcised by exceptional priests who give their lives
—struggles with these exceptional men with incredible tenacity	—resists priests with tenacity
MEANS	
—teeth, strength, speed	—strength, multiple powers
—surprise attacks on unsuspecting, vulnerable bathers	—hides in the body of a young girl
SCENE	
—seaside resort which refuses to acknowledge danger	—suburban Washington where people do not acknowledge existence of devil
—water in which shark is at home and people helpless	—girl's house which devil possesses as well
MOTIVE	
—hunger, malevolence	—possession of soul

If you make a complete list for one item first (here we began with *Jaws*), you can follow its outline when you make up your list for the second item (as we did for the list on *The Exorcist*).

After you think out your brainstorming list, you should study it in terms of your purpose—here, to find significant similarities. Then you should select the particular similarities you wish to focus on, that is, the ones that will explain the two films' similar ability to scare people and similar success at the box office.

Selected Similarities

1.	Devil and shark are both malevolent forces	(agents)
2.	Victims are innocent—forces enter their lives unexpectedly	(acts)
3.	Hunters go forth and force dramatic confrontations with evil creatures	(acts)
4.	Resolutions temporary	(acts)

Having selected these similarities and determined that additional research will not be necessary, you can now formulate the central statement for the essay. Although this statement should logically acknowledge that the films are dissimilar in many ways, it should primarily focus on the important features that they share.

Statement

> Widely separated in their locale, characters, and theme, both *Jaws* and *The Exorcist* portray an uncontrollable evil force that arbitrarily preys upon unsuspecting victims. Both films celebrate the exceptional men who overcome it, although the resolution they bring about is only temporary.

After you have composed the central statement, you need to consider the strategy for your introduction. In this case you might use the pentad to develop your topic from a slightly different perspective. You might consider that these two films were made by filmmakers—agents—whose motive was profit. They wanted to produce popular films and discovered an effective formula—one that underlies both films. Therefore, the filmmakers used devices that would scare audiences; they created these malevolent forces as a *means* of drawing people to the theaters. You should indicate in your introduction that the similarities the films share explain their similar impact on American audiences.

Introduction

> The movie business has traditionally been one in which the secret of box-office success is elusive. Recently, moviemakers have found the public's taste to be more and more unpredictable—so much so that no single formula for success seems to exist anymore. When one considers the diversity of such box-office money-makers as *Rocky, The Sound of Music, The Godfather,* and *Carrie,* one can begin to appreciate the problem that the film industry faces. But a comparison of two seemingly dissimilar successes—*Jaws* and *The Exorcist*—

> reveals some common characteristics that can make movies popular. Widely separated in their locale, characters, and theme, both *Jaws* and *The Exorcist* portray an uncontrollable evil force that arbitrarily preys upon unsuspecting victims. Both films celebrate the exceptional men who overcome it, although the resolution they bring about is only temporary.

Since your central statement gives you the sequence for your supports, you can formulate your topic sentences easily.

I. Introduction and Statement

II. Topic Sentence 1: In both *Jaws* and *The Exorcist,* an evil force preys upon innocent people.

III. Topic Sentence 2: Because these evil forces are so mysterious, only the strongest and most exceptional of men can deal with them.

IV. Topic Sentence 3: Despite the heroism of the individual men, the resolutions in both movies are far from final.

After formulating your topic sentences, you should consider your concluding strategy. Since you point out in the introduction that both of these films made money by scaring people, you might want to refer again to this similarity. In the body of the essay, you will talk about significant likenesses between the two films, so in your conclusion you might address how these common features are actually the means by which the filmmakers ensured the films' popularity. Having written your introduction, central statement, and topic sentences, and having determined the strategy for your concluding paragraph, you can proceed to write the essay. As you read the following sample essay, note the form of the body paragraphs.

Jaws and *The Exorcist*

> The movie business has traditionally been one in which the secret of box-office success is elusive. Recently, moviemakers have found the public's taste to be more and more unpredictable—so much so that no single formula for success seems to exist anymore. When one considers the diversity of such box-office money-makers as *Rocky, The Sound of Music, The Godfather,* and *Carrie,* one can begin to appreciate the problem that the film industry faces. But a comparison of two seemingly dissimilar successes—*Jaws* and *The Exorcist*—reveals some general characteristics that can make movies popular. Widely separated in their locale, characters, and theme, both films portray an uncontrollable evil force that arbitrarily preys upon innocent victims. Both films celebrate the exceptional men who

overcome it, although the resolution they bring about is only temporary.

In both *Jaws* and *The Exorcist,* an evil force preys upon innocent people. In *Jaws* the evil force is a great white shark that snacks on bathers at a seaside resort. In *The Exorcist* the evil force is Satan himself; he decides to possess a young girl and forces her into all kinds of unnatural and grotesque acts. Despite their dissimilarities—one an actual animal and the other a supernatural being lacking any stable physical form—both the shark and the devil represent forces that people cannot control, and these forces terrify us. Both the shark and the devil strike unexpectedly and choose their particular victims for no apparent reason. Although aware of the presence of these forces, people cannot predict attacks or defend themselves from them. The young girl in *The Exorcist* can no more understand what has happened than the quickly disappearing victims of *Jaws*.

Because these evil forces are so mysterious, only the strongest and most exceptional people can deal with them. In *Jaws* the shark hunter, the oceanographer, and the police chief are the only men in the community perceptive enough to understand the danger and courageous enough to seek it out. In *The Exorcist* only the priest recognizes that the girl does not have a psychological or physiological disorder; he alone is courageous enough to seek out the devil that has possessed her. As the shark hunter risks and suffers a horrible, violent death, so too does the priest. Thus the similarity between the evil forces in these movies leads to a similarity in those who recognize and, at tremendous cost, fight the evil.

Despite the heroism of the individual men, the resolutions in both movies are far from final. In *Jaws* one shark is destroyed, but others clearly lurk in the ocean. In *The Exorcist* the devil apparently leaves the girl, but is in no way killed or banished from the earth. Audiences leave both films with an awareness of the possibility that malevolent powers exist in the world. Typically people who watch *Jaws* forego swimming in bodies of salt water; people who watch *The Exorcist* may find their way to church a bit more often. In both films one senses that the sacrifice of the hero—the shark hunter in *Jaws,* the priest in *The Exorcist*—has only briefly sated the evil force.

Why are *Jaws* and *The Exorcist* such great box-office successes? The simple answer is that, despite their dissimilarities, they scare people. Both movies prey upon our basic fears and insecurities, even as they reassure us that heroic, wise individuals can win temporary victories over evil. More specifically, these two movies scare us because they portray evil forces that are mysterious—that strike unexpectedly, uncontrollably, and

> irrationally. These films scare us because they portray only the most heroic of us as capable of dealing with evil forces, and then only at great cost and with no conclusive effect.
>
> When "Bruce" strikes his first victim in *Jaws,* we do not see him. We see only a young girl's puzzlement, her horrible recognition, her helplessness, and her terror. The shark, though a fearful physical specimen, does not terrify us so much as his mystery does, a fact which the makers of *Jaws* recognized and exploited by not letting audiences see Bruce until the second half of the movie. In *The Exorcist,* audiences never see the devil, but only his influence. For this reason many people feel that *The Exorcist* is an even more horrifying movie than *Jaws,* despite the latter's special effects. Once we see Bruce, we can deal with him. Unseen, he is as horrifying as the devil, and only the bravest dare challenge him. But whichever film is scarier, the combination of mysterious evil, brave heroes, and partial resolution of the conflict produced long lines, record box-office receipts, and prosperity for the makers of both movies.

In this sample essay, the student discusses both movies in each of the body paragraphs. This method of comparison-contrast development is called the *alternating pattern*. In Chapter II we discussed the use of the alternating pattern in writing comparison paragraphs; this same pattern can be used on a larger scale in writing comparison essays. In outline form, an essay built on the alternating pattern looks like this:

I. Introduction and Central Statement

II. Similarity 1: Evil force and innocent victims
Jaws / The Exorcist

III. Similarity 2: Exceptional individuals combat evil
Jaws / The Exorcist

IV. Similarity 3: Temporary resolution
Jaws / The Exorcist

V. Reason for success
Jaws / The Exorcist

VI. Nature of the evil force
Jaws / The Exorcist

The discussion keeps alternating between the two films; each paragraph discusses one feature both films share.

Another method of development—the *divided pattern*—is also available to you. We have already discussed this pattern on a smaller scale in the section on comparison paragraphs. To use this pattern in essays, you divide your discussion, writing first about one subject and then about the other. In outline form an essay built on the divided pattern looks like this:

I. Introduction and Central Statement
II. *Jaws* Evil force and innocent victims
III. *Jaws* Exceptional individuals combat evil
Temporary resolution
IV. *Jaws* Reason for success
Nature of evil force
V. *The Exorcist* Evil force and innocent victims
VI. *The Exorcist* Exceptional individuals combat evil
Temporary resolution
VII. *The Exorcist* Reason for success
Nature of evil force
VIII. Conclusion

When the discussion focuses first on one film and then the other, you must make sure that you discuss the same points in the same order. In the discussions of both films, you must start with the evil force, go on to the innocent victims, then bring in the exceptional individuals, the temporary resolution, and your theory for the film's popularity and ability to frighten people. The danger of this method is that, if you are not careful to refer to the first subject throughout your discussion of the second, you might seem to be writing two separate essays. If you were to write the *Jaws-Exorcist* essay in the divided pattern, you would have to keep referring back to *Jaws* as you made your points about *The Exorcist*. You would also have to use transitional phrases such as *similar to* Jaws, *as in* Jaws, and *like* Jaws.

The alternating pattern is a more popular form than the divided pattern because by using it you can more easily give a clear, balanced treatment to the two items you are comparing. You are in no danger of separating your subjects since you must deal with both in each paragraph. The only danger of the alternating pattern is that your paper can resemble a tennis match if you bounce back and forth between items too quickly. A way to avoid the tennis-match effect when using the alternating pattern is to divide your body paragraphs in half; devote half of the paragraph to one subject, half to the other, and make a transition in midparagraph. A general rule to remember for both patterns is that you must give both subjects equal treatment. You should say as much about *The Exorcist* as you do about *Jaws*.

Many professional writers combine the alternating and divided patterns when they write comparison essays. You will not combine these patterns for the short, five-paragraph essay as much as you will for longer essays, but you have the option. You should allow your central statement to dictate your pattern as much as possible.

One more word about the form of your introduction and central statement. We have been focusing on comparison in the *Jaws-Exorcist* example, but elements of contrast do show up. If you are emphasizing similarities, you need to recognize differences at some point in your paper since you are doing comparison *and* contrast. You might therefore make your central statement in the form of a complex sentence, so that you can acknowledge differences in your dependent clause and then assert similarities you will emphasize in your independent, or main, clause. Observe this sentence structure in the second sentence of the following sample essay, written by a Florida student about a campus controversy. Each year, students hold a Halloween Ball on a centrally located field called the Plaza of the Americas. Recently, public nudity (students wear Saran Wrap costumes), excessive drinking, and open drug-trafficking have caused the university to consider canceling the ball. But this student writer criticizes this possible measure by comparing the activities at the ball to the activities that take place in the stands at Florida football games. She points out that the officials would never consider canceling the football games. This essay, then, points out similarities between two items that seem very different. The student's purpose is clear—she is using this comparison to justify the retention of the Halloween Ball. Note that she mainly uses the *divided pattern,* devoting one central body paragraph to the football games and one to the Halloween Ball. Note too that she keeps her essay unified by providing clear references to the football games throughout her discussion of the ball.

A New Look at the Halloween Ball

Administrators at the University of Florida are trying to get rid of the Halloween Ball, but would they be just as willing to do away with Florida Gator football games? Although this question might seem a bit drastic, these two campus activities actually have a lot in common. Both events attract thousands of people—spectators at one and participants at the other. Students use drugs and drink alcoholic beverages, whether at Florida Field or the Plaza of the Americas. Various safety hazards are also evident at both of these traditional Gator affairs. Yet university officials are trying to banish the Halloween Ball in an effort to eliminate its negative effects. The administrators should recognize that football games cause as many problems as the ball does. The faults of the Halloween Ball are simply over-emphasized by its opponents.

Of course, Gator football does bring money in to the university, while the Halloween Ball does not. But, as long as the ball does not cause a loss of money, the lack of revenue should not cause administrators to cancel it. Many people enjoy attending the ball, and this should be reason enough for it to continue.

In Gainesville, football games bring thousands of rambunctious spectators to the Gators' Florida Field. The smell of funny cigarettes fills the air, and fans frequently fill their Gator cups with rum. Occasionally someone can be seen spilling the contents of a colorful capsule into a Coke. At best, people act wild and obnoxious; at worst, they pass out in the stands. The drinkers often dispose of their bottles by leaving them on the ground with other debris, and the broken glass creates a safety hazard for other fans. Also, the fans often endanger themselves and the football players by flinging Gator cups, minifrisbees, and minifootballs at each other and onto the field. The "game" called "over the top" is also potentially dangerous. In this game the fans on the first row hold a woman over their heads and pass her upward toward the fans on the last row of the stadium in an attempt to throw her "over the top." The unfortunate woman is not only excessively handled by her male passers, she also risks being dropped and suffering serious injury. But since thousands of people participate in such activities at the games, the potential dangers are often overlooked.

The Halloween Ball is a campus activity that also attracts thousands of students, but at the Plaza of the Americas rather than Florida Field. The participants drink beer, smoke marijuana, and pop pills just as many football fans do, and nobody forces anyone to take part in these activities. Careless students will get drunk or overdose, but most of the students will not. The hazards that accompany the ball are usually minor. No one will be permanently damaged from exposure to Saran-Wrap costumes or an occasional manifestation of lewd behavior. Every year the Halloween Ball enthusiasts look forward to this traditional event, just as Gator fans look forward to the football games. Football fans will not be disappointed come fall; the games will continue no matter how excessive fan behavior becomes. Halloween Ball participants should not be disappointed either; the ball elicits behavior no worse than the behavior at the football games.

Football games and the Halloween Ball are both favorite attractions that the University of Florida offers its students. Misuse of drugs and alcohol, in addition to safety hazards, has been cited by university officials as reason enough to discontinue the ball; yet football games create the same problems. The main objective of the administration should

> be to curb excessive behavior rather than to ban entire activities. If they compare Gator football and the Halloween Ball and hope to achieve any kind of consistency, administrators will realize that they cannot criticize or ban the ball without doing the same to football games.

ILLUSTRATION

Without doubt, the most efficient, effective way there is of backing up general statements is to give examples. In fact you instinctively call for examples whenever you read or listen to generalizations that are in any way unclear or shaky. If your friend Judith advises you not to date Hugh since all her evenings with him have ended in disaster, you will naturally want at least one "for instance." After she goes on to describe how he spilled a jar of mustard on her new slacks, bit her lip when he kissed her, and slammed his car door so hard he broke the window, you will probably decide that Hugh is, after all, a man to avoid. Similarly, if you hear a news commentator say that the president's indecision often escalates minor crises into major ones, you will undoubtedly want the commentator to cite some particular crises and explain how the president was indecisive in each one. If the commentator can provide examples as convincing as those that Judith gives concerning Hugh, you might indeed agree that the president has a problem. In the same way, if you want to convince your parents that you must have a car at school to avoid the onset of scurvy and malnutrition, you might describe three meals you were forced to eat because you had no way to get to a store or reputable restaurant. Certainly your parents will be moved by your accounts of the gummy ketchup-covered noodles that the cafeteria calls spaghetti, the popcorn and tuna feast that your roommate prepares nightly, and the soggy buns and limp fries served by Beagle Burger, the only fast-food place within walking distance of campus.

When you write essays, you can use examples to support certain kinds of central statements—ones that do not call for reasons, but for specific illustrations. For instance, suppose you have observed the tendency to save and restore old neighborhoods and buildings in many cities, and you wish to comment on this trend. Your central statement might read:

> With federal funding for renovation at $60 million this year and new federal, state, and local laws being enacted to preserve historic landmarks, the country is witnessing what *Time* magazine calls "the recycling of America."

After reading this statement, your audience will naturally expect you to provide instances of such restorations. Suppose you go on to cite the renovation of the 130-year-old governor's mansion in North Carolina, the reclaiming of slum areas in Sacramento, and the building-protection laws in New York City. In doing so, you adequately support the claim in your central statement. Note that the statement does not prompt readers to ask for reasons—it merely states the existence of a trend and does not involve readers with *why* the trend came about. If you altered your central statement to raise the question of *motive,* your supports would have to be different.

> The current U.S. interest in reclaiming and renovating old buildings and slum areas can be attributed to our growing concern with energy conservation, environmental protection, and economic stability.

This statement calls for body paragraphs that give detailed commentary on the three *motives* Americans have for "recycling" old buildings. The statement cannot be supported by illustrations alone.

In a pure illustration essay, the central statement *can* be supported by examples alone. Read the following sample statements:

1. Americans have reason to distrust so-called experts.
2. The much awaited and publicized Super Bowl games frequently prove to be tedious and unremarkable.
3. Rock concerts endanger their patrons almost as much as they entertain them.

Each of these statements calls for examples to back it up. For statement 1, we might cite the Three Mile Island accident, the DC-10 air crashes, and the Ford Pinto explosions as instances when experts should have found major flaws in their equipment but did not. For statement 2, we could remind readers of the interminable games that were Super Bowls V, VII, and XII. For statement 3, we could describe catastrophes at concerts by the Rolling Stones, the Who, and the Sex Pistols. As these central statements and examples indicate, the illustration model encourages you to focus on specific *acts* or *scenes*—disasters, football games, events at concerts. Note that each of these sample statements is of limited scope, that is, each of them requires only a few pertinent examples to satisfy readers. If we make central statements too broad in scope, we might find supporting them with examples alone a considerably more difficult task. Look at the following: "American college students are more apathetic than ever before." If we chose to back this up with only three examples—Teresa Morales, Anthony Jones, and Lee Moran—we would hardly be convincing. Teresa, Anthony, and Lee simply cannot be made to represent *all* American college students. If, however, we limited the statement to "Students in Dr. Osborne's History of Ideas course are frequently dazed and bored" and we cited Teresa, Anthony, and Lee as examples, we would have a more plausible statement and more effective supports. Readers can accept Teresa, Anthony, and Lee's boredom as representative of this much smaller group.

When you plan an illustration essay, you must first be sure that your central statement is one that can be supported by examples alone. Then you should brainstorm. Almost necessarily, your central idea will spring from your own observations or your reading. Probably you will already have at least one example in mind which prompted you to make the statement. If this is the case, your brainstorming task is to find at least two other similar examples. If, for instance, you witness your friend's frenzy as he battles a computer error in the registrar's office, which has dropped him from all his classes, you might be prompted to comment on your school's inept registrar. You could make the following statement:

> The university registrar frequently makes errors that cause innocent students untold hassles and worries.

Your friend's case would be your first example, but you must brainstorm, or search for related *acts,* to prove your point. Perhaps you remember your own frustration when the central computer continually denied your requests for financial aid. Perhaps upon questioning fellow students you hear several other horror stories involving brutal secretaries or mile-long lines. Examine these instances, choosing as examples those that have the most details and about which you can say the most. Having selected the appropriate examples, you can go on to formulate your topic sentences.

Before you begin to flesh out your paragraphs, test your central statement and examples once more. Be sure that your central statement is limited enough so that the examples you select will convince your readers. In addition make certain that your examples fit your central idea, that they are pertinent to the point you want to support. For instance, if your central statement is, "Many television advertisers appeal to our desire to be popular," and you choose as an example a commercial that relies on a sexy model, you will have problems with unity; the topic of sexiness will conflict with the topic of popularity. Each example must directly support the central idea.

Note the following sample illustration essay, "The Recycling of America." As we recommended, its central statement can be supported by examples alone, and the statement is limited enough so that three detailed examples can convince readers. The three examples are all pertinent to the central idea of the essay.

The Recycling of America

Until recently, the "pull-down-and-build-over spirit," as Walt Whitman called it, characterized America's attitude toward old buildings, landmarks, and neighborhoods across the country. Few people appreciated the historic, or simply old, structures that were falling into disrepair yearly in many U.S. cities. Historical societies had long fought to preserve the old landmarks that gave character and continuity to American communities, but such groups had never found the financial support or political clout to reverse America's preoccupation with the new. In the past decade, however, growing interest in the environment, energy, and the economy has reversed the assault on the old. This reversal is best seen in the restoration and preservation projects that are now flourishing in over 500 American cities. With federal funding for renovation at $60 million this year and new federal, state, and local laws being enacted to preserve historic landmarks, the country is witnessing what *Time* calls "the recycling of America."

In Raleigh, North Carolina, the controversial restoration of the 130-year-old governor's mansion is a tribute to the joint efforts of historians, architects, and concerned citizens across the state. Many modernists in the legislature believed the $200,000 price tag for restoration was too high; others objected to the outlandish gingerbread facade of the Victorian mansion. Disregarding the preservationists' concerns for historical integrity, the legislature authorized new plans for modernization. When the intended fate of the old house became clear, a powerful coalition lobbied successfully for the mansion's preservation. Historians found century-old designs for the house, and architects drew up plans to restore it to its former majesty. Architects were able to save the ornate exterior with its dozen gables, while they strengthened the roof and foundation to meet safety standards. In 1977 the two-year restoration project was completed, and Governor Jim Holhauser opened the mansion to the public. North Carolinians had watched the step-by-step project with growing pride, and thousands were eager to see the new face of an old favorite.

Raleigh's efforts were small compared to the multimillion dollar project in Sacramento that recycled 28 acres into an economically solvent business district. In 1965 this skid row was in physical and moral decay, yet businessmen saw financial potential in the area's restoration. Today that potential has been realized, with over 160 businesses thriving along quaint, well-designed streets. Architects retained the original "old west" character of the buildings, and made the area a desirable place to tour and shop. "Old Sac" is now visited by families, tourists, and most recently, 100,000 music lovers for a jazz festival.

New York City has come from behind to lead in the recycling movement. After allowing the demolition of such classics as the Metropolitan Opera House and Pennsylvania Station, the city now protects over 1200 buildings as historic landmarks in 37 districts. Manhattan's Soho district is one of the best-known restoration projects in the country. Soho had earned its sobriquet "Hell's Hundred Acres" as a dismal conglomeration of defunct factories and warehouses. In the 1960s, artists migrated to Soho because of the low rents for lofts, and they began to improve what they found. Ten years later Soho was a fashionable area of 8,000 residents; it boasted 85 art galleries, 30 restaurants, 60 boutiques, and two museums. Soho is what the "recycling of America" is all about.

What has been termed a trend may become a way of life if America continues to support such projects as Soho, "Old Sac," and Raleigh's governor's mansion. The "pull-down-and-build-over spirit" is being replaced. With money, talent, and care America has seen what a little recycling can do.

If you consider the paragraph structure of this sample essay, you'll see that the writer not only puts together an effective illustration essay, she also obeys the general rules for writing good essays of any kind. Her introduction gives sufficient background for the central idea and gains the reader's interest. Her topic sentences refer to the central idea, since they announce the example that each paragraph will discuss. They also provide subtle transitions from one paragraph to the next. Note as an example the topic sentence for the second body paragraph: "Raleigh's efforts were small compared to the multimillion-dollar project in Sacramento that recycled 28 acres of slums into an economically solvent business district." The writer uses the word *recycled* to remind us of the central idea, and she refers to the previous paragraph by citing *Raleigh's efforts.* Notice that she does not need to use a bulky, mechanical topic sentence to perform these tasks. By repeating a key word and using a comparison, she writes more efficiently; she makes the sentence serve as both a topic sentence and a transition. She doesn't have to write: "Another city that is also taking part in the recycling movement is Sacramento, which is developing 28 acres of slums into an economically solvent business district." Finally, in the conclusion the writer successfully reiterates the central idea and adds a clinching statement to round out the essay.

A reminder is necessary here. In this chapter we have discussed organizational principles for the short illustration essay. You will, however, use examples in most of the essays you write, especially longer ones that are making more complex points. Illustration will be part of almost any essay you write.

EXERCISE 3

Read the following illustration essay and evaluate it in terms of content, organization, style, and agent prose. Ask yourself the following questions.

1. Is the central statement clear and can it be logically supported by examples? Is it of limited scope?
2. Are the examples selected by the student appropriate? Do they convincingly support the central statement?
3. Does the writer give enough details about each example? Does the writer develop all the body paragraphs well?
4. Does the introduction give sufficient background information leading up to the central statement?
5. Does the conclusion refer to the introduction and round out the essay?
6. Do the topic sentences meet the requirements of agent prose? Do they meet the standards we set for topic sentences in Chapter II; that is, do they tell specifically what topic the paragraph will discuss and do they provide some form of transition?
7. Do all the sentences meet the standards of agent prose? Are they clear and precise? Do they define agents and acts?
8. Is the essay effective or ineffective?

Textbooks Get an *F*

Statistics show that over sixty percent of a college student's education is provided by textbooks, which seemingly would be written in a clear, comprehensible style. The books used by many general education classes at the University of Missouri, however, suggest that good writing seldom appears on the shelves of a campus bookstore. These texts obscure important facts and concepts with Latinate, meaningless, and technical diction, awkward sentences, and unnecessary words, thereby decreasing the reader's understanding and interest in learning.

Ellis and Gulick's *Calculus with Analytic Geometry*, the textbook used by the general calculus classes at the University of Missouri, is as appropriate as a sourcebook of examples of awkward sentences as a mathematics publication. The long, complex sentences, such as the following, must be read several times to be understood: "Despite the various methods that exist for calculating integrals—those we have described and many we have not—it is frequently difficult or impossible to express an indefinite integral in terms of the familiar functions and thereby compute the corresponding definite integrals." Test scores, however, are a better representation of Ellis and Gulick's awkward writing and the difficulty a student has reading it. Mathematics professors complain that the most frequently missed questions are those pertaining to the reading material. Obviously, the use of poorly written mathematics textbooks has a serious effect on the learning process.

Meaningless words and phrases make William Fleming's *Arts and Ideas,* a typical humanities textbook, even less understandable than the average mathematics book. Fleming employs terms out of proper context in meaningless discussions of art. A description of the Pazzi Chapel suggests that in the cloister "mystery and infinity have yielded to geometric clarity." Similarly, Botticelli's *Birth of Venus* is said to be dominated by "incisiveness of outline" and "ballet-like choreography of lines." Passages containing unrelated technical words grouped into nonsensical gobbledygook are more confusing: Botticelli's paintings become "reflections of a neopagan atmosphere with its Christian concordances" while Masaccio's are "in the iconographical tradition." Meaningless studies of art in typical humanities textbooks are perhaps contributory to the unpopularity of classical art with college students.

To assure proper understanding and performance of dangerous experiments, special care would presumably be taken in clearly and concisely writing a chemistry laboratory manual. John Baxter and George Ryschkewitsch's *General Chemistry* laboratory manual is quite ambiguous, however, as important facts are obscured with Latinate or technical diction. Medicine droppers, common household implements, are confusingly renamed "micro-pipets." The simple principle that the greater the extent of reaction between two substances, the more concentrated are the products is restated: "the more strongly the water molecules are deformed, the more acidic and less basic their gelatinous hydroxides will be." As absurd is the description of electrons changing position under the influence of a positive charge as "mutual polarization caus[ing] shifts in electron distribution evoking induced dipoles." The Latinate, technical syle in which chemistry textbooks and laboratory manuals are written is one reason why chemistry classes typically give the lowest grades at a university.

> The textbooks used by general education classes in mathematics, humanities, chemistry, and other subjects at the University of Missouri are notable for a poor writing style. In many cases the writing in these texts deserves an *F*. They confuse students and make learning disinteresting, or even odious. The increasing use of such works is probably a major factor in the decreasing general knowledge of graduates and the decline in the number of college applicants.

CLASSIFICATION

People who face an unorganized group of things instinctively eliminate chaos by grouping them. Most people, for instance, keep their cleaning products in one cabinet, their canned goods in another, their dishes in another. Only in the most chaotic of homes would you find frying pans next to the roach killer. In the same way, newspaper editors do not put their stories together at random. When you pick up the paper to read about your school's last basketball game, you flip directly to the sports section; you do not have to begin at page one and search for the story on the game. Similarly, university officials, faced with a mass of people of differing ages, majors, financial situations, races, and religious beliefs, group students a number of ways—usually according to the colleges they enter and their academic year. In college you find yourself identified according to these classifications—for instance, as a 3CHEM or a 4LA, meaning that you are a junior majoring in chemistry or a senior in the liberal arts school.

Classification, therefore, is a process that you expect universities to use in identifying students, editors to use in the newspaper, and everyone to use in the kitchen. That people do this simplifies your life. You will find that you, too, naturally employ classification to organize all kinds of activities. When you do the laundry, you may separate the white clothes from the colored clothes, the cottons from the permanent press fabrics, the regular clothes from the delicate ones. When you begin your studies for the evening, you might separate the more difficult assignments from the easier ones or the ones due tomorrow from the ones due in a few days.

Just as you use classification in these familiar ways, you can also use classification to organize your writing in special situations. Whenever your purpose for writing is to examine a collection of things (agents-acts-scenes-means-motives) and to discover how they can be grouped or categorized, you should organize your paper according to the principles of classification. Let's go through these principles with a specific example in mind. Suppose you are asked to write an essay on the *means* that television advertisers use to appeal to the public. You would begin by brainstorming, by simply listing all of the television advertisements you have seen recently.

Zenith
Coke
Pepsi
McDonald's
Burger King
L'Oreal
Avon
Gillette Foamy
Wilkinson Sword blades
Close-up
Chrysler
Mercury Monarch
Volkswagen
Curtis Mathes
Revlon Mascara
Ivory Liquid
Federal Express
Nabisco Shredded Wheat
Publix
Winn Dixie
Pizza Hut
Grecian Formula 16
NyQuil
Maytag
Xerox copiers
Easy Off
Sears radial tires
local restaurant
Miller Lite beer
Budweiser
local car lot
Mr. Coffee
Butter-Up popper
L'eggs panty hose
Excedrin
Bayer aspirin
Dr. Pepper
Crest
Mustang II
Mazola
Prell
Right Guard
Dial
Irish Spring
Allstate Insurance
Metropolitan Life
Old Spice
Contac
Merrill Lynch
E.F. Hutton
Prudential Insurance

After you make up your list, you should decide on one principle of classification, one characteristic or feature that you will use to set up different categories. These first categories need not be directly related to *means.* They are a way for you to continue the brainstorming process by organizing your data. For example, you could differentiate between local and national advertisements; in this case your classification principle would be the *source* of the commercials. As you do this, you should record your categories on a classification chart to keep track of your divisions. Note the following:

Television Advertisements
(source)
National Local

Your chart is correct at this point for three reasons. You have divided the large class (television advertisements) into at least two subclasses (national and local). You are using one principle of classification (*source*) to set up these subclasses, and these subclasses are all-inclusive. By *all-inclusive* we mean that all the television advertisements on your list belong to either one subclass or the other. But you can't end your chart here if you want to write an interesting essay; the subclasses are so broad they include many different kinds of television advertisements. You need to continue brainstorming and establish additional subclasses. At this point you can also begin to focus your chart. Since in a short essay you will not discuss all kinds of advertisements, you will probably want to develop only one side of your chart. Let's work with the *national* advertisements. Since you must set up additional subclasses, you must decide on another principle for division. Guided by the pentad, you might choose the advertiser's *motive*.

Television Advertisements

(source)

National

(motive)

To sell a product	To ask for a contribution	To provide a public service message	To support a candidate

Again, these subclasses work because they meet the three criteria that we said a valid classification must follow. The larger class has been divided into at least two subclasses (four here), the principle of classification (*motive*) is consistent, and these subclasses are all-inclusive—all of the national advertisements on the list fit into one of these four groups.

Now you must decide whether you want to stop at this point and write an essay on the four types of national television advertisements determined by motive or whether you want to divide one of these four into subclasses and close in on your paper topic still further. You might decide that these four types of advertisements are so obvious they leave little room for development, and that you need to continue brainstorming. If you choose to divide into subclasses those national television advertisements that sell a product, you again have to search for a principle of classification. Again using the pentad, you could choose *means*. Keeping the three criteria for valid classification in mind, you might divide the subclass in the following way:

Television Advertisements

(source)

National

(motive)

Those selling a product

(means)

Those appealing to our emotions	Those appealing to our logical faculties	Those appealing to both

Since the subclasses of this division are still too obvious, you would probably want to carry your brainstorming one step further and split one of these subclasses into smaller categories. For example you could subdivide those national television advertisements selling a product by appealing to our logical faculties. If your principle for classifying these advertisements is the claims they make (again, *means*), your chart might look like this:

Television Advertisements

(source)

National

(motive)

Those selling a product

(means)

Those appealing to our logical faculties

(means)

Those claiming that their products give us quality and efficiency	Those claiming that their products save us money or add to our financial security	Those claiming that their products improve or save our health

Making sure that you have again followed the three criteria for logical classification, you can finally stop dividing your subclasses into smaller categories. Your chart is now specific enough to serve as the basis of a short essay. But before you begin to write, you must look at your brainstorming list and decide which commercials you can use as examples of the subclasses you have created. All effective classification includes illustration. You must cite sample members of the subclasses if your essay is to be really specific and concrete. Therefore, to complete your chart, fill in examples under your most specific subclasses.

Those national television advertisements
that sell a product by appealing to our
logical faculties

Those claiming that their products give us quality and efficiency	Those claiming that their products save us money or add to our financial security	Those claiming that their products improve or save our health
Curtis Mathes Maytag Xerox copiers	McDonald's Prudential Insurance Sears radial tires	Bayer aspirin Mazola Nabisco Shredded Wheat

Once you have brainstormed—that is, once you have made your list, formulated your chart, and selected your examples—you can plan your classification essay. Your essay will develop your chart by focusing particularly on your most specific class and subclasses. In this case, the advertisements trying to sell a product logically are the most specific class, and the three "claims" are the most specific subclasses. The introduction to your essay should explain the characteristics of your most specific class and indicate the sequence of your body paragraphs. As always, in the introduction you should indicate your purpose, that is, the point you wish to make by classifying your topic. You should make it clear that you will be discussing the *means* by which certain advertisers achieve their purpose, which is selling the product.

After you establish your purpose, explain the characteristics of your specific class, and indicate its subclasses, you will have set up the organization for the rest of your essay. Each body paragraph should deal with one of the subclasses. In each of these paragraphs, you should discuss the distinguishing features of the subclass—those features that set it off from the other members of its class. Then you can make your discussion concrete by citing one or more of the examples from your chart and showing how they fulfill the characteristics of the subclass. For the example essay we are developing, you would devote one body paragraph to those ads claiming their products give us quality or efficiency, and you could cite the Curtis Mathes and Xerox commercials as examples. Your next body paragraph would discuss those ads claiming their products save us money or add to our financial security; the McDonald's and Prudential Insurance commercials would be examples. In your final body paragraph, you would talk about those ads claiming their products improve or save our health, and you would use the Nabisco Shredded Wheat and Bayer aspirin ads as examples. In your conclusion you could reassert your purpose for classifying and perhaps draw pertinent conclusions from your divisions. Remember that your concluding paragraph should never leave your readers asking, "So what?" It should remind them of the essay's main idea. Your outline would look like this:

I. Discussion of Main Class: Television commercials
   —Indication of subclasses: "Logical" commercials
   —Indication of purpose: How television has manipulated us

II. Discussion of Subclass 1: Commercials claiming quality and efficiency
   Example(s): Curtis Mathes, etc.

III. Discussion of Subclass 2: Commercials claiming economy
   Example(s): McDonald's, etc.

IV. Discussion of Subclass 3: Commercials claiming health benefits
   Example(s): Bayer, etc.

V. Conclusion—reassertion of purpose: Hidden persuaders

We followed this outline as we composed our sample essay on television advertisements, but it is an outline that you can profitably follow no matter what your topic. Note that while you might come up with more than three subclasses, if you had only two, you would have a short essay much like a comparison essay. Be sure to develop your examples thoroughly. You should not be satisfied simply to cite the example; you should *explain how* the example specifically fits the characteristics of the subclass. The principles of effective classification are all evident in the following sample essay.

Television Commercials

Americans watch advertisements—nine and one-half minutes of them per one-hour show—so that they can enjoy the television programs these advertisements make possible. Most advertisements are designed to sell products to the American public, coaxing them to buy anything from new tires to dandruff shampoo. The most flashy of the advertisements appeal to the passions and irrational impulses of Americans—their sexual fantasies, their cravings for adventure, their conflicting desires to belong to a group and at the same time to assert a rugged individualism. Some advertisers, however, are moving away from appeals to our passions and are making commercials that appeal to our logical faculties. They base their advertisements on facts and seemingly ask us to *reason* rather than *feel*. These supposedly rational commercials make three basic claims and so fall into three divisions: those claiming that their products give us quality and efficiency, those claiming that their products save us money or add to our financial security, and those claiming that their products improve or save our health.

The television commercials that claim their products give us quality and efficiency certainly appeal to our reason. They do not link their products with macho heroes or slinky models; they do not promise us fame or adventure. They simply show us that we will benefit in tangible ways if we select their product, and they back this claim up by offering us demonstrations, reports, testimony, and facts. Maytag is one company that uses this approach. Their lonely repairman bemoans his inactivity and goes on to explain that Maytag washing machines and dryers are so well built that they never break. He elaborates on their special features and mentions Maytag's confident guarantee. Then an announcer breaks in to remind us that Maytags are "dependable" machines. By the close of the ad, we are assured that if we buy Maytags we will never have to pay the Maytag repairman. In a similar ad, Xerox has Brother Dominic confronted by stacks of manuscripts that his abbot has asked him to reproduce. Brother Dominic faces long weeks of tedious hand-copying, but, fortunately, the Lord provides a miraculous expedient—a Xerox copier. The grateful Dominic completes his task in moments rather than weeks. And as we watch the copier whip out copies, collate them, and perform back-to-back reproductions, we, like the abbot, can truly marvel at this "godsend" of a machine. We too can envision the ways in which it would save us time and energy if we had one.

Another type of commercial that appeals to our reason promises us economy or financial security. This type of advertisement is especially effective in these days of endlessly escalating prices and ever shrinking savings and salaries. When Americans are shown that by purchasing a particular product they will spend less than they might have or when they are shown that by investing in a certain way they will guard against financial ruin, they are likely to believe. These advertisements offer facts, statistics, and assurances about the value and affordability of the products in question—all rational considerations. In one such advertisement, McDonald's reminds us that we can still buy a complete meal—hamburger, fries, and drink—for under a dollar.

We see an amazed customer staring at his change while a happy voice says, "At McDonald's you can get a meal and come away with change in your pocket." The customer exits, flipping the money in the air and whistling the McDonald's theme. Prudential Insurance doesn't promise to save us money, but they do promise to provide funds in case of unexpected accidents or expenses. In one of their ads, a car careens through city streets causing a series of catastrophes. It smashes through a fruit stand, breaks a window, and knocks a light pole across the top of a limousine. Of course, the fruit stand owner, the house owner, and the car owner all have "a piece of the rock," which will help them avert financial ruin. They are dismayed, but not destroyed. Thus Prudential coaxes us to consider whether *we* would be destroyed by such disasters and then offers a soothing, reasonable description of programs they offer to make sure we are not.

While this type of commercial plays on our money worries, another type directs its message to concerns about our health. These advertisements assume that we all wish to be slim, avoid cholesterol, maintain regularity, and ease pain as quickly as possible. They offer doctors' reports, scientific findings, chemical analyses, diagrams, models, and case studies to help us come to the rational conclusion that we need their products. The Nabisco advertisers, for instance, sell their Shredded Wheat through a logical, no-frills approach. They show us a close-up of a shredded wheat biscuit, and as we gaze at this fibrous rectangle, a confidential voice whispers the long list of nutritional ingredients that it contains. The voice assures us that this shredded wheat contains no salt and no sugar and that it provides the fiber so important to digestion and elimination. We haven't watched Farrah Fawcett downing the cereal; rather we have received a straightforward presentation of the benefits that it provides and that all thinking people should desire. Bayer aspirin also lists the ingredients of its product and promises us that it will reduce fever and help us through bouts with cold and flu. Additionally, Bayer's advertisers call our attention to doctors' reports and recommendations. The claim that "four out of five doctors recommend Bayer" asks us to *think* and buy Bayer. These statistics are accompanied by an opening view of a man with blatant flu symptoms coming in from an evening thunderstorm. He is coughing, aching with fever, and chilled. After his concerned wife gives him Bayer aspirin, we see him lying comfortably in bed and smiling. Obviously, his wife gave him an effective medicine—Bayer.

In all of these "thinking people's" advertisements, advertisers appear to use a straightforward approach; they seem to give us

> the facts and invite us to draw logical conclusions. Therefore, we tend to accept their claims and their products more readily than we do the claims and products of advertisers appealing to our passions. When Joe Namath recommends panty hose or when a sexy model appears each time a man uses Noxema Shave Cream, we readily see that we are being manipulated—we know that Joe is no expert on hose and that the sex symbol is not going to appear in our bathrooms. But when we are told that "four out of five doctors recommend Bayer" or that "a piece of the rock" will help us meet disaster, we do not always question the commercials as we should—they seem to be giving a straight story without gimmicks. This sense of security can be a mistake, however, and the public should not let down its guard just because a commercial seems to make a rational appeal. How many doctors were actually surveyed about their preference for Bayer aspirin? The company need only have asked five to say "four out of five doctors recommend Bayer." This would hardly have been a valid sample. How much does "a piece of the rock" cost? How many of us are going to have a little old lady driver knock a pole across our cars? How does Prudential perform for ordinary accidents and claims? These kinds of questions are appropriate no matter how logical commercials seem. And with an apparently endless stream of advertisements appealing to our rational faculties, we need to remember to ask them.

Note that the introduction in this essay reflects the narrowing-down process we went through when doing the chart. The introduction raises questions of *motives* and *means,* introduces the most specific class—advertisements appealing to our logical faculties—and gives its characteristics. The introduction then names the three subclasses of this class. Each of the three body paragraphs deals with one of these subclasses, giving its characteristics and then providing examples. Notice that the examples are not just stated, they are presented in detail so that the reader can see how they exhibit the general characteristics of the subclass. The conclusion repeats the main points from the introduction and states more strongly the purpose for the classification. You should follow this pattern for the "short"—five-to-ten paragraph—classification essay because it helps you fit extensive material into an economical form.

The essay on advertisements is an example of *pure classification*. We began our brainstorming by *listing* all the members we could think of belonging to the *broad* class of commercials. Only after studying this list did we begin to group certain television advertisements together because of key similarities. Another method of grouping things is *division.* This method is often mistaken for pure classification but is actually quite different. In division you cite a class and divide it without first referring to a list of specific members of the class. Only after you finish your general division into subclasses do you search for particular members of those subclasses.

This method works well if you already know how you wish to divide a class into subclasses and do not need to explore and experiment as you do when you brainstorm for pure classification. For instance if you know you want to divide the class *apartments* into efficiency apartments, garden apartments, studio apartments, and townhouse apartments, you need not list all the apartments in your community and study that list before beginning to classify. Your own common knowledge has already provided you with the subclasses. Therefore, *division* is appropriate when you *thoroughly know* the class and the subclasses. *Classification* is appropriate when you want to *explore* a broad class for the subclasses within it, and discover, with the help of the pentad, categories that are not immediately obvious or part of your common knowledge.

Many times you will find stating a purpose much easier in pure classification than in division, since in pure classification you are probably informing your readers about groupings that they have not noticed. In division the categories that were so clear to you before you began to write are most likely equally clear to your readers before they begin to read. They probably all know the different types of apartments. Many of them, however, might not have noticed that commercials fall into patterns; they are bombarded by too many different kinds of ads to pay close attention.

The process of division can also lead you to certain dangers with your brainstorming chart. Because you do not have the list of particulars in front of you, you can easily fail to make your subclasses all-inclusive. For example the student who wrote the following sample essay, "Wash and Dry," wanted to identify the kinds of people who frequent 24-hour laundromats. He divided the people into three basic types: the intellectual, the cheerleader, and the coin-op addict. Study his chart.

People Who Use Laundromats

Intellectual   Cheerleader   Coin-op addict

Obviously, his subclasses are not all-inclusive since these three types are not the only ones who use laundromats—the rest of us folks do too. If he had used the classification process, he would have listed all the people he saw in the laundromat over a given time period and then worked out categories that accounted for every person there. Or, if he had still wanted to focus on the three types he chose, he would have seen that he had to change his general class to colorful or distinctive characters in the laundromat to make his subclasses all-inclusive. Even then he might still have had to adjust his subclasses because his list might provide other "colorful types" he could have added to his chart. As you read his essay, note that while he minutely describes the characteristics of the intellectual, the cheerleader, and the coin-op addict, he does not offer examples. These logical problems mar an otherwise witty, original piece of writing. As you read it, you should mark the points in the essay at which it strays from the principles of agent prose—of which there are many—just to keep in practice.

Wash and Dry

It has been said by many that if you were to die and go to hell you would find yourself in a 24-hour laundromat. Needless to say, you will never meet your future husband, wife, or lover in a laundromat. They are forsaken by God and inhabited briefly by humankind. Although countless thousands have found themselves in a laundromat, they remarkably boil down to three basic types: the intellectual, the cheerleader, and the coin-op addict. Of course, they all come to perform the same basic task of cleaning dirty laundry. But how they approach their task and those around them is well worth observing.

The intellectual stands out like a polar bear in Hawaii. He could never be confused with a coin-op addict because he is wearing clean clothes. He is wearing a lab coat, black rim glasses, short hair, and in his breast pocket he has every writing instrument known to man. His attitude is one of efficiency, practicality, and a general sense of detachment. He starts the "experiment" by measuring just the right amount of Cheer, which can be used with three different temperatures, into a cup that has metric measurements that only a scientist could love. He then reads the washer lid, and then carefully punches all the right buttons. Our man then sits down and thumbs through *Scientific American* until his wash is done. The intellectual then places his clothes in the dryer. He knows how long the average dryer takes to dry clothes and has the exact change in his hand. In his mind he is planning a paper on What is Truth? His clothes finish drying and he folds his clean clothes into neat squares and hangs the lab coats on hangers. He collects his books, thoughts, clothes and starts to leave. He feels sorry for the others because they will never understand life, love, and the world around them in the truest sense of the word.

The cheerleader could not be taken for the intellectual because you know instinctively that she has never taken advanced chemistry 309, and that she wouldn't know what a *Scientific American* was if it came in and looked her in the face. She is wearing the latest in laundry wear. Gym shorts with matching shoes, bandanna, and a designer T-shirt. It would have been a dress, but after all, she's "only going to the laundry." On second glance you notice her face. It reads of disbelief: disbelief that her clothes are dirty, disbelief that she has to wash them herself, and disbelief that she came into a room with no one of any merit to notice her "laundry outfit." She has decided to make laundry day as painless and quick as possible. She haphazardly pours her Dynamo into the little blue cap that goes with the little blue gym shorts. Our cheerleader then dumps her trunk of clothes into the washer and pushes buttons at random. She then sits down and writes a letter on her pink Holly Hobbie stationery to one of several of her best friends in the entire world. She then starts another letter, this one to her boyfriend in Texas. She asks him if he ever gets lonely like she does, and if he ever wants to date other people like she does. Her clothes come out of the machine brilliant and unwrinkled. She tosses them into a hamper and starts to leave. She feels sorry for the other people in the room because they will never understand life, love, and the world around them in the truest sense of the word.

The coin-op addict could not be mistaken for anything but what he is. No sane person could ever mistake him for an intellectual or a cheerleader. He is, thank God, in a class by himself. He is wearing a gray Fruit of the Loom T-shirt with plaid double-knit pants that end just where the ankle and white socks begin. He has a look of joy about him. He loves the smell of mildew, the haze of steam, the noisy machines, and everything involved with making the laundry the living hell that it is. He cannot wait until his clothes get dirty so that he can once again go to the laundry. He has no cup, he just pours his Oxydol into the washer. The coin-op addict savors every moment. He punches the buttons slowly to prolong his mission. He finally sits down and starts to look at the pictures in *Popular Mechanics* and *Hot Rod*. He continues to read them long after the machine has stopped. He puts the money and clothes in the dryer and continues to read *Hot Rod*. When the clothes are dry they come out a dull gray, and he folds his 30 pairs of T-shirts and 19 pairs of underwear into loose gray balls. He then tosses them in front of the cheerleader who smiles because, "one must be nice to inferiors."

The coin-op addict wonders why everyone doesn't want to stay in the laundromat. He starts to feel sorry for them because they will never understand the world around them, life, love, and laundromats in the truest sense of the word.

Exercise 4

Read the following classification essay. Mark the points at which it lacks agent prose, and then criticize its content and organization. Be sure to test it according to the logical rules of classification.

The Tucker Band Program

Students take advantage of Tucker University band courses for various reasons. Usually, if a musician in one of the bands can be classified as good, mediocre, or bad, his or her reason for joining the band can be known. Participants in the program can be divided into two major groups, music majors and non-music majors, and they can be further categorized as those who take band for fun, for credit, or for practice.

The people who take a band course at Tucker University for credit shouldn't be referred to as musicians, because in most cases, they're not. These members of the music world are almost exclusively found in the marching band. This band is their choice because to be a member in one of the other performing groups would require extra time and practice on their own. Also, in an organization of this size, when performing, difficulty arises in trying to separate the good players from the bad. This is to their advantage because they are rarely blamed for mistakes which are their own. They can enjoy the glamour of the uniform, the popularity of the performer, and get an easy *A* to boost their grade point average while being undecided on a major, without having to do even their fair share of the work. (These people hardly ever learn the music or their parts in the halftime show.) Mike Stedman is a good example of this type of person. He often draws away from the band's spirit with his lacking performance and absence of esprit de corps.

Many students are in the program for the excitement of the bands. Paramount reasons for the membership of persons like this include the popularity, free admission to football games, and also free admission to music festivals. Musicians in this category are usually enthusiastic, and do their part very well, considering that they rarely are found to be among the better musicians in the band. Charlie Hicks can be found in this category. He is often a credit to the band because of his working spirit.

A few band members are in the University Band program for practice because they may someday look to music as a livelihood. Musicians such as this are usually more serious about their music and performances than those previously mentioned. They can often be found in more than one performing group. Their reason for membership in the program is maintenance of their musical knowledge and ability. This group sometimes includes jazz band members and scholarship recipients. Chris Pickel can be associated with this category. Chris is a fine musician, and she holds music to be a very important part of her life. She realizes that if her major course of study doesn't turn out as she wishes she could probably go into music as a profession and be successful.

The Tucker University band program includes a variety of members. The reasons for their participation are as diverse as the members themselves. There is no doubt that if members from all of these categories shared goals pertaining to the program, the bands would show a definite improvement.

DEFINITION

Many times in your college courses and future professions you will be called on to define terminology or clarify certain key words. Your economics professor might ask you to explain terms such as *laissez-faire* and *gross national product,* your history professor might ask for definitions of *theocracy* and *Manifest Destiny,* or your literature professor might ask you to define *novella* or *intrusive narrator.* Doctors constantly have to learn new terms for diseases, treatments, and surgical techniques and have to define these terms for other doctors. Lawyers must learn legal language—a mass of Latinate terms and their complex definitions—and, in the same way, businessmen must learn the language of the marketplace. To master their fields, engineers, sociologists, psychologists, research scientists, mechanics, and pilots all must learn complicated sets of specialized terms. You will frequently have to use the techniques of definition yourself and rely on others' use of these techniques as you study your chosen field.

These techniques of definition are quite accessible to you because you employ them almost instinctively, at least with certain kinds of terms. Test yourself for a moment. Jot down quick definitions of the words *martyr, democracy,* and *integrity.* Now compare them. Probably your definition of *martyr* closely agrees with the following: "a person who suffers or dies for his or her beliefs." If we were to check the definitions of *martyr* that other students in your class wrote, they would probably be similar to yours. As a class all of you could produce one definition of the term that everyone would accept. The reasons for this concurrence are twofold: first, *martyr* is a *concrete* term applied to only one kind of person; second, all of you instinctively used the same techniques to define a concrete term. You put the term into the *class* or the *group of like objects* to which it belongs; a *martyr* is a *person* first of all—he or she belongs to that general class. Then you gave the particular characteristics of martyrs that separate them from all other people. You can't stop with the statement that "a martyr is a person" since all of us belong to that class, and we are not all martyrs. You have to go on to explain how martyrs differ from all other kinds of people. The process you intuitively employed can be put into a simple formula.

Term = Class + Particular Characteristics
A martyr = a person who suffers or dies for his or her beliefs.

You also might have illustrated your term as part of your definition, although giving examples is not crucial for this type of formal definition. However, if you added "such as the early Christians in Rome," your definition would be even more effective.

The definition of *martyr* is relatively easy because it clearly brings the pentad into play. You group an agent with other agents, just as you might group a scene with other scenes and so on. But your definitions of *democracy* and *integrity* will both present difficulties. These words are abstractions, not agents, and you will tie them to the pentad only with great difficulty; you will continually have to refer to illustrations and examples as you offer your definitions. Whereas in the case of *martyr* the example of "early Christians in Rome" was a nice extra touch, in the case of *democracy* such an example is essential. You and the other students in your class will probably all agree that *democracy* is "a form of government." But when you begin to give particular characteristics, you will most likely lose consensus. The term has been used so frequently to describe so many different governments that you will be hard put to agree on the particular characteristics that fit *all* the governments we call democracies. Some of you might say a democracy is a representative government; others might say it is a government by individuals in which each person participates directly. Many governments that we term socialist or communist consider themselves democracies. Therefore, while you still could use the T = C + PC formula for this term, the cutting edge of your definition will be in your examples.

The word *integrity* presents another type of problem. Study closely the definition you have jotted down for this term. Very possibly, you had difficulty since you could not place *integrity* in a class that everyone agrees upon. You might have said it is a "type of behavior" or a "personality trait" or a "way of acting." Or you might have avoided putting the term in a class at all. You might have given a synonym for the word such as "soundness" or "honesty" or "moral uprightness." Of course the problem with this method is that your audience might be no more sure of the meaning of *honesty* than they are of the meaning of *integrity*. In essence you are defining one abstraction with another. The fact that *integrity* is an abstraction is, of course, the root of your difficulty with the term. You cannot put an abstraction into a set class, nor can you give it particular characteristics that everyone will accept. You might say that people who have integrity behave honorably. But what is honor? Different societies will have different notions about what constitutes honorable behavior. Again, the examples you cite will prove crucial.

First, let's discuss ways to gather and organize material for a *formal* definition of a *concrete* term. The key is to choose a term that warrants an extended discussion. If a one-sentence dictionary definition is all you need to clarify the term for your reader, then you will probably not want to write at length on it. For example, we would not want to read a full essay defining *desk*. We can be satisfied with the terse dictionary definition—"a table for writing, reading, or studying." The same goes for words such as *chair, automobile, snorkel, sweater, bobsled,* and *beach*. When we speak of *extended definition,* we refer to a thorough discussion of a concrete term about which people might have misconceptions or hazy ideas. The term must be concrete—you must be able to put it in a class and give it particular characteristics—but it must also *need* to be clarified and discussed. Terms such as *psychosis, sonata, theocracy, impressionism, anxiety, democracy, capitalism, fascism, scuba diving, manslaughter,* and *reggae* fit this description. They can all be put into classes, and all of them are probably terms we have *heard* but cannot define precisely. Therefore by defining them and stating their particular characteristics, we are writing with a purpose. None of us would profit from reading the obvious—a treatise defining a toothbrush, for instance. But all of us would profit from clarification of an overused term that no longer means exactly one thing (*democracy*), or an explanation of an unfamiliar term (*reggae*), or an explanation of an often-used term that we still might not be clear about (*manslaughter*).

To compose a *formal extended definition* of such terms, you should write out a core definition sentence. Let's use the word *myth* as an example. Before you can formulate your core definition, you will first have to determine the most specific class to which the term belongs. You might know immediately, but more than likely you will need to set up what we call a *ladder of generalization.* You will put your specific term, *myth,* at the bottom of this ladder, not knowing the most specific class to which *myth* belongs. You will want to brainstorm by finding the most general class, which will go at the top of the ladder. Probably it will be *literature.*

Literature

↑

Myth

Having determined the most general and specific terms on the ladder, you can brainstorm by working from one to the other. Ask yourself, "What kind of literature is myth a part of?" It belongs in the class of *oral literature.*

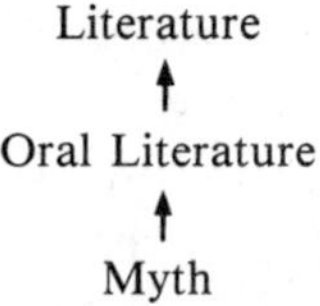

Now you must determine if you can find an even more specific class than *oral literature* to which *myth* belongs. You have to see if you can divide *oral literature* into subclasses and if *myth* will fit into one of these. You can discover, possibly with some research, that epics, ballads, and folktales are all types of oral literature and that a myth is a type of folktale. With this step, you will have completed your brainstorming chart because you have arrived at the immediately broader class to which your term belongs.

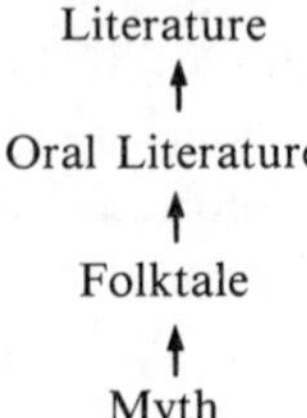

You can now go on to formulate your core definition, following the T = C + PC formula:

A myth (T) is a type of folktale (C) that explains a mystery of existence in terms that human beings can understand (PC).

To extend this definition, you should devote a portion of your essay to classifying *myth,* and a portion to contrasting it to other members of its class. To do this, you would first state the characteristics of folktales, then you would explain the particular features of *myth,* and then you would show how *myth* differs from other kinds of folktales, say *legend* and *fable.* To complete the definition, you might discuss an example of the term that fulfills the general characteristics you have described. You might, for example, cite the story of Pandora's box as a myth since it explains the presence of evil in the world by saying that a curious woman opened a box, letting human troubles escape.

An outline for a paper based on the definition essay model would look like this:

I. Introduction
   a. Discussion of general class to which term belongs
   b. Focus on term

II. Core definition of term
   Particular characteristics

III. Term contrasted with other member of its class

IV. Term contrasted with other member of its class

V. Example of term

VI. Conclusion

Specifically, then, our outline for a paper on *myth* would look like this:

I. Discussion of folktales
   Focus on *myth*

II. A myth is a type of folktale that explains a mystery of existence in terms that human beings can understand.
   Particular characteristics

III. A myth differs from a fable in that . . .

IV. A myth differs from a legend in that . . .

V. An example of a myth would be the story of Pandora's box . . .

VI. The term *myth* needs clarification because . . .

Let's talk more specifically now about each step in the essay. We are actually suggesting that you combine three models you are already familiar with—classification, comparison and contrast, and illustration—to produce the definition essay model. You will need to recall the basic principles of these three models to complete each step of definition effectively.

When you *classify myth* you must first give the general characteristics of the class—*folktale*—to which *myth* belongs. Only then can you narrow your focus to your term, make your central statement, and further explain the particular characteristics of *myth.* Unless your readers understand what a folktale is, they will not be informed by your statement that "a myth is a type of folktale," and they will not understand the significance of the term's particular characteristics.

When you *contrast myth* with other members of its class, you are really making a negative definition. You are telling what your term *is* by telling what it is *not.* But you must never lose focus on your main term; if you forget your purpose—to define *myth*—and give equal discussions to *fable* and *legend,* you will end up with a classification of types of folktales, not a definition of *myth.* Therefore, you should cite only the characteristics of *fables* and *legends* that contrast with the characteristics of *myth;* you should connect your points about them to your central definition of *myth* at all times.

When you *illustrate* your term, you must choose an example that fits the term as you have described it. Since your central point about *myth* is that people use it to explain the mysteries of existence, you should choose a specific myth that clearly illustrates this point. We have suggested the story of Pandora's box since it clearly attempts to explain the presence of evil in the world. Always make sure to connect your example with your whole definition. You can also use illustration within the definition essay by integrating examples throughout your classification and comparison-and-contrast sections. You might want to cite Pandora's box as you state the particular characteristics of *myth;* you could then contrast the story of Pandora's box with the legend of Davy Crockett and one of Aesop's fables as part of your contrast paragraphs.

In the outline, we suggest that you specify the reason for defining your term in the conclusion, since your introduction should focus on the class to which your term belongs. But many writers, to gain the reader's attention, prefer to state their purpose in the introduction and then move into classification. In that case your conclusion could reassert the need for a clear definition of the term, or it could take on other tasks. An introduction in which you state your purpose and gain reader attention is particularly appropriate when the class to which your term belongs is so well known or familiar that you do not need to cite its characteristics. This would probably not be the case with *folktale.* Though many people have heard the term, few could give its distinguishing features without research. But for a paper defining the term *psychosis,* you might not need to explain at length the characteristics of the class to which it belongs—personality disorders—since most of us are aware of what these entail.

Consider the following introduction.

> Increasingly, people are engaging in the formal and informal study of psychology. Record numbers of students are enrolling in psychology courses, and psychology-related self-help books such as *I'm OK, You're OK* are perennial best-sellers. As a result we are seeing a corresponding increase in the layperson's use of psychological terminology. Frequently, however, people use psychological terms incorrectly. For example we often use the term *psychotic* in place of the terms *neurotic* or *psychopathic* when we're describing someone we perceive to have a personality disorder.

This introduction, as we have noted, avoids an obvious explanation of personality disorders and, instead, gives purpose to a definition of the term *psychosis.* This introduction also focuses on the term to be defined and so prepares the reader for the central statement to follow at the start of the first body paragraph. Now look at the rest of this definition essay.

> Psychosis is a personality disorder characterized by the individual's loss of contact with reality. Psychotics become so overburdened with daily conflicts and anxiety that they give up the struggle to cope with everyday life. As a result, they may lapse into a fantasy world or respond to events in the real world with exaggerated emotions. For example, they may imagine voices talking to them in abusive language, or they may respond to constructive criticism with violence. Because they have lost touch with reality, psychotic individuals require hospitalization and/or protective care.
>
> In contrast, neurotics are less severely disturbed than psychotics. Neurotics also experience severe conflicts in daily life, but unlike psychotics they desperately try to cope with the resultant anxiety. Therefore, neurotics rarely require hospitalization, and they are not usually dangerous to themselves or others, as psychotics often are. Whereas neurotics can usually hold down a job and get along to some extent with their families and friends, psychotics' social functioning is greatly impaired. Obviously then, when we refer to a neurotic individual as "psychotic," we are not only using

the term inaccurately, but we are also doing a gross injustice to an already troubled individual.

The layperson also misuses the term *psychotic* to refer to someone with a psychopathic personality disorder. Since their disorder is manifested by a lifelong pattern of socially deviant behavior, psychopaths differ from psychotics. While psychotics may appear normally adjusted until their personality disorder arises, psychopaths seldom acquire any moral development and consistently seek the immediate gratification of their desires. Although both psychotics and psychopaths are prone to violent acts, psychotics strike out at the perceived cause of their anxiety, while psychopaths, who do not usually experience anxiety, act impulsively. Clearly, we must also learn to distinguish between these two personality types.

Among the many psychotics who have influenced the course of history, Adolf Hitler was a prime example. True to the psychotic personality, Hitler existed in a fantasy world. For instance he envisioned the German people as a master race of pure Aryan stock, and therefore the only people suitable for earthly existence. Hitler's psychotic delusions caused him to fear and despise other racial and ethnic groups and compelled him to wage a world war to exterminate them. In April 1945 with Berlin under the siege of American and Russian troops, Hitler spent the last days of his life raving like a maniac. Perhaps if the German people of the 1920s and 30s had understood the dimensions of Hitler's psychosis, they might have averted his atrocities. Likewise, if people were able to recognize psychotic disorders, they might be able to help troubled individuals before they harm themselves and others.

Note that the writer gives the particular characteristics of psychosis after the central statement and that the central statement follows the T = C + PC form that you use intuitively. The two contrast paragraphs maintain a focus on the main term *psychosis* even as they discuss the ways it differs from other kinds of personality disorders—neurosis and psychopathic behavior. The conclusion offers an example of a famous psychotic, Hitler, and reasserts the importance of defining the term. The only failing in the essay is that it does not give other, less controversial examples of psychotic behavior. Not all psychotics are inhuman mass murderers; many of them are not even violent.

In the essay on psychosis and in our example on myth, we assume that you know what term you wish to define. We assume that to brainstorm you will need to make a ladder of generalization and place your term in the most specific larger class to which it belongs. We assume, then, that you will be working *from* your term up the ladder of generalization. But this might not always be so.

If you are not sure of which specific term you will define, you might want to take the opposite route and choose a general class that interests you. Using the principles of division that we discussed in the classification section, you can construct a brainstorming chart to explore this general class, narrowing it down until you arrive at a definable term. For instance, perhaps you are interested in television shows and wish to explore this general category. You might begin by dividing the shows in an obvious way.

Television Shows

Prime-time   Daytime   News

You might then decide that since you watch prime-time shows most frequently, you will go on to divide them.

Prime-time

Dramatic shows   Comedies   Variety shows

Again, in your quest for specificity you will need to choose one of these still-too-general categories and divide it. Let's say you are more inclined to watch dramatic series than comedies. After recalling as many dramatic shows as you can, you will want to work out some all-inclusive subclasses.

Dramatic Shows

Traditional Action-mystery series	Prime-time Soap opera	Traditional Dramatic-character series
Hart to Hart	*Dallas*	*The Waltons*
The Fall Guy	*Knots Landing*	*Trapper John, M.D.*
Magnum, P.I.	*Hill Street Blues*	*Little House on the Prairie*

Here you can probably stop your brainstorming since prime-time soap opera seems a viable term for definition. We hear this term applied to shows, but how many of us are sure of exactly what it means? Therefore, you can profitably define it. Also, you can put *prime-time soap opera* (your term) in a class and state its particular characteristics (T = C + PC).

> A prime-time soap opera (T) is a type of dramatic series (C) that uses continuing plot lines and changing characters (PC).

After arriving at your term and formulating your central statement, you can easily set up the outline for your definition essay.

I. Introduction
(You will probably want to focus on the influx of prime-time soap operas into the nightly television schedule and the new twists they bring to the dramatic series format. You won't have to define *dramatic series* as you had to define *folktale.*)

II. Core definition of prime-time soap opera
—particular characteristics further detailed

III. A prime-time soap differs from a traditional action-mystery series in that . . .

IV. A prime-time soap differs from a traditional dramatic-character series in that . . .

V. The show *Dallas* is probably the clearest example of a prime-time soap.

VI. Conclusion
(You might want to speculate on where dramatic series go from here or on what the popularity of the prime-time soap reveals about television audiences.)

The definition essay you would write from this brainstorming chart and outline would be the same type as the ones on *myth* and *psychosis.* They all are examples of the *formal extended definition* essay.

If you need to define an abstract term, you cannot use the formal definition model, but we suggest that you use some of its principles. More specifically, we suggest that you use illustration alone to define the term, although you may also in subtle ways differentiate your abstract term from others like it. Using the first suggestion—illustration—you might give several examples of instances or situations that fit your term. For example, if you are defining *courage,* you might cite three examples in which people display courage and then sum up the characteristics illustrated by each case. You might cite an athlete's determined recovery from an apparently crippling injury, a soldier's risking his or her life to aid an injured comrade, or a blind student's successful career at a large, confusing university. All of these people could be called courageous. You must search your examples, see what traits they share, and then draw conclusions about what behavior deserves the label of *courage.*

Another special type of definition essay is the *etymological definition* essay. To write this type of composition, you would choose for your term a word whose meaning has changed dramatically through the centuries. You would explain the present meaning of the term and then contrast this meaning with past meanings. Words can change in both denotation (their literal meaning) and connotation (the associations they evoke). Words can also change from one part of speech to another—they can come into the language as nouns, for example, and evolve into verbs. We now typically use the word *gossip* as a verb that means "to spread rumors about others." But in the eighteenth century, the word was used as a noun and meant "an old woman." The word *shambles* used to refer to a slaughterhouse; now we principally use *shambles* to describe a messy, disordered condition. Some words have changed only slightly in denotation but have shifted dramatically in connotation. For example, *hussy* has always been a term applied to women—and it has remained a noun—but over the years its connotation has changed. Initially *hussy* was applied to respectable women and was a synonym for *housewife;* gradually, it came to mean "a woman of low morals." Today the word is most often used in a humorous context. This change in meaning is *pejorative:* the word has gone from a positive to a negative connotation. If the word had gained a more respectable meaning through the years, it would have undergone an *ameliorative* change, a change for the better. For example, the words *primitive* and *natural,* understood in the sixteenth and seventeenth centuries to denote lack of learning and taste, are today often synonymous with *wisdom* and *virtue.* An etymological definition essay traces the changes that a term has gone through; this kind of essay is, in fact, a history of the development of a word. Consider the following sample essay on the changes in the word *hussy.*

Would You Call Your Mother a Hussy?

During the sixteenth century, it would have been proper to call one's mother a "hussy." This word, like many others, has undergone a change in meaning over a period of years, and today it means something quite different from what it meant originally. For approximately 200 years now, the word *hussy* has been defined as "a woman of low or improper behavior," or "a pert, mischievous girl." However, during the sixteenth century the word *hussy* was used in reference to the mistress of a household. Developing from a phonetic reduction of *housewife, hussy* was used as neutrally as *housewife* is today. Being a gentleman's hussy was as respectable as being a gentleman's wife; indeed, they were the same.

In succeeding years a gradual shift occurred, and by the eighteenth century, the word *hussy* had taken on a new meaning. *Hussy* became a "rustic" or "rude" way of addressing a woman. Although the degree of rudeness depended largely on the user's intention, to be addressed as "hussy" during this period was to be addressed with some disrespect. For instance, a man who felt superior to a woman might familiarly address her as "hussy."

The changes in *hussy*'s meaning can be seen in characteristic expressions used during different periods. Spelling changes also occurred but were unrelated to the changes in meaning. In sixteenth-century Scotland a man might say to his servants: "No servants shall take other clothes than their master's and hussy's and their household's clothes to wash." Here *hussy* implies no disrespect toward the mistress of the house. But by the middle of the eighteenth century, we hear in Fielding's *Tom Jones:* "Hussy, . . . I will make such a saucy trollop as yourself know, that I am not a proper subject of your discourse." Or, a bit later in the eighteenth century, we encounter a woman using the term, somewhat humorously, of herself: "He . . . patted my cheek, and genteely called me a little hussey." Here *hussy* has become more of an address and more of a label for a woman of frivolous character. By the nineteenth century, this meaning of the word had become standard, as in George Eliot's: "The naughtier the little huzzy behaved the prettier she looked."

The evolution of the word *hussy,* then, has been a downward one morally. Reduced from the respectable sixteenth-century term *housewife, hussy* gradually took on varied connotations of disrespect until it came to mean "a woman of ill repute." Today the word seems to be taking on a humorous connotation. Thus you might overhear in contemporary conversation: "My father is so antiquated he believes any woman who asks a man out is a hussy." But you would never, under normal circumstances, say to your mother, "Mom, you're a terrific hussy!"

To write a paper of this type, you will obviously have to do research. Your likeliest source of information will be the *Oxford English Dictionary,* available in all college libraries. The *OED* provides a thorough history of each word, recording its changes in meaning and giving sample sentences to illustrate how it was used at various stages of its development. The student who wrote the paper on *hussy* took his example quotations from the *OED.* You can illustrate an etymological definition by using a few of these sample quotations to put the word in context.

EXERCISE 5

Read and criticize the following definition essay. Notice the essay's style and the writer's use of agent prose. Then ask yourself the following questions.

1. Does the writer place the term logically into its class?
2. Is the description of the general class in the introduction adequate?
3. Does the central statement provide the class and the term's particular characteristics?
4. Is there adequate elaboration on these particular characteristics?
5. Does the writer maintain the focus on her main term in her contrast paragraphs?
6. Does the example fit the term and truly illustrate its characteristics?
7. Does the conclusion clearly state the purpose for defining the term?

Outside the Body

Dreaming is a natural function of all human beings. Dreaming refers to the experience of recalling scenes that seem to occur in a purely imaginary and sometimes absurd world. Usually this world is part of the sleeping unconscious. There are several types of dreams, and perhaps the most unusual one is the out-of-body experience, or OOBE (standard abbreviation). In the OOBE, dreamers feel themselves located at some point other than where they know their physical bodies to be. An out-of-body experience is a type of dream that has a deeply emotional and sometimes religious effect on people, unlike dreams such as the high dream or lucid dream.

A high dream, unlike the OOBE, has a pattern similar to the induced state of consciousness of a psychedelic drug. People experience intensified perceptions of colors and "vibrations" that are not usually present in the OOBE. Feelings of immediate insight into life are experienced, but they differ from the insightful experience of the OOBE because their effect is only a temporary feeling of ecstasy.

The lucid dream differs from the OOBE in that dreamers possess a state of consciousness in which they are able to think and reason. People may actually think, "I am dreaming," even though they remain in the dream world. The lucid dream in itself is more of a conscious analysis of a dream than the philosophical or religious feeling experienced in the OOBE. However, lucid dreams can turn into out-of-body experiences.

Most OOBEs occur either spontaneously or because of an accident or illness that brings the dreamer close to death. In one particular incident, a pilot became a minister after an OOBE. It seems that Burris Jerkins had been in the midst of an explosion. He was in serious condition with a slim chance of survival. Jerkins recovered, however, and during his recuperation experienced an OOBE.

In the OOBE Jerkins floated into the clouds, looked down, and saw himself lying in bed. Soon he found himself accelerating through intergalactic space. He became aware of great numbers of beings in communion with one Great Being and assumed that he must be dead. Jerkins felt comforted as he realized that his wife would join him someday. It became clear, though, that he would continually move faster than any being behind him and slower than any being ahead of him. Jerkins stated, "It had a profound religious effect on me, in that it shook my view that the universe is made up of what we can see, touch, and feel."

The OOBE occurs neither in a waking state nor in an ordinary dream state. It is a state of consciousness that is experienced in no other type of dream. The OOBE is a unique phenomenon in any lifetime and has a profound effect on dreamers that no other type of dream state produces.

Exercise 6

When you write a central statement for a formal definition essay, you must be sure to put your term into its correct class and to state particular characteristics that clearly distinguish the term from all other members of its class. Study the following central statements to determine if they are acceptable.

1. A tragedy is a type of drama in which sad events take place.
2. Flip-flops are a type of sandals usually made of rubber and worn for casual occasions.
3. Avant-garde is a type of music played by weird musicians.
4. Soccer is a type of game in which players kick a round ball up and down a field until someone scores a goal.
5. A lie is a statement that people know to be false even as they say it.
6. A cross-country skier is a person who skis for long distances.
7. A theocracy is a government by theocrats.
8. A network is anything reticulated or decussated, at equal distances, with interstices between the intersections.
9. A chair is an object usually found in homes and offices.
10. A satyr is a mythological being who is part human and part goat.

ANALYSIS

Whenever you analyze anything, you divide it into its component parts and study them closely to determine how they fit together or how they work. If you analyze a problem, for instance, you look at all of the circumstances that contribute to it and only then determine its main causes and a possible solution. When batting instructors analyze a baseball player's swing, they break it down into the movements that the player uses to prepare the swing, make contact with the ball, and follow through. After such an analysis, they may help the player improve on one movement or several.

Often your purpose for writing an essay will be to analyze your feelings, events happening around you, other people's writings, or events in the past. You can perform such analyses by *classifying, defining, illustrating,* and *comparing,* since each of these processes calls for you to break down your topic and explore its parts. But two other types of analysis are important. They are *process analysis* and *causal analysis.*

You write *process analysis* whenever your purpose is to teach how to do something or to explain how something works. If you want to teach your reader how to write an effective essay, how to assemble a kite, or how to start a band, you will use the process model. If you want to explain to your reader how a ski jumper can float down a mountain, how a newspaper is put together every day, or how a rotary engine works, you will use the process model as well. Process analysis always asks you to focus on *acts.*

The process analysis essay proves quite easy to organize for two reasons. For one, your purpose is direct and clear. Your goal is to explain an act or process to readers, or to instruct readers so that they can perform a particular act or process. Also, when you teach or explain a process, it usually falls into logical steps, automatically providing a clear sequence of ideas. For instance, if you are teaching your readers how to write an effective essay, you will tell them to begin with brainstorming, then to formulate a central statement, to organize their supports, and only then to begin writing. This teaching essay should proceed chronologically with the steps building on one another. Therefore, the order of the body paragraphs is already determined; each will deal with one step in the process you are describing. The same is true with an essay that explains a process. For example, if you are describing how a ski jumper can float down a mountain, you will probably divide the process into logical steps: the run down the slope to pick up speed; the moment of takeoff, when the snap of the knees and the positioning of the skis are so crucial; the actual flight, when the jumper's body uses the air in the same way that an airplane wing does; and finally the all-important landing with the knees bent. The order for your body paragraphs here is obvious too; each will describe one facet of the whole jump. Again you will organize the essay chronologically, putting the steps in the order in which the jumper performs them.

In the process essay, your introduction will probably describe the process or *act* as a whole, its purpose, and its end result. Typically your central statement will indicate the steps in the process that you will discuss in your body paragraphs. In this way you set up your sequence. Each body paragraph will discuss a major step in the process, and your conclusion might return to a general view of the difficulty of the process or the importance of the end result.

Look at the following sample essays. The first analyzes the process people should go through to determine whether a pizza is truly worthwhile. The writer advises the readers that they must make three tests to judge accurately.

Judging Pizzas

Although it originated in Italy, the pizza has achieved its greatest popularity in America. Industry studies show that last year Americans downed more than 50,000,000 pizzas, frozen and fresh, in restaurants or at home. Pizza parlors, palaces, inns, and huts dot American roadways—roadways crowded with various pizza vans delivering the ever-popular pie. As happens with all good things, however, the popularity of pizza is not without its drawbacks. With so many pizzas being produced, the quality of pizza, at least in the United States, has tended to decline. Many merchants, interested in profit more than quality, have conspired to produce a pizza that bears little relation to the delicious Italian original. Pizza lovers, looking forward to enjoying their favorite meal, often find themselves disappointed by cut-rate imitations. In fact, despite the wide variety of pizzas in America, pizza lovers may have trouble finding a true pizza. Luckily, however, they are usually well aware of the tests they must make to spot the genuine article. They know they must first examine the crust to make sure it is crunchy and chewy. Then they must determine whether the tomato sauce is thick and tasty. And finally they must test the cheese topping, which must be rich and succulent.

Novices may debate the merits of anchovies and jalapeño peppers, but true pizza lovers know that the pizza is only as good as its crust. In Italy the dough for pizza crusts is made lovingly and carefully by hand. American pizza makers, all too interested in mass production, have tried to modernize the crust-making process. They usually go one of two ways:

they make a very thin crust, not unlike that of frozen fruit pies, or they make a very thick crust, not unlike frozen dinner rolls. People who have eaten a standard American frozen pizza, only to discover that they mistook the pizza crust for the cardboard box the pizza came in, know how far the thin crust deviates from the crust of true pizza. People who have gagged on the crust of pizzas produced by many nationwide chain restaurants know the dangers of the thick crust. These chain restaurants often bill their pizza as "Chicago style." Actually, no such thing as Chicago style pizza exists. These pizza makers have simply discovered that they can take what was essentially a spongy dinner roll and substitute it for pizza dough, thus clearing the way for mass production. Since this pizza would bear only the faintest resemblance to real pizza, they had to justify the change; "Chicago style," with its connotations of Godfather authority and midwestern vitality, was their answer. The true pizza dough that pizza lovers seek is handmade by an expert. It is thick but light, crunchy but chewy, and provides a firm but not overwhelming base for the toppings. Pizza purists either find a crust like this or dispose of the inferior pie in the nearest trash can.

If the crust is the heart of the pizza, tomato sauce is its soul. In searching for a true pizza, pizza lovers look for a sauce that is thick and tasty. They know that the Italians make their sauces from only the ripest, plumpest tomatoes. American pizza makers, again in the interests of mass production, do not want to waste time selecting tomatoes. They buy tomatoes by the ton, reduce them to sauce, and spread a scant glaze of the mixture on their pizzas. The sauce, full of second-rate, often unripe tomatoes, is usually thin and watery. Also, since the appeal to mass taste requires that no taste be offended, American mass producers add few spices to their sauce. They let the bland tomato taste stand by itself in order to save money and spare sensitive customers. Anyone who has ever eaten mass-produced pizza has encountered this watered-down sauce. Even before eating one of these pizzas, true pizza lovers immediately notice the sauce is more orange than red. A true pizza, on the contrary, will be decidedly red in color. The dull color of the mass-produced pizza only adumbrates its insipid taste. Faced with an orange pizza, pizza purists turn away in disgust.

If crust is the heart of the pizza and sauce its soul, then its body—the stuff that holds it together—is cheese. True pizza lovers look for only the finest natural cheeses, the kind used by Italian pizza makers. American mass producers substitute skim-milk whey and processed cheese for Mozarella and Gouda. People who have dropped a frozen pizza, only to have it bounce back into their hands, know how rubbery and second-rate these cheese substitutes are. Since cheese is expensive, American mass producers not only use substitute ingredients for it, they also thin it out. A true Italian pizza is a cheese pie; the cheese is so thick that eaters can sink their teeth into it before they hit the crust. The American frozen pizza is a cheese cookie that breaks with every bite; the "Chicago style" pizza is a cheese puff that offers only cheesy-tasting dough. If purists do not discover just the right amount of fresh, natural cheese on their pizza, they cry "take this away."

Pizza lovers must seek a pizza that, whatever the toppings, has a crunchy, chewy crust, a thick, tasty tomato sauce, and a rich, succulent cheese layer. American mass producers—the frozen pizza makers and the nationwide chain restaurants—usually do not offer true pizza. In the interests of mass production, they have modified the crust, thinned out the tomato sauce, and made substitutions for the cheese. True pizza lovers should not deign to eat these products; if a pizza fails to meet the three tests, consumers should rant and rave rather than passively eat. The disgruntled can usually escape to one of the local, family-owned restaurants that still take the time and trouble to make their own dough, to select the best tomatoes, to pay for real cheese. They make not a product, but a work of culinary art that passes all tests administered by pizza purists.

The essay on true pizzas tells readers how to evaluate this Italian dish—it gives instructions. Another kind of process essay describes a process that has already taken place. This type of essay is almost invariably more formal than the fairly commonplace "how to" essay. The following essay clearly delineates the steps (or acts) by which slaveholders tried to make slaves willingly accept their fate. The author, Kenneth Stampp, is not instructing us how to keep slaves subservient; he is describing a past process by breaking it down into its component parts. Note how he maintains unity in the essay by first describing the slave owners' problem (how to foster the "ideal" of subservience in their reluctant slaves), then questioning how this subservience might be engendered by southern whites, and then breaking down their methods into five steps. Throughout the rest of the essay, he proceeds logically from one step to the next. Note, too, that he occasionally pauses to provide quotations or examples that support his claims.

To Make Them Stand in Fear

A wise master did not take seriously the belief that Negroes were natural-born slaves. He knew better. He knew that Negroes freshly imported from Africa had to be broken in to bondage; that each succeeding generation had to be carefully trained. This was no easy task, for the bondsman rarely submitted willingly. Moreover, he rarely submitted completely. In most cases there was no end to the need for control—at least not until old age reduced the slave to a condition of helplessness.

Masters revealed the qualities they sought to develop in slaves when they singled out certain ones for special commendation. A small Mississippi planter mourned the death of his "faithful and dearly beloved servant" Jack: "Since I have owned him he has been true to me in all respects. He was an obedient trusty servant. . . . I never knew him to steal nor lie and he ever set a moral and industrious example to those around him. . . . I shall ever cherish his memory." A Louisiana sugar planter lost a "very valuable Boy" through an accident: "His life was a great one. I have always found him willing and obedient and never knew him to fail to do anything he was put to do." These were "ideal" slaves, the models slaveholders had in mind as they trained and governed their workers.

How might this ideal be approached? The first step, advised those who wrote discourses on the management of slaves, was to establish and maintain strict discipline. An Arkansas master suggested the adoption of the "Army Regulations as to the discipline in Forts." "They must obey at all times, and under all circumstances, cheerfully and with alacrity," affirmed a Virginia slaveholder. "It greatly impairs the happiness of a negro, to be allowed to cultivate an insurbordinate temper. Unconditional submission is the only footing upon which slavery should be placed. It is precisely similar to the attitude of a minor to his parent, or a soldier to his general." A South Carolinian limned a perfect relationship between slave and his master: "that the slave should know that his master is to govern absolutely, and he is to obey implicitly. That he is never for a moment to exercise either his will or judgment in opposition to a positive order."

The second step was to implant in the bondsmen themselves a consciousness of personal inferiority. They had "to know and keep their places," to "feel the difference between master and slave," to understand that bondage was their natural status. They had to feel that African ancestry tainted them, that their color was a badge of degradation. In the country they were to show respect for even their master's nonslaveholding neighbors; in the towns they were to give way on the street to the most wretched white man. The line between the races must never be crossed, for familiarity caused slaves to forget their lowly station and to become "impudent."

Frederick Douglass explained that a slave might commit the offense of impudence in various ways: "in the tone of an answer; in answering at all; in not answering; in the expression of countenance; in the motion of the head; in the gait, manner and bearing of the slave." Any of these acts, in some subtle way, might indicate the absence of proper subordination. "In a well regulated community," wrote a Texan, "a negro takes off his hat in addressing a white man. . . . Where this is not enforced, we may always look for impudent and rebellious negroes."

The third step in the training of slaves was to awe them with a sense of their master's enormous power. The only principle upon which slavery could be maintained, reported a group of Charlestonians, was the "principle of fear." In his defense of slavery James H. Hammond admitted that this, unfortunately, was true but put the responsibility upon the abolitionists. Antislavery agitation had forced masters to strengthen their authority: "We have to rely more and more on the power of fear. . . . We are determined to continue masters, and to do so we have to draw the rein tighter and tighter day by day to be assured that we hold them in complete check." A North Carolina mistress, after subduing a troublesome domestic, realized that it was essential "to make them stand in fear"!

In this the slaveholders had considerable success. Frederick Douglass believed that most slaves stood "in awe" of white men; few could free themselves altogether from the notion that their masters were "invested with a sort of sacredness." Olmsted saw a small white girl stop a slave on the road and boldly order him to return to his plantation. The slave fearfully obeyed her command. A visitor in Mississippi claimed that a master, armed only with a whip or cane, could throw himself among a score of bondsmen and cause them to "flee with terror." He accomplished this by the "peculiar tone of authority" with which he spoke. "Fear, awe, and obedience . . . are interwoven into the very nature of the slave."

The fourth step was to persuade the bondsmen to take an interest in the master's enterprise and to accept his standards of good conduct. A South Carolina planter explained: "The master should make it his business to show his slaves, that the advancement of his individual interest, is at the same time an advancement of theirs. Once they feel this, it will require but little compulsion to make them act as it becomes them." Though slaveholders induced only a few chattels to respond to this appeal, these few were useful examples for others.

The final step was to impress Negroes with their helplessness, to create in them "a habit of perfect dependence" upon their masters. Many believed it dangerous to train slaves to be skilled artisans in the towns, because they tended to become self-reliant. In the Richmond tobacco factories they were alarmingly independent and "insolent." A Virginian was dismayed to find that his bondsmen, while working at an iron furnace, "got a habit of roaming about and *taking care of themselves.*" Permitting them to hire their own time produced even worse results. "No higher evidence can be furnished of its baneful effects," wrote a Charlestonian, "than the unwillingness it produces in the slave, to return to the regular life and domestic control of the master."

A spirit of independence was less likely to develop among slaves kept on the land, where most of them became accustomed to having their masters provide their basic needs, and where they might be taught that they were unfit to look out for themselves. Slaves then directed their energies to the attainment of mere "temporary ease and enjoyment." "Their masters," Olmsted believed, "calculate on it in them—do not wish to cure it—and by constant practice encourage it."

Here, then, was the way to produce the perfect slave: accustom him to rigid discipline, demand from him unconditional submission, impress upon him his innate inferiority, develop in him a paralyzing fear of white men, train him to adopt the master's code of good behavior, and instill in him a sense of complete dependence. This, at least, was the goal.

But the goal was seldom reached. Every master knew that the average slave was only an imperfect copy of the model. He knew that some bondsmen yielded only to superior power—and yielded reluctantly. This complicated his problem of control.

Causal analysis establishes the relationship between effects and causes. Typically for this sort of essay, you will focus on one effect and examine its causes (usually motives or means) or focus on one cause and examine its effects (usually acts). For example, you may note that you have great difficulty parking your car on campus—an annoying "effect." Exasperated, you might begin to question the causes. You discover that the campus police oversell parking stickers, that they allow visitors to park in student spaces, and that one of the old parking lots is now the site of the new gymnasium. You have discovered three causes that produce the unpleasant effect of not being able to park your car. If you wrote an essay on the problem, you would order the three causes according to their degree of importance. Possibly visitor parking and the destruction of the old parking lot are only contributing causes, while the fact that the campus police sold ten thousand stickers for three thousand spaces is the chief cause of the problem. In that case you should probably discuss the minor causes first and build toward a more detailed examination of the major cause in your later body paragraphs. Your conclusion could very well be a call for action. Look at the following student essay that follows this pattern. In it the student analyzes an effect—the lasting popularity of the Beatles—to determine its causes. He begins the essay by establishing the enduring success of the group—that is, he describes the effect. He discusses minor causes first and then finally explains the major causes of the group's success at the close of the essay.

The Beatles
An Analysis of the Act
You've Known for All These Years

During the summer of 1964, "Beatlemania" was at its peak. The Beatles' record sales had easily eclipsed all existing sales plateaus for both singles and albums, and vast stadiums, once considered too large for the staging of pop music events, had been crammed to capacity with screaming young fans. Even the name *Beatles* had become a household word, thanks largely to the group's exposure on television's most popular hour, "The Ed Sullivan Show." On one particular August night, thousands of school-aged adulators poured into New York's Shea Stadium several hours early, anxiously awaiting the event that they had each paid almost six dollars to see: the Fab Four in concert. The Beatles themselves arrived at the ballpark in armored cars; they dared not venture out unguarded anymore for fear that overzealous fans might rip them to shreds. At last, Ed Sullivan took the stage to announce the Beatles' arrival, but his words, like the sparse thirty minutes of music to follow, were rendered inaudible by the screams that erupted from sixty thousand pairs of lungs. When it was over, the Beatles quickly departed, one hundred and sixty thousand dollars richer, having earned close to one hundred dollars a second for their evening's performance.

Just as the Beatles had set new precedents with their live performances, so too did they sell more records at a faster rate than ever before. On April 4, 1964, the legitimacy of Beatlemania could no longer be disputed or ignored as the top five spots on *Billboard* magazine's Hot 100 singles chart were graced by the following Beatles songs: "Can't Buy Me Love," "Twist and Shout," "She Loves You," "I Want to Hold Your Hand," and "Please Please Me." The Beatles' virtual monopoly of the American record sales charts was a phenomenon in pop music that had never occurred before and that, most likely, will never be duplicated. There was still more to come—the innovative studio techniques, the elements of lyrical depth and musical sophistication, and the call to a war-torn world to "give peace a chance." But in the summer of 1964, Beatlemaniacs were gleefully content with another chorus of "yeh, yeh, yehs."

Why were the Beatles so popular with young audiences of 1964, and why do their records continue to be popular to this day, almost fifteen years after the group disbanded? Certainly the Beatles' stateside arrival in February of 1964 could not have been better timed. Weary from the strain of the Cuban Missile Crisis and shocked by the horror of the Kennedy assassination, Americans were in desperate need of a diversion, "a bit of light entertainment" as Anthony Burton of the *New York Daily News* wrote of the Beatles at the time. But for millions of teenagers, the Beatles meant much more than a few giggles to get one's mind off the cold war. By embracing a quartet of long-haired foreigners who were young and brash and boldly independent, young Americans were able to free their own rebellious spirits. And of course, the music the Beatles produced had much to do with their initial success. Backed by Ringo Starr's propulsive beat, the Beatles poured out their infectious pop sound with a bouncy exuberance that proved to be a shot in the arm for the dismally bland American pop music scene. Unlike most other pop stars of the era, the Beatles were considered competent enough to write and perform their own material. Each new Beatles album provided eager fans with a collection of Lennon/McCartney originals, usually odes about adolescent love. Fans could both dance and listen to their music—a rare combination at a time when most pop albums were a dumping ground for banal filler. Still, these factors cannot fully explain the phenomenon that was the Beatles.

Much of the Beatles' popularity today as well as in the sixties can be attributed to the unique "chemistry" that existed among the four individuals in the band. While most pop bands of the pre-Beatles era consisted of a single star backed by a group of faceless musicians basking in reflected glory, the Beatles were all stars in their own right—each one a distinct personality and each one an essential component in the overall makeup of the group. Of the four, the personalities of John Lennon and Paul McCartney were clearly dominant; while Paul was the Beatles' heart, John was the Beatles' soul. Often described as the Beatles' diplomat, Paul was easily the most suave, articulate, and charming of the four, as well as the prettiest. Musically, Paul was the most versatile as both a vocalist and instrumentalist, and he was the first of the Beatles to compose timeless melodies that transcended all social and cultural bounds. John, at the opposite extreme, was every bit as cynical as Paul was cheery. Rumored to have the highest IQ of the four, John was notorious for lashing out with his razor-sharp wit at those who provoked him. Unlike Paul, who was always eager to fill the "Mr. Showbiz" bill, John was not content with the notion that pop stars should radiate "mindless good cheer," and this trait often surfaced in his biting lyrics. Although he was not as adept as Paul at writing beautiful melodies, John was the first Beatle to write sensitive, serious lyrics as well as the one most willing to experiment. While Paul caught the fancy of many a starry-eyed romantic, John appealed most to those world-weary intellectuals who were Beatles fans.

The two remaining Beatles, while not as influential in shaping the direction the band was to take, also contributed to the group's multifaceted image. As the youngest Beatle, George Harrison was somewhat shy and withdrawn, particularly in the early years; consequently, he was the last of the four to emerge as an individual. However, as the group matured, so too would George, and the Eastern influences that permeated his music and philosophy would make him the "mystic" of the Beatles. George's virtuosity on the guitar and later on the sitar (an instrument that he introduced to the rock world) distinguished him from the other Beatles, who were competent but seldom outstanding instrumentalists. Ringo Starr, on the other hand, had not been blessed with the technical skills or the capacity for songwriting that the other three Beatles possessed. However, his goofy features, highlighted by his prominent nose, and his self-effacing mannerisms stirred a certain protective instinct in many fans, making Ringo perhaps the most lovable of the Beatles. Content in his role as the Beatles' drummer, Ringo was generally happy to remain in the shadows of John, Paul, and George, inspiring one writer to call him "one of history's most charming bit-part players." With four different heroes to choose from, Beatles fans could follow the ups and downs of their favorite Beatle's daily existence through the wonders of mass media—almost as if they were keeping in touch with a close friend away from home.

While John, Paul, George, and Ringo shared a unique chemistry that made them seem like brothers, their appeal as the Beatles would never have endured had their music not been exceptional. Simply stated, the Beatles were the greatest innovators in the history of pop music, and through their contributions to style and technique, they transformed the pop music genre from the simplistic dance music of their idols

(Chuck Berry and Buddy Holly) to a highly sophisticated art form. With the release of *Sgt. Pepper's Lonely Hearts Club Band* in 1967, the Beatles' music earned the praise of distinguished intellectuals and members of the avant-garde as well as the all but unanimous approval of the underground press. Widely acclaimed as the most influential pop album of all time, *Sgt. Pepper* inspired many critics to write elaborate dissertations about the underlying "concept" of the album and the "hidden meaning" of the songs' imaginative, often surreal, lyrics. From that point on, every album released by a major artist would receive the same analytical scrutiny that had formerly been afforded only to novels. The *Sgt. Pepper* album was also heralded as a masterwork of engineering; the clarity and "presence" of the voices and instruments surpassed anything else of the day. Interestingly, critics have made much of the fact that a recent reworking of *Sgt. Pepper* by some of today's top stars lacks the presence and freshness of the original, despite the use of recording equipment far more sophisticated than that which the Beatles had at their disposal in 1967.

If the music of the Beatles still sounds fresh, the songs themselves have as much to do with that as do the recording techniques employed, for the Beatles, especially Lennon and McCartney, were gifted songwriters. Many of the Beatles' most beautiful melodies are easily adaptable to any style of music, which accounts for the phenomenal number of "cover" versions that Beatles songs have inspired. Paul McCartney's genius for composing irresistible pop melodies has made him the most widely interpreted songwriter of the day. One of his ballads, "Yesterday," has been recorded by over one thousand artists ranging from folksinger Joan Baez to "the Champagne Music King," Lawrence Welk. Although most of the Beatles' timeless works were penned by Paul McCartney, George Harrison's "Something" was lauded by Frank Sinatra as "the greatest love song of the last fifty years" and had the distinction of replacing "My Way" in Ol' Blue Eyes' repertoire. However, the Beatles' influence has not been lost on the young pop musicians of today; we can discern elements of the Beatles' style in the music of many new wave acts such as Elvis Costello and the Knack. The inventiveness of the Beatles' music and the timeless essence of many of their melodies will make their contributions to pop music important for some time to come.

While the significance of the Beatles' innovations in pop music cannot be overestimated, the legend of the Fab Four has grown to mythical proportions in the years since the band's breakup. The Beatles are the embodiment of the excitement and wide-eyed naiveté of the lost youth of yesterday's "flower children," now approaching middle age and very much a part of the "establishment" they once scorned. Their nostalgic perceptions have smoothed out the rough edges of the Beatles' mystique. For the young Beatle fans, many of whom were still in diapers when the first wave of Beatlemania washed over American shores, interest in the Beatles legend has flourished in the absence of a comparable phenomenon that they could call their own. And the assassination of John Lennon in 1980 has made all our memories of the Beatles even more poignant and compelling than before. The fact that the Beatles are now only a memory preserved in vinyl has enhanced their legend. While many of the Beatles' comtemporaries have been reduced to self-parody as time erodes their talent and vitality, the Beatles broke up while they were still at the height of their influence and creative powers. As Yoko Ono wrote in her parable of "The Golden Temple," "That's why the Beatles will stay a beautiful myth, because they ended before they deteriorated."

This causal analysis essay, which explores the reasons for the popularity of the Beatles, and the process analysis essays on slavery and judging pizzas are just two specialized forms of analysis. Remember that you perform analysis of some sort any time you break something down into its component parts. In our final sample, a student analyzes three writers' use of psychological mumbo jumbo in an issue of *New Woman* magazine. While the essay follows the illustration model, its essential purpose is to *analyze* the *motive* for abstract diction in certain kinds of magazine articles.

Magazine Psychology

In his essay, "Politics and the English Language," George Orwell makes critical observations about modern prose style. He notes that most modern prose lacks "concreteness," and he identifies political writing as the major offender. Today, decades after Orwell wrote his essay, we can still largely agree with his point, for most modern political writing continues to avoid precise and evocative diction. However, we can now place a second culprit beside political writing as we experience yet another body of writing that abounds with "party-line" prose and imprecise expressions. This type of writing, which usually appears in magazine articles dealing with the new pseudopsychology, is "psychological mumbo jumbo."

Three articles in the February 1980 issue of *New Woman* magazine are filled with this psychological mumbo jumbo. Kenneth Wydro's article, "Everything that Happens Does So

For a Reason,'' assures us that we can overcome loneliness by ''turning to our creative psyche self.'' Although the phrase ''psyche self'' is not new (magazine psychologists love to use it), readers still have no more than a vague notion of what it means. Wydro defines one's psyche self as ''his or her creative soul''; thus he gives us one abstraction in exchange for another. Still, readers proceed, hoping Wydro will provide them with an illustration of this ''creative soul.'' What they find, however, is far from illustrative. Wydro explains, ''If you begin to take your inner life seriously, and consciously develop your talents, and commit yourself to your inner light and to your voice within, a creative strength, confidence, and creative rejuvenation will emerge.'' Orwell would shudder and rightly so.

Yet Mr. Wydro's article is not the only source of mumbo jumbo in *New Woman;* Dr. Gerald G. Jampolsky's article, ''If You're Feeling Unloved, Depressed and Empty Inside . . . ,'' provides another good example. Because most readers experience feelings of depression at one time or another, the article's title gets their attention. However, attention wanes as Dr. Jampolsky attempts to define love and fear. He begins, ''Where do love and fear fit into the scheme of things?'' He continues, ''Love is the total absence of fear. Fear distorts your perception and confuses you as to what is going on. Love asks no questions. Its natural state is one of extension and expansion, not comparison and measurement. Love, then, is really everything that is of value, and fear can offer you nothing because fear is nothing.'' Readers can extract nothing from Dr. Jampolsky's article save a renewed confidence in the old saying that love is impossible to define. Love is really *everything* and fear is *nothing?* Spare us, Dr. Jampolsky.

Dr. Irving Oyle's article, ''Something to Do to Heal Yourself,'' provides additional examples of psychological ''nonspeak.'' Dr. Oyle begins his article by saying that although in medical school most students are repeatedly reminded of the body's self-repairing abilities, in actual practice many doctors overlook this principle. Then, instead of explaining ''self-healing'' by citing actual cases that illustrate this ability of the body, Dr. Oyle offers a lengthy abstraction: ''You can create the conditions which will allow the healing process to occur, but this autonomous healing factor is under the complete control of your psyche which, by varying its rate of vibration, can cause disease or initiate healing. The therapeutic efficacy of any healing system is directly proportional to your inner faith in that system.'' Baffled by such abstractions as the *psyche* and its *rate of vibration* and such sentence subjects as *therapeutic efficacy,* we can but hope that our language has its own "self-repairing abilities" since Oyle is cruelly violating it here.

In all of the *New Woman* articles, the writers use lengthy explanations filled with abstract words and phrases to explain their concepts. Surely this is what Orwell referred to when he stated that the tendency of modern prose is away from "concreteness." In his essay Orwell states that politicians use abstractions to mask unpleasant realities. Apparently, pseudo-psychologists use abstractions to mask the essential emptiness of their discussions. They have found a complicated, ostentatious way of writing about nothing.

Summary The essay models that we have discussed in this chapter—comparison, illustration, classification, definition, and analysis—are usually considered types of *exposition,* writing that explains and reports. But as you will see in the next chapter, these models also are essential to *argumentation.* In trying to persuade an audience to take an action or change their ways of thinking, you will necessarily *compare* things (The Sentra gets better mileage than the Rabbit), *classify* things (Calvin Kleins are top-line jeans), *define* terms (Pornography means more than just adult-rated books and movies), *illustrate* your points (*The Producers, Duck Soup,* and *Bananas* all demonstrate movie audiences' desire to laugh their troubles away), and *analyze* (Nixon was a successful propagandist because of his knowledge of what moves Americans and his ability to manipulate language and circumstances to mask unpleasant facts). Therefore in the discussions of argumentative techniques and patterns of organization that we will present in Chapter IV, we will return again and again to the so-called expository models of essay writing.

EXERCISE 7

Criticize the following analysis essay, which traces the causes for the success of *Star Wars*. Look for points at which the author fails to write agent prose. Ask yourself the following questions.

1. Does the writer clearly state the effect before discussing causes?
2. Does she state the most obvious causes first and then move on to subtler ones?
3. Does she provide good transitions in her topic sentences so that her readers can follow her thought progression?

4. Does her conclusion state the most elusive, most subtle cause, or does it at least refer again to the effect and round out the essay?

Analysis of *Star Wars*

George Lucas is one of Hollywood's youngest and most successful producer-writers. By age 35 he had created two huge box-office successes. His first major film success, *American Graffiti,* became the eleventh highest money-maker of all time. However, his 1977 success, *Star Wars,* broke all income records, and within one year it had become the number one money-maker among the all-time greats.

No one in Hollywood, not even George Lucas himself, had anticipated that *Star Wars* would gross over 3.6 million dollars in its first nine days, nor had anyone expected *Star Wars* to gross $267 million by January 1978, surpassing *Jaws'* previous record of $200 million. *Star Wars* was a monstrous success, similar to the creatures that filled its script. Audiences around the world flocked to theaters to watch the woolly "wookie," a pair of noisy robots, a has-been general, Han Solo, and the fair-haired, blue-eyed Luke Skywalker attempt to save Princess Leia from her captor, Darth Vader. Leia is Vader's prisoner on the Death Star, the mobile command station of the Galactic Empire, and behind his cloak and fiery red eyes, Vader represents everthing that is evil.

As a young rebel, Skywalker is bound to his duty to save Leia and destroy the Death Star; he is the Romeo of *Star Wars.* Vader, however, is more machine than human, and he is determined to quell the rebels. This type of machine versus human plot is typical of many science fiction films, including Stanley Kubrick's *2001: A Space Odyssey.*

Kubrick's film captured a similar audience only not with the same computerized ingenuity as Lucas. While *2001* had its share of laser duels, battleship chases, and grotesque creatures, *Star Wars'* intense use of computer technology gave Lucas the advantage of 363 individual special effects compared to Kubrick's 35. *Star Wars'* Obi-Wan Kenobi duels to the death with Vader using laser swords. Spaceships maneuver with split-second accuracy in and out of planetary ravines, spitting balls of light at each other. A foot chase on the Death Star leads Skywalker and Leia to a dead end where the two battle fiercely with Empire guards; beams of red light flash into puffs of smoke vaporizing everything they hit. Throughout the entire film, Lucas creates spectacular scenes with his array of computers, and all for half a million dollars less than the technically limited *2001.*

And *Star Wars* did not end with the actors' parting lines as did *2001*. Beyond the theater doors, a *Star Wars* culture emerged, characterized by plastic Death Stars, Vader, wookie, and Skywalker dolls, and radio-controlled robots resembling R2-D2 and C-3PO. From the *Star Wars* set, 6000 color transparencies were stolen and sold on the open market for five dollars each. Hordes of plastic models used in the filming were stolen and are now considered priceless collector's items. A female teenybopper fan club idolized Skywalker in much the same way as teenage girls swooned over Clark Gable in *Gone With the Wind*. In fact, Ben Bova, editor of a leading science fiction magazine, *Analog,* calls *Star Wars* "a galactic *Gone With the Wind.*"

Why has *Star Wars* entranced millions of people, young and old alike? What is it that brought audiences back four or five times to see the Death Star annihilated and Skywalker and company jet off into the galactic horizon? What was so fascinating about a six-foot, gold-plated man whose double could be the Tin Man in *The Wizard of Oz?* Certainly our populace has within it a sizable science fiction fan club who would undoubtedly pay to see any cloned creature terrorize an unsuspecting planet. But this group of cybernetic sadists obviously doesn't account for some $267 million of tickets sold. *Star Wars* presents special effects never before attempted or made possible. R2-D2 projects Princess Leia in a holographic form onto the floor. The 3-D effect is spectacular. No less spectacular is a scene when R2-D2 and his friend, Chewbacca, play a space-age form of chess, using 3-D holographic forms in place of the usual plastic pieces. Rather than a bishop capturing a knight, a dinosaur devours a small blue-eyed monster. Monsters are common in the film and thanks to Rick Baker, makeup expert for the 1976 remake of *King Kong, Star Wars'* audiences are treated to a time-honored, John Wayne barroom scene, complete with a freak from every galaxy and a brawl. The special effects are remarkable and a definite force behind the movie's appeal, but the main reason for *Star Wars'* success lies even deeper.

Star Wars gives one man's insight into the future. Do creatures like these really exist? As we experiment with nuclear power and laser light, *Star Wars* suggests that beings more extraordinary than ourselves may exist. Some believe that humans, as we know them, rule our universe. But others are drawn to *Star Wars* to see what may lie in other universes, to see what type of beings already enjoy the mechanized world that our population desperately seeks. Is *Star Wars* impossible?

A fine line must be drawn between what is probable and what is possible. *Star Wars'* creatures are drawn by the human hand, and they are a consequence of imagination more than reality. The veritable success of *Star Wars* rests on stronger foundations. *Star Wars,* in actuality, is not science fiction, but a fantasy that combines *Flash Gordon, The Wizard of Oz,* Errol Flynn movies of the 30s and 40s, and every western ever created. The film evokes our childhood, when the Hardy Boys stole our imagination. Director George Lucas says, "The word for this movie is fun." He recreates a fantasy of freaks and gives us the comedy team of R2-D2 and C-3PO. Remarkably similar to Laurel and Hardy, the incomprehensible midget and his pessimistic friend constantly face the same type of nonsensical situations as did the 20s comic team. Their humor is simple. R2-D2 speaks in what *Time* magazine calls an "eloquent blend of Tarzan's ape and John Silver's parrot." His cohort, C-3PO, faces danger like a wet noodle. He constantly repeats, "We're doomed, we're doomed," at every crossroad with danger. But as a fantasy, *Star Wars* also relies on the traditional good-guy, bad-guy theme.

Like the humor, the plot is simple. The good guys are those who oppress the rebel Tatooine people. The theme is unadulterated by sexual overtones, and very little, if any, blood is shed throughout the film. Tragedy is not a part of *Star Wars; Star Wars* is an antitragedy.

For Lucas and his movie, the return to simplicity and fantasy has created an enormous success. Some see *Star Wars* for its sci-fi intrigue and others pay only for its special effects. But the movie has successfully combined these elements into a traditional movie plot. *Star Wars* is a fantasy that releases us from the tensions of our lives and returns us to the simple days of our childhoods, when good always conquered evil, and there was always a happy ending.

IV Moving from Exposition to Argument: the Shaping Role of the Audience

In most essays you write, you start with your personal experiences and opinions. Then if you use the expository essay models we have described, you can stretch your experience and make it relevant to a broader audience. So far in this book, we have been focusing mainly on expository writing—writing that simply explains or reports. Although you usually direct an expository essay to an audience, you do not have to consider the nature of this audience. It can remain general and unspecified since you are not trying to persuade people one way or the other or convince anyone of anything. When you write an argument, however, you attempt to persuade a specific audience to accept your views—you tailor your essay to your audience. At first glance, argumentative writing is more complicated and difficult than expository writing, since it adds another dimension to the writing process. But this sense of audience can give direction and a clear point of view to your writing. In appealing to a specific audience, you will tend to use the expository models with increased precision. Although argumentative writing requires an extra step in the writing process, that step may ultimately make your essay more effective.

An excellent way to start practicing argumentative writing and to experience its power is to use it in your academic work. Papers, essays, and exam questions you write as arguments will be much more effective than a mere regurgitation of facts set forth in no particular order. Like all readers, teachers do not enjoy trying to figure out what a writer is saying; they look for clarity and reward the rare exam that develops a persuasive point of view in a logical sequence. Your relationship with your teachers is unique and, in a sense, artificial—you will never again have such a captive audience. Whether you enter the world of law, business, politics, medicine, social work, or art—whatever field you pursue—you will need to use writing to gain the attention of your readers. You will need to persuade people, and basic to your persuasiveness will be your ability to make well-organized, complete statements. You can prepare yourself for the working world by beginning to argue with your teachers now. Do not merely list ideas, facts, and examples in your exams and papers; rather try to use the appropriate essay model to convince your teachers of your point of view.

In order to write persuasively, you must always consider what particular kind of audience you are addressing. Of course, you can never know the exact nature of every audience you will encounter. But we can suggest two general criteria by which you can gauge an audience. We will then analyze how your estimation of the audience should shape your argument. The first judgment you should make about your audience is whether it will be sympathetic to your views. You can locate any audience on this scale:

Sympathetic	
Disinterested	Uninformed
Uninterested	
Hostile	

Note that *disinterested* and *uninterested* have very different meanings. *Disinterested* is synonymous with neutral; a disinterested audience may be interested in your topic but brings no prejudices to the argument. *Uninterested* means that your audience has no interest in your topic; you will have to make a special effort to capture audience attention before you can begin to argue. An *uninformed* audience is unfamiliar with your topic and holds no opinion until you give out some kind of information; then it may fall into any of the other categories. For this kind of audience you will have to provide more extensive background information than for the others.

The second characteristic of an audience that you should assess is its sophistication. By sophistication we do not mean taste in books, clothes, or sports cars. We refer instead to the willingness of audience members to listen to an argument, make judgments on the information given, and, if the evidence is convincing, change their views. As we use it, *sophistication* describes the relative ability of an audience to be receptive to complex logical demonstration. The scale on which you can locate the sophistication of an audience looks like this:

Sophisticated

Persuadable

Unsophisticated

Persuadable refers here to audience members who respond to logic and reason if you first win their sympathy, but whose sophistication is not powerful enough to overcome their own hostility or lack of interest.

Obviously, a sympathetic and sophisticated audience is the easiest to appeal to. Often your teachers will have these qualities but, of course, there is no guarantee that they will always be your audience. Once you leave the artificial classroom situation you will encounter few such audiences. Perhaps your most important and surely your most difficult work will be with people who are hostile to or uninterested in your ideas.

What kinds of essay organization will work with different kinds of audiences? How will you proceed if you face a sophisticated but hostile audience or if you face an unsophisticated and uninterested audience? To answer these questions, you should recognize some important connections between the expository models you have studied and some basic argumentative procedures.

How Expository Models Become Argumentative: Four Examples

Definition Essays with Deduction

In Chapter II we discussed the deductive paragraph—one which you begin with the generalization you wish to discuss. In argumentation the word *deductive* is used similarly; it describes a process of reasoning which judges a particular case in light of a widely accepted generalization. In its most basic form, deduction allows you to interpret a new and unfamiliar experience by placing it against a background of familiar knowledge you have already gained. For instance, even if you have never been in a head-on collision at seventy miles per hour, common human experience has given you the generalization that such accidents are usually fatal. If, then, you someday find yourself traveling at seventy miles per hour confronting an oncoming car in your lane, your immediate thought will doubtless be, "If I hit that car, I'm dead." Although the point is a little academic in this situation, we can note that your instantaneous reaction is a valid deduction. You began with an unspoken generalization:

> All head-on collisions at seventy miles per hour are fatal.

You then considered your particular case in light of that generalization:

> I am about to have a head-on collision at seventy miles per hour.

Then you came to the conclusion:

> I am about to die.

The basic form of deductive reasoning is called a *syllogism.* As in our car-crash example, a syllogism consists of three parts: a *major premise* (or generalization), a *minor premise* (a particular case), and a *conclusion.* We should mention that we are using the term *conclusion* here in a specific way. Up to this point, we have used the term to refer to the final part of an essay. You can think of this kind of conclusion, then, as a structural conclusion. The kind of conclusion you reach when you formulate a syllogism, however, is a logical conclusion. Sometimes logical conclusions appear in the structural conclusion of an essay, but sometimes they do not. What is important at this point in our discussion is to realize that the term *conclusion* can refer to two different concepts.

Usually in conversation people do not make full, formal use of the syllogism. Most often, as in the car-crash example, we leave the major premise unspoken—it is behind our reasoning but only implicit in our statement—and we take a shortcut to the conclusion. Look at the following statement:

> Gary Carter is a superstar; he's been in ten All-Star games.

This may seem harmless enough, but the full reasoning behind it runs as follows:

> Major Premise: Anyone who has been in ten All-Star games is a superstar.

Minor Premise: Gary Carter has been in ten All-Star games.
Conclusion: Gary Carter is a superstar.

Spelling out this syllogism in its entirety may seem unnecessary. However, much reasoning in ordinary conversation is nothing more than a syllogism with a premise left out, and sometimes this reasoning is debatable or even false. Compare the following statement with the one about Gary Carter.

Choo Choo Coleman was a superstar; he played for the '62 Mets.

To an informed sports fan, this statement is ludicrous, but only because its unspoken major premise is impossible to accept.

Major Premise: Anyone who played for the '62 Mets (probably the worst major league baseball team ever) was a superstar.
Minor Premise: Choo Choo Coleman played for the '62 Mets.
Conclusion: Choo Choo Coleman was a superstar.

To discover the truth or falsity of statements like these, you must uncover the full syllogism lurking behind them and scrutinize its validity. As our claim for Choo Choo Coleman reveals, many of the partially expressed syllogisms of ordinary discourse will lose force when you spell them out fully. If you work your way back to the major premise, you might discover that it is not acceptable.

EXERCISE 1

Work out the syllogisms that are implicit in the following statements. Find the premise that goes unspoken, and determine if you can accept it.

1. Mr. Haskell was a great teacher; what a wild sense of humor he had.
2. Southgate Schaeffer is the top high school in the area; last year their football team won the city championship.
3. Did Nixon go to Russia and China? You bet he did. That's greatness, I tell you, greatness.
4. What a lousy class! We have assignments due every day, and papers are due at the end of every week.
5. With its styling and comfort, the Cadillac Seville is the car of the future.

How can the ability to set up syllogisms help you write an essay? You should recognize that the major premise in a syllogism usually depends on a definition—a definition of a concept like *superstar* or *great teacher* or *lousy class*. When you want to make a deductive argument, you can use the basic definition essay model, but you will apply the definition model in a very precise way. The requirements of the syllogism will shape and link the three parts of your essay. Your introduction will give background on the topic and then state your major premise. In the body paragraphs, you will develop your minor premise by discussing a particular case (or group of particular cases) in light of your major premise. The structural conclusion of your essay will restate your major premise and then state your logical conclusion, or judgment on the particular case(s) you have discussed.

Major premises come in two kinds: *single* and *multiple.* The *multiple major premise* defines something in terms of multiple characteristics, and those characteristics become the topics of body paragraphs. In an argument about athletic shoes, for example, you might begin with the multiple-premise definition: "A good athletic shoe should be comfortable, durable, and inexpensive." Having set up this multiple premise, you also set up a sequence for your essay; both you and your reader know what your body paragraphs will discuss: comfort, durability, and economy. The *single major premise* isolates one characteristic and declares it to be of crucial importance. Suppose you want to turn an expository essay on English teachers into an argument for the greatness of one particular English teacher whose outstanding virtue was her infectious enthusiasm. You might open with the single-premise definition: "Above all else, English teachers must be enthusiastic about their work." In your body paragraphs, your topic sentences could repeat the key word *enthusiasm* as you go on to describe the different ways in which your teacher exhibited this virtue.

There are two very effective and clear sequences you can use to make a deductive argument. With a multiple premise, your essay will look something like this.

Essay Sequence with Multiple Premise

Introduction:	*Background information:* growing popularity of athletic shoes; now worn by almost everybody almost everywhere
	Statement of premise in parts: look for comfort, durability, and low cost
Body Paragraphs:	Section 1: the comfort of particular shoe(s)

	Section 2: the durability of particular shoe(s)
	Section 3: the cost of particular shoe(s)
Conclusion:	Restatement of premise
	Summary of findings
	Final judgment (conclusion) on particular shoe(s)

With a single premise, your essay will look roughly the same, but you will repeat one key word in your topic sentences rather than introduce new words.

Essay Sequence with Single Premise

Introduction:	*Background information:* importance of English teachers; almost everyone, at one time or another, has had dealings with one
	Statement of premise: the truly great teacher brings an infectious enthusiasm to his or her work
Body Paragraphs:	Section 1: first illustration of enthusiasm
	Section 2: second illustration of enthusiasm
	Section 3: third illustration of enthusiasm
Conclusion:	Restatement of premise
	Summary of findings
	Final judgment (conclusion) on particular teacher(s)

EXERCISE 2

Here are two introductory paragraphs for essays that would make successful deductive arguments. Identify the premise in each one, and compose a series of possible topic sentences for the body paragraphs that would follow from these introductions. Then choose one list of topic sentences and write a complete essay by providing both illustrations and a conclusion.

1. In what has become an almost yearly event, tennis fans are once again arguing about the character of John McEnroe. His supporters and detractors are equally vociferous, and, in the midst of all the noise they create, the average fan may have

great difficulty coming to a rational, intelligent decision. Before people come to blows, however, they should consider what any tennis player should be and should do. Of course, opinions vary widely, but most people agree that a great player must have a powerful service and strong ground strokes, must play with stamina throughout long matches and with courage at the big points—points that determine championships. Rather than fight and shout about John McEnroe, tennis fans would do better to measure him against these standards.

2. Writing is as individual an effort as painting or sculpting. Each budding writer will have a different background and outlook and should, during his or her education, receive the same individualized, specialized attention that fine arts students receive. For this reason, the skill of the teacher is of paramount importance. It is difficult to set any universal standards of excellence for writing teachers and still keep in mind the different expectations and goals of the students, but most people look for a teacher who is enthusiastic about teaching and generates some of that enthusiasm in the students. Enthusiasm normally grows into motivation, motivation into accomplishment.

As you no doubt have recognized by now, the key to a deductive argument is how you introduce the premise. If you can set up a valid premise correctly, particularly a multiple premise, your essay organization will immediately be clear; the premise will provide you with topic sentences, and you will need to worry only about offering sufficient illustration and development within the body paragraphs. In our experience, however, students often have two problems with premises. First, they sometimes confuse conclusions with premises. Second, they sometimes introduce their premises too abruptly and in a dogmatic, categorical manner—a manner that may alienate their audience.

To avoid confusing conclusions with premises in a deductive essay, you should remember that the premise is at a higher level of generalization than the conclusion. In the premise you do not actually refer to your particular case but rather to the *class* that includes your particular case. On the other hand, the conclusion links your particular case to the general class presented in the premise. In an essay that concludes, for example, that John McEnroe should be acclaimed as a great tennis player, the premise could be a generalization about what makes a good tennis player.

Thus, in your prewriting, you will begin with your particular case (for example, John McEnroe) and then figure out the general class that includes your particular case (in this instance, tennis players). Recall the standards for classification that we developed in Chapter III. You do not want to get too far away from your topic with your generalization. Generalizations can be made on many different levels. John McEnroe is also, among other things, a son, a man, and a person. But premises about being a son, a man, and a person would lead nowhere in this essay. Ideally, the premise should be at a level of generalization once removed from the particular case. The following series of generalizations may help you to grasp this point.

apple pie	Ohio State University
dessert	state universities
food	educational institutions
basic human needs	U.S. institutions

A successful deductive argument for the virtues of apple pie would probably not open with a premise about the human need for food. More appropriately, the essay would open with a premise about dessert—a definition of what constitutes a great dessert. An essay that attacks dessert as wasteful and extravagant might open with a premise about human needs, but would probably begin more effectively with a premise about food—what it should do or how we should use it. On the other hand, an essay by a gourmet or gourmand in praise of food could open very well with a premise about basic human needs. Similarly, if you want to write a deductive argument that praises or attacks your state university, you should not open with a generalization about educational institutions; rather you should try to define what a state university should be and should do. Then you can consider your state university in light of that definition.

As we've mentioned, the second problem students have with premises is introducing them too abruptly or categorically. A premise is a definition you ask your audience to accept, not a conclusion that you need to prove, and if your audience does not accept your premise, you will lose your argument at the very start. Therefore, you must introduce your premise with both tact and modesty. You must not appear dogmatic and inflexible. Admit that opinions may vary, but then offer your definition as one that most people can accept. When you introduce your premise you will find it useful to make some kind of qualification.

> Of course, opinions vary widely but most agree that a great tennis player . . .

> Educators have difficulty setting universal standards of excellence for writing teachers that will allow for the different expectations and goals of the students, but most people look for a teacher who is . . .

This strategy is particularly necessary if you suspect any hostility in your audience. It allows you to briefly acknowledge the point of view of hostile readers and perhaps prevent them from immediately rejecting your case.

EXERCISE 3

Study the following two sets of introductions. In each set try to find the one example that states a premise and does so with modesty and tact. In the first set of introductions, the subject is a revision of the Florida Constitution to legalize casino gambling. In the second the subject is Levi's jeans.

Set A: 1. Florida voters will soon decide a very controversial issue. The dispute is about casino gambling. Supporters of Let's Help Florida, an organization in favor of casino gambling, claim gambling will produce millions of dollars for the state, triple tourism, and create eighty-nine thousand new jobs. On the other hand, sponsors of No Casinos, a Tallahassee-based organization against casino gambling, say that casino gambling will do no good and will undoubtedly harm Florida. Everyone knows that anything that is detrimental to tourism, industrial growth, and the economic well-being of Floridians is not in the best interest of the voters.

2. The children of the United States deserve to receive a good education and to grow up in a safe environment. This may not be possible for the children of the state of Florida. With the present lack of funding for schools and law enforcement agencies, the children of this state are being shortchanged. The voting adults of Florida must take responsibility for these problems and find an effective remedy as soon as possible. Most voters agree that any proposition that will increase funding for education and law enforcement, add to the general welfare, and result in no new taxes certainly merits careful attention.

3. Florida residents must make a decision about the future of casino gambling in Dade and Broward counties. The outcome of the November 7 referendum will have a great impact on the type of tourism in the state. The legalization of gambling would lure organized crime into the state, encourage the delinquency

of minors, and turn away respectable tourists. Casino gambling will also contribute to windfall profits for shady hotel entrepreneurs.

Set B: 1. Today, pants are made out of many different fabrics. Cotton pants are the most comfortable, since cotton is both cool and pleasant to wear. The Levi Strauss Company makes most of its jeans out of cotton. Its jeans are worn by people all over the world. Levi's are comfortable, stylish, and durable.

2. Jeans are very popular today. People of all ages have started wearing them for comfort as well as for style. Until recently, however, jeans were worn only as "bum-around" pants. Now people wear jeans for almost any occasion. Every household probably has at least one pair of jeans per family member. Throughout the years one brand of jeans has outshone most other brands in popularity. People generally agree that this brand, Levi's, is the best pair of jeans money can buy.

3. Some of society's most remarkable accomplishments within the last one hundred years have been in the areas of technology and production. Never before have people had the capability to produce so much in such a limited amount of time. Competing manufacturers try to produce top-quality merchandise for as little cost as possible, while consumers choose from this array and decide which brands to buy. The accomplishment of mass production has but one fault—a slight decrease in the quality of goods. A market in which this decrease in quality is very evident is the clothing market. People have come to rely on the convenience and economy of mass-produced clothing, but are not willing to sacrifice quality. Consumers are constantly searching for clothes that are durable, stylish, and yet moderately priced—in short, for a dependable brand of clothing unsurpassed in practicality. While there are many adequate brands of clothing on the market, many have come to rely on the Levi's brand as one of the few that consistently meets these high standards.

You can write a lucid, well-organized essay using deductive argument if you have the syllogism clear in your mind. In the introduction to your essay you should state the major premise in such a way that your audience will agree to it; you must avoid sounding overconfident or arrogant. Often this introduction will define crucial evaluative terms like *good, great, weak,* or *evil.* You cannot use words like these in an argument without defining the standards on which you are basing your judgment. *You cannot leave your major premise unstated.* The body of the essay will develop the minor premise and relate particular cases to the premise. If you treat the major and minor premise successfully, you can write the conclusion almost effortlessly. Simply restate the premise and summarize how the particular case or cases measure up.

You should be aware that deductive argumentation does not work to full advantage with every kind of audience. Since it requires you to begin with a generalization—a statement that does not raise the immediate point of controversy—deduction can be unexciting. It does not always capture and hold the attention of an uninterested audience. This does not always have to be the case—recall Exercise 3, Set B, number 3, in which the author offered a conclusion as well as a premise. But, in general, deduction is not the best kind of argument to use with an uninterested audience.

Deduction is also risky with a hostile audience. Such an audience, particularly if it understands the conclusion to which you are leading, may challenge your premise or refuse to accept it. One important exception to this rule, however, deserves mention. Sometimes if you face an extremely hostile audience, you may use deduction to delay a negative reaction. Remember, when you introduce a premise, you need not mention your specific subject. In some cases you can *float a premise*—that is, start with a premise members of a hostile audience will accept, but then use it to reach a conclusion they would otherwise reject. If you look back to Exercise 3, Set A, number 2, you can see how a clever arguer floats a premise. Here the writer wanted to argue for the casino gambling proposition, but her audience was strongly opposed to it. So, instead of immediately introducing the subject of casino gambling and evoking the wrath of the audience, she begins by talking about funding for education and law enforcement and offers an almost incontestable premise: anything that increases funding for education and law enforcement, without increasing taxes, merits the careful attention of Floridians. Of course, a hostile audience may still reject her argument, but by floating a premise, she at least gets otherwise hostile people to listen to her, to agree with her on one point, and, perhaps, to question their own premises.

Using a deductive argument is also difficult with unsophisticated audiences who are not always impressed by the careful linking of major and minor premises. Unsophisticated audiences may also object to the long time a deductive argument takes to come to the point. On the other hand, precisely because it emphasizes logical sequence, deduction will tend to impress sophisticated audiences. A sophisticated and sympathetic college professor will probably be very pleased by a well-organized deductive argument; if you can set up a multiple major premise when you write an essay exam, you will very likely receive a good grade.

Exercise 4

Here is an example of a deductive argument. Find the premise, and note how it converts an expository essay into an argument. Write your own topic sentences based on this premise; then see if you can find something like your sentences in the essay. Then divide the essay into paragraphs.

Chuck Taylor All Stars: Still the Best?

Today athletic shoes have moved out of the gym and into almost every part of American life. Americans buy more athletic shoes than they ever have before, and famous athletes endorse a wide variety of them. The Juice says that Spot-bilt are the best, while Dr. J recommends Pro-Keds. Walt "Clyde" Frazier wears Pumas, while Stan Smith prefers Adidas. Consumers, bewildered by all the claims and all the endorsements, may find selecting a new pair of athletic shoes a difficult task. Rather than listen to all the celebrities, purchasers may want to ask what exactly makes a good athletic shoe. Of course the needs of people differ quite widely: the weekend athlete may not want the same shoe that the professional does; the shopper who wants to wear jogging shoes around town may not want the same shoe that the confirmed tennis nut does. Still, most people will agree that a good, all-purpose athletic shoe should be durable, comfortable, relatively inexpensive, and stylish. If people use these standards to select a shoe, they may discover that an old favorite—Converse Chuck Taylor All Stars—may still be one of the best buys around. Chuck Taylor All Stars wear like iron; their durability is legendary. Basketball star Jerry Jones was able to play a game in a pair of All Stars that his brother had worn for an entire season. When Lakemont High School basketball coach Joe Stevens had his budget cut, he put his team in All Stars and did not have to replace any shoes over the course of an entire season. The reason for the remarkable durability of the All Stars is the reinforced canvas from which they are made. Other manufacturers, particularly Europeans, have tried to find substitutes for canvas, principally to improve the comfort and appearance of their shoes. But the most popular substitute—velour—rips and tears quite easily, and over time its nap wears down. Shoes by Puma and Adidas are also less durable because their manufacturers stretch the velour over padding. This inevitably increases the friction on the fabric and hastens its aging. All Stars do not have extensive padding in their shoes, and as a result they last longer. The reason the Europeans add a great deal of padding to their shoes is to make them more comfortable, and the shoes do, indeed, feel more like slippers than athletic shoes. But the real test of a shoe's comfort comes during the contest. Converse cushions the instep and heel of the All Star with a thick, lightweight urethane padding. A specially vulcanized rubber reinforces the sole of the All Star, making it lightweight and flexible—comfortable. In the shoe store the All Star will not feel as luxurious as the shoes by Adidas, Puma, and Keds. But on the court—be it basketball, racquetball, tennis, or squash—All Stars both pad and protect the feet. Comfort in a shoe depends on the quality of the sole and the instep, and it is in those crucial areas that the All Star has no match. Of course, a shoe's durability and comfort are meaningless if no one can afford the shoe. With their extra padding and the excise duties they face, European imports are very expensive in America. Adidas models range from thirty-five to sixty-five dollars; Pumas are slightly more expensive. The Pro-Ked imitation of the European shoes retails at about thirty dollars. Because of their inexpensive material and simple design, Chuck Taylor All Stars are much more affordable. They usually retail for about eighteen dollars and often go on sale for as little as twelve. People with large families know that they can buy three pairs of All Stars with the money they would pay for one pair of Pumas. With the money he saved by putting his team in All Stars, Coach Joe Stevens was able to buy a projector for game films—even though his budget had been cut. The only real problem with All Stars is their appearance; they look clunky and old-fashioned. The European shoes are much more stylish—they resemble regular streamlined shoes and sport handsome emblems that add status appeal. The Adidas emblem—three parallel lines—is world famous, as is the Puma emblem, which is a long, sleek curve. All Stars only have a little patch with a star at the ankle. At one time All Stars only came in white and black, and this limited their stylishness. Now like the European shoes, they are available in all colors. Still, someone who wants an athletic shoe to cruise in will not choose All Stars. As athletic shoes have grown in popularity, the European styles have become increasingly dominant; they have contributed greatly to the variety of choices that shoe buyers now have. Consumers who are confused by this abundance of shoes, however, may want to remember that durability, comfort, low cost, and stylishness are the qualities of a good shoe. Remembering this, they may want to look again at the Converse Chuck Taylor All Stars. Although their appearance is old-fashioned, All Stars offer durability and comfort at an unbeatable price. If your shoes slip and slide, get the ones with the stars on the side!

Illustration Essays with Induction

In Chapter II we discussed the inductive paragraph—one that you conclude with a general principle you arrived at by examining particulars. In argumentation the word *inductive* is used similarly; it describes a process of reasoning that establishes a generalization by observing similarities among particular cases. As we have discovered, deductive reasoning judges a particular case by noting its conformity to a generalization. Inductive and deductive forms of argumentation, however, are not exact opposites. In a deductive argument, the generalization is a definition, a premise, that a writer *asks* an audience to accept; in an inductive argument the generalization is a logical conclusion that the writer must *prove*.

When using inductive argument to prove a point, the writer does not have to wait until the end of the essay to mention the generalization; in fact, as we shall see, the generalization, or logical conclusion, often appears at the beginning of an inductive essay. In this way, the inductive essay differs from the inductive paragraph, in which the generalization always comes at the end. What distinguishes an inductive argument is that the writer must prove a logical conclusion to be true by using particular cases—illustrations—to support it. The burden of proof in an inductive argument is much greater than in a deductive one. While writers who proceed deductively direct their efforts toward establishing a premise and pay less attention to specific cases, writers who proceed inductively should have a wealth of illustrations (evidence) at their command. But despite the difficulties of inductive reasoning, induction is a much more natural, common form of reasoning than deduction.

Few of us state or recognize all our premises, but almost all of us constantly arrive at generalizations on the basis of our observations. Some of these generalizations are valid; many are not. Claims that "doctors are unfeeling" or "opera singers are temperamental" are false because sensitive doctors and serene opera singers have been known to exist. Closer to validity might be statements like "most doctors are unfeeling" and "most opera singers are temperamental." Still we must test these generalizations with certain questions. For instance, have we examined a sufficient number of doctors and opera singers in a sufficient number of appropriate situations? Were the doctors and opera singers that we observed a fair sample of their respective professions? In other words, will our illustrations convince our audience that our generalizations are true?

Great dangers—oversimplification, superficiality, bias—threaten the writer who would reason inductively. Consider the following paragraph.

> I'm telling you health fanatics are harmful to your health. I used to live with someone who jogged, did yoga, meditated twice a day, popped twelve organic vitamins with each meal, and ate only macrobiotic food. I developed an ulcer. Health fanatics are perhaps the only Americans left who truly appreciate our Puritan heritage. Their mission is to make you feel guilty for eating, drinking, smoking, sitting, and every unaerobic breath you take. They are annoying and nosy, self-righteous and smug. My ex-roommate never passed up an opportunity to read out loud the list of ingredients in my breakfast cereal as I guiltily crunched away. But the harm caused by a little artificial color, partially hydrogenated vegetable oil, BHT, and the dreaded sugar couldn't possibly equal the gastrointestinal disorders caused by these ill-humored nags. All of this might perhaps be tolerated were it not for the messianic zeal with which health fanatics approach all human activity. Not only do they try to perpetuate their ilk through blatant, boring proselytizing, they are determined to achieve immortality for all their members. Health freaks are a dangerous and hypocritical bunch. They see absolutely no contradiction in going through life giving others high blood pressure, guilt complexes, and other stress-related diseases, while they themselves continue on the pious path of everlasting perfection.

A few of the strengths and many of the weaknesses of induction are evident in the example passage. Whether you decide to believe the writer or not will depend on how convincing you find his illustrations. But despite these dangers, induction remains a necessary method of writing and thinking. Given human inability to experience and know everything, we must inevitably arrive at generalizations on the basis of limited samples that we hope are accurate.

The basic logical movement in inductive reasoning is from particular examples to a generalization. In an essay you can make this movement in two different ways, each of which will have a different effect on your audience. You can either open your essay with a compelling case (a narrative) or with a logical conclusion. When you open an essay with a logical conclusion, you have arrived at this conclusion mentally by examining particulars. In the body of the essay you will prove your logical conclusion true by using these particulars as illustrations.

In our discussion of inductive essays that begin with logical conclusions, we will first demonstrate the difference between an inductive essay opening with a logical conclusion and a deductive essay opening with a premise. Note that logical conclusions can be either single or multiple. In an *inductive* essay on casino gambling you could state the single logical *conclusion* this way:

> Casino gambling will ruin Florida's family tourism business.

Compare this to opening a *deductive* essay with a single *premise:*

> Anything that threatens Florida's family tourism business is not in the best interest of Floridians.

In an *inductive* essay on Levi's, you could state the multiple logical *conclusion* this way:

> Levi's are durable, stylish, and inexpensive.

Compare this to the multiple *premise* in a *deductive* essay:

> Pants should be durable, stylish, and inexpensive.

The differences between the premises and the logical conclusions may seem small, but they are crucial. A premise is something you ask your audience to accept; a logical conclusion is something you must prove to your audience. In the deductive essay, illustrations are less important than the premise; you will come to specific cases, but their number may be quite small. Often, if you set up the right premise, you will have to consider only one specific case. (Thus, in the casino gambling essay, once the author described one way in which casinos could threaten family tourism, she needed to say no more. To make her essay even stronger, however, she also described several other threats.) But in the inductive essay, the illustrations will be essential. By opening with a logical conclusion, you commit yourself to offering numerous relevant examples.

The sequence for the single or multiple conclusion essay is similar to the sequence for the single or multiple premise essay. Once again your introduction will give background about the topic; then it will move on to state a logical conclusion. If the logical conclusion is single, your body paragraphs will simply multiply illustrations that support it, and your topic sentences will repeat one key word. If the logical conclusion is multiple, then your body paragraphs will divide into sections devoted to each part of the logical conclusion. Your topic sentences will begin each new part with the appropriate key word. In the structural conclusion of the essay, you will restate your logical conclusion and summarize the evidence in support of it.

Essay Sequence with Single Logical Conclusion

Introduction:	*Background information:* the origin and history of the movement for casino gambling in Florida *Statement of logical conclusion:* Floridians should oppose casino gambling because it will *threaten* family tourism
Body Paragraphs: (Note: the length of this section will depend on the number of your illustrations.)	Paragraph 1: illustration of one way in which casino gambling will *threaten* family tourism Paragraph 2: illustration of a second way in which casino gambling will *threaten* family tourism Paragraph 3: illustration of a third way in which casino gambling will *threaten* family tourism
Conclusion:	Restatement of your logical conclusion; summary of illustrations

Essay Sequence with Multiple Logical Conclusion

Introduction:	*Background information:* the growing popularity of jeans; now worn by almost everybody almost everywhere *Statement of logical conclusion:* Levi's remain the best, most popular jeans because they are *comfortable, durable,* and *stylish*
Body Paragraphs:	Section 1: paragraph(s) illustrating the *comfort* of Levi's Section 2: paragraph(s) illustrating the *durability* of Levi's Section 3: paragraph(s) illustrating the *stylishness* of Levi's

Conclusion: Restatement of your logical conclusion; summary of illustrations

Generally, you will devote a paragraph to each illustration. But if you have several illustrations of Levi's durability, for example, you may devote several paragraphs, rather than a single one, to that topic. If the discussion of your illustrations is very brief, you may combine illustrations in one paragraph.

Since it establishes a clear sequence, a logical conclusion at the opening of an essay can be effective with sophisticated audiences. If the logical conclusion is surprising or provocative, it may capture the attention of an uninterested audience. Opening with a logical conclusion, however, is not effective with a hostile audience. With a hostile audience, you will do much better to float a premise.

Another type of inductive argument, sometimes in the form of a narrative, begins with a lengthy description of one particularly compelling case. This case should cut to the heart of the matter; it should capture all or most of the questions that a subject raises. The following paragraph illustrates an inductive argument that uses *one compelling case.* The paper's title is "The Persistence of Racism in the South." The author argues that, although much progress has been made, an almost vestigial racism still haunts the states of the old Confederacy.

> Route 29 south of Charlottesville, Virginia, takes motorists through one of the loveliest regions in the state. From the highway the driver can see the peaks of the heavily forested, translucently green and gray Blue Ridge mountains. Passing two miles south of Covesville, Virginia, the motorist also sees a sign so worn by time that its letters are difficult to read. The sign is an advertisement for the old Albemarle Hotel for Colored People. The hotel itself was torn down in 1973. The need for a hotel like this disappeared with the emergence of the modern inns (Holiday, Ramada, Family) that serve people without regard to race. But as the sign provides a haunting reminder of past injustice, it also brings up the question of continuing if less blatant racism that still afflicts this part of the country. In the midst of natural beauty and modern convenience, the sins of the Old South still shadow us.

Here a particular weather-beaten sign, not a premise or a logical conclusion, becomes the focus of an essay. The inductive example allows the writer to begin her essay with a narrative—an attention-getting mode that most people find easier to write than a deductive introduction. Since a narrative is basically a story, subject specificity and predicate condensation are easier to develop because the writer can describe specific people and events. After this particular example and the generalization she derives from it, the writer can go on to elaborate her case. Since her narrative does not establish a sequence, she must tie her essay together by linking the body paragraphs to the narrative. As she talks about advances and setbacks for blacks in housing, education, and employment, she must organize her discussion by referring to the sign and its meaning. The writer must continually refocus on the conjunction of progress and enduring racism. The basic sequence for this type of essay, then, looks something like this.

Essay Sequence with Narrative

Introduction:	Narrative leading to generalization: an old weather-beaten sign
Body Paragraphs:	New topic: housing; reference to sign
	New topic: education; reference to sign
	New topic: employment; reference to sign
Conclusion:	Return to particular case; assert its general validity

The inductive essay that opens with a narrative can stir interest in an uninterested audience. It can also create sympathy in a hostile audience, particularly if the conclusion to which it leads is not immediately clear. A sophisticated audience, however, may be skeptical of this kind of argument. Sophisticated people will be wary of arguments made on the basis of one illustration alone. "How much," they might ask, "can one decrepit sign tell us about the people of a region as large and diverse as the South?"

The following selections illustrate the two types of inductive argument. In the first, the writer uses one compelling case to organize her discussion of Florida's Functional Literacy Test. Note how she then links the compelling case to the topic she raises in her body paragraphs. Although the introduction does not establish a sequence, the essay develops unity and a clear point of view through its references to the narrative. The second essay, which you have already encountered in Chapter III, begins with a single logical conclusion and then documents it. Note the wealth of illustration that this author brought to her subject.

A Blessing in Disguise

Controversy over the FLT (Functional Literacy Test) has become a part of life in Florida. Eleventh graders take the test to determine if they will graduate from high school with a diploma or with a mere certificate of attendance. Opponents of the FLT feel it singles out one group of students and makes them suffer for the years of poor education they received in Florida's public schools—poor education for which the state, not the student, should bear the blame. Advocates feel the test will stop public schools from graduating students who cannot read, write, or compute simple arithmetic. In judging the validity of the FLT, one might consider the case of Larry Petersen. Larry worked hard, behaved well, and never missed a day during all his years at school. He passed from grade to grade, even though he could not learn simple math and communication skills. Despite these problems Larry graduated from high school and felt very proud and secure about his future. But now that Larry is in the working world, he finds that his diploma means nothing because he cannot hold jobs requiring that he read instructions or add figures. He is bitter and resentful toward the people who kept him on the path to graduation because all his years at school are no help to him now.

Larry knew his reading ability was below average. He worked hard to improve it but made little progress. Consequently, he faces many problems in all the jobs he tries. Simple reading materials such as instruction manuals, policy memos, or even one-sentence directions present great difficulty to him. Hundreds of thousands of workers probably face the same problem. According to calculations made by the Florida Department of Education (calculations based on the number of people who failed the FLT last year), 350,000 people have graduated from Florida's public schools with little or no skill in reading. This means 350,000 workers are likely to lose job after job because they cannot read the simple material that their work requires.

Larry also finds writing anything a frustrating task. No one in high school warned him of the problems he might encounter after graduation because of his poor writing skills. He always asks friends to help him fill out job applications, credit forms, or anything that requires him to write more than his name and yes or no. Larry is not alone. According to Dr. Francis McHugh, the director of Florida's Adult Education Board and a leading adult writing consultant, 21.7% of Florida's adults below the age of thirty-one with high school diplomas cannot write well enough to do basic office work.

Larry lost his most recent job as a clerk because he continually shortchanged or gave too much change to customers. Lacking the ability to do basic computations, he has even lost jobs in the seemingly nonintellectual field of construction. Larry's bosses liked him, but when he ordered twice as much lumber as a job required, he had to go. Larry's case may be a bit extreme, but it is not atypical. Florida's Council for Adult Mathematical Competence surveyed 1,600 recent graduates from Florida's public high schools. The council found that 31% of the graduates could not add three-digit numbers, 38% could not calculate percentages, and 43% could not perform long division. Like Larry, these graduates are probably candidates for unemployment and all the bitterness it brings.

Larry, along with countless other Florida high school graduates, is angry. He was passed through school and given a diploma for work he felt he completed. He and many others thought they could handle most jobs because they possessed a high school diploma. Now, to them the diploma is nothing more than a worthless piece of paper, signifying only wasted time.

Larry Petersen and thousands of other Florida high school graduates lack skills in reading, writing, and basic math; therefore, they have difficulty holding down jobs and functioning in society. The "uneducated" graduate feels a deep and dangerous cynicism. If Floridians could see how their system of public education fails to impart basic reading, writing, and arithmetic skills, they would demand improvement. The FLT shows people that many graduates lack basic intellectual skills and consequently cannot be productive members of society. By illustrating the problem, the FLT can provide the impetus for change and improvement in Florida's public schools. Some argue that the FLT is cruel, and it certainly has caused a group of high school juniors considerable tension and anxiety. But the reality of Larry Petersen's fate is also cruel, a fact that today's high school juniors should realize. The truth about the quality of education in Florida may hurt, but students should face that truth before they leave school, not after. Whatever its short-term effects, in the long run the FLT will have a profound and positive influence upon public education in Florida.

Textbooks Get an *F*

Statistics show that over sixty percent of a college student's education is provided by textbooks, which, you would think, should be written in a clear, comprehensible style. The books used in many general education classes at the University of

Missouri suggest, however, that good writing seldom appears on the shelves of a campus bookstore. These texts obscure important facts and concepts with Latinate, meaningless, and technical diction; awkward sentences; and unnecessary words. Their impenetrable writing styles decrease the reader's understanding and interest.

Ellis and Gulick's *Calculus with Analytic Geometry,* the textbook used in general calculus classes at the University of Missouri, could just as easily be a sourcebook of awkward sentence examples as the mathematics publication it is. Long, complex sentences, such as the following, must be read several times to be understood: "Despite the various methods that exist for calculating integrals—those we have described and many we have not—it is frequently difficult or impossible to express an indefinite integral in terms of the familiar functions and thereby compute the corresponding definite integrals." Test scores, however, are a better proof of the difficulty Ellis and Gulick's awkward writing creates for students. Mathematics professors complain that the most frequently missed exam questions are those pertaining to the reading material. Obviously, the use of poorly written mathematics textbooks has a serious effect on the entire learning process.

Meaningless words and phrases make William Fleming's *Arts and Ideas,* a typical humanities textbook, even less understandable than the average mathematics book. Fleming employs terms out of proper context in obscure discussions of art. A description of the Pazzi Chapel suggests that in the cloister "mystery and infinity have yielded to geometric clarity." Similarly, Botticelli's *Birth of Venus* is said to be dominated by "incisiveness of outline" and "ballet-like choreography of lines." Passages containing unrelated technical words grouped into nonsensical gobbledygook are more confusing: Botticelli's paintings become "reflections of a neopagan atmosphere with its Christian concordances" while Masaccio's are "in the iconographical tradition." Unintelligible descriptions of art in typical humanities textbooks perhaps contribute to the unpopularity of classical art with college students.

To ensure the proper understanding and performance of dangerous experiments, writers of chemistry laboratory manuals would presumably take special care to express themselves clearly and concisely. Yet John Baxter and George Ryschkewitsch's *General Chemistry* laboratory manual is quite ambiguous. Latinate and technical diction commonly obscure important facts. Medicine droppers, common household instruments, are confusingly renamed "micro-pipets." The simple principle that the greater the extent of reaction between two substances, the more concentrated are the products is restated: "the more strongly the water molecules are deformed, the more acidic and less basic their gelatinous hydroxides will be." Equally absurd is the description of electrons changing position under the influence of a positive charge as "mutual polarization caus[ing] shifts in electron distribution evoking induced dipoles." The Latinate, technical style in which chemistry textbooks and laboratory manuals are written is one reason why chemistry students typically receive low grades at the university level.

The textbooks used by general education classes in mathematics, humanities, chemistry, and other subjects at the University of Missouri all share obscure writing styles. In many cases the writing in these texts deserves an *F*. These books confuse students and make learning uninteresting or even odious. The increasing use of such works is probably contributing to the decreasing general knowledge of college graduates.

Comparison by Way of Analogy

Analogy is a process of reasoning in which you set up parallel cases. In analogy you note that one specific case is similar to another and then infer that what is true for the first case will also be true for the second. Since no two things are exactly alike, you can also use analogy to highlight important differences. Writers use two types of analogy: explanatory and logical. The *explanatory analogy,* which is really a metaphor, explains one class of things by reference to another, usually more familiar, class; it thus compares two different things. This kind of analogy is useful for explaining but less useful for persuading, mainly because it rests on a resemblance that is only superficial. One of the most common and misused explanatory analogies is the hackneyed comparison of running a government to running a ship. Politicians generally use this analogy to argue for strong executive leadership. Incumbents talk about the need for an experienced captain and warn voters of the dangerous and uncharted seas that lie ahead. The fallacy of this argument is that running a government is only vaguely like running a ship. The concerns of a state government, let alone the federal, are much more extensive and complex than those of a supertanker. The comparison breaks down. A similar breakdown occurs in the once popular comparison between serving as president of the United States and coaching a football team. References to "game plans," "winning records," and "toughness" do not impress the sophisticated reader, who knows that a nation cannot win an economic crisis as a football team can win a game, amd who knows that a president's vision and compassion are probably as important as statistics about performance.

The *logical analogy* is a much more reputable method of reasoning, for it demonstrates similarities between two things. An argument by logical analogy might take this shape. Imagine you want to argue against a treaty between the United States and another nation. You discover that this nation has repeatedly broken past treaties when it served its interests to do so. You may organize your essay by summarizing the past treaty obligations and violations, pointing to similarities between the new treaty and the old ones, and then concluding that the latest treaty will suffer a fate similar to that of the old ones. As this example illustrates, an analogy argument is a comparison-contrast essay with a purpose. If you look back to the essay comparing the University of Florida's Halloween Ball to its football games (pp. 125–127), you can see very clearly how a comparison essay can become an argument. By showing that behavior at the ball is really no different from behavior at football games, the author argues that the ball, like the football games, should remain a part of university life. The form an analogy argument takes, then, is very similar to the model for the comparison-contrast essay we described in Chapter III—with one exception. The introduction to the analogy essay must establish a purpose, an end, for the comparison or contrast. When you write an analogy argument, you must have a clear sense of the conclusion to which the analogy will lead your audience.

To write a successful analogy argument, you must understand what type of analogy you are using. If you are using an explanatory analogy, then you must indicate to your reader that the analogy is a tool not a truth, and you must not try to base your entire essay on the analogy. Emphasize that you know the analogy is useful only for purposes of illustration and debate. This will prevent you from losing your argument when the analogy breaks down. If you have a logical analogy argument, your introduction must outline the features you will compare and reveal the purpose for your comparison.

EXERCISE 5

The following two newspaper columns focus on a famous Supreme Court ruling and use analogy argument. In the William Raspberry column, try to find both an explanatory and a logical analogy. In the Jesse Jackson column, analyze the analogy with care. Jackson presents an explanatory analogy and bases his entire argument on it.

Sow's Ear Case into Silk Purse
by William Raspberry

WASHINGTON—Bakke was, from the beginning, a bad case on which to hang the future of affirmative action. The special-admissions program of the University of California Medical School (Davis) was not the best one to defend, based, as it was, on too-specific numerical set-asides.

And while Allan Bakke's allegation was that he was a victim of "reverse" discrimination based on race, it seems clear that he was more accurately a victim of age discrimination. He was turned down 13 times by 12 different medical schools, not because he was white but because he was 10 years older than the average medical school freshman.

With such a sow's ear of a case to work with, the wonder is not that the U.S. Supreme Court failed to produce a silk purse, but that it did manage to fashion a serviceable, disposable handbag.

The outcome of the celebrated case is widely interpreted as an awkward compromise that pleases no one. The Court ruled that Bakke had been discriminated against, but agreed that it is constitutional for admissions officers to give some consideration to race.

I, for one, welcome the ambiguity. A clear-cut decision that race may not be considered would have denied the reality of the American racial experience. Minorities, and blacks most particularly, have been crippled by racism—including racism that has been condoned by earlier Supreme Court edicts.

On the other hand, a clear-cut rule that because of that racist history, blacks and other minorities could be forever spared the necessity of competing with whites, would have struck too many Americans as unfair.

While the Court majority ruled against the Davis plan of setting aside for minorities 16 out of 100 freshman seats in the medical school, five members took pains to praise the Harvard approach to the problem.

Harvard, like Davis, has decided that it is educationally valuable to have a student body that is diversified with respect to geographic origin, background and interest, income—and race. Without setting any target numbers for any single category, Harvard looks at its list of admissible applicants, awarding "points" here for ethnic background, there for perseverance or special talent, and comes up with recommendations.

But every applicant competes with every other applicant. There is no special preserve for minorities, as there was at Davis.

What strikes me as particularly sensible about the Harvard plan is that it permits screeners to look at individuals, without dependence on rigid formulas. It is, of course, what sensible screeners always do.

They neither assume that identical scores reflect identical applicants or that membership in a minority group is automatic proof of the need for special consideration.

Suppose a black applicant to Harvard Law School, a product of the inner-city slums who attended substandard public schools and graduated from a mediocre black college, scores 650 on his law school admissions test. Can anyone suppose that such a person is the mere equal of a white applicant who, having graduated from Groton and Columbia, also scores 650? The Harvard plan permits admissions screeners to give special weight to the black youngster's special achievement.

On the other hand, suppose it is the black student whose law-professor father sent him to Groton and Columbia, while the white applicant, the child of an unemployed coal miner, attended substandard public institutions. The Harvard plan would permit the screeners to award no bonus ponts whatever to the black applicant and perhaps offer a point or two to the white one.

In both cases, they are free to look at race, but only as one of several pertinent factors.

And as years go by and racial conditions change, they will tend to give less and less consideration to race. Which, again, is as it should be.

For not even the most adamant of affirmative-action supporters, who agree wholeheartedly with Justice Thurgood Marshall's recital of the legacy of slavery, would insist that blacks should forever be granted special consideration. At some point, people will be expected to sink or swim on their own.

But when? The answer is a lot easier for a screening committee with a fair amount of discretion than for a technician trying to come up with a set formula.

Last week's Supreme Court ruling raises some questions in cases involving minority set-asides—the Philadelphia Plan requiring that 10 percent of construction jobs go to blacks, for instance, or the District of Columbia rule mandating that 25 percent of the city's construction contracts go to minority contractors.

But it is by no means clear that the ruling makes these plans unlawful.

In general, the Court—for all the differences of outlook reflected in its six separate opinions—emerged from a stinking quagmire of a case wearing the distinct aroma of roses.

Closing the Gap for Blacks
by Jesse L. Jackson

The Allan Bakke case has returned to the news because it has finally worked its way through a full review to the Supreme Court.

The court's decision in the Bakke case will be discussed in another column; right now it is important to talk about the facts of American life that make affirmative action necessary and just.

If you will, allow your mind to wander with me to an imaginary one-mile foot race between two world-class athletes. Each is anxious to win a sub-four-minute mile.

The race begins and, sooner than expected, one runner falls behind the other. Suddenly, officials notice the trailing runner has weights attached to his ankles. They stop the race, ordering both athletes to hold their places.

The weights are removed; the officials fire the starting gun again and each runner continues from the point where he was stopped. Not surprisingly, the runner who had run part of the entire distance without ankle weights comes in first. The fundamental moral question here is: Was it a fair race? The obvious answer is simple: no. If the second runner could be compensated—perhaps by comparing the times of the two runners' final lap and then projecting that time over the entire race, a more accurate appraisal of each runner's ability and performance could be calculated.

If a reasonable means of compensation could be devised, no one would say that it constituted "reverse discrimination" against the first runner or "preferential treatment" for the second. All would agree that some adjustment was only fair and just.

It's possible to work out an easily accepted, reasonable and moral solution to the runners' "problem" because racial attitudes are not involved—which makes all this similar to the position in which blacks find themselves in the United States. Blacks have been running the race with weights on their feet—weights they didn't want or choose. Weights of "no rights which a white must respect," weights of slavery, of past and present discrimination in jobs, education, housing, in poor health care and more.

Affirmative action programs have been an extremely reasonable, even conservative, approach to compensating blacks for past and present discrimination. (A recent study by an agency of the federal government indicated that at the present rate of "progress" it will take 43 years to end job discrimination—hardly a reasonable timetable or a pace too reckless.)

Blacks are far behind. Blacks do not have their share of the nation's architects or engineers, bank tellers or electricians, social scientists or insurance brokers, lawyers or anything else. Affirmative action must help blacks to catch and close these and other gaps.

There is much confusion about the goals and timetables of affirmative action, and quotas. Again, discussions about affirmative action usually are confused because people begin at the end—rather than at the beginning.

The media have chosen to use such code words as "reverse discrimination" and "preferential treatment" in discussing affirmative action rather than the fact that affirmative action is not "reverse discrimination" but "reversal of discrimination."

The Bakke Case may be the legal focus of resistance to affirmative action and to blacks' upward mobility, but "Bakke-ism" is the political climate in which we are operating. The question isn't how the Supreme Court decides the Bakke case, but how to overcome "Bakke-ism."

Those opposed to blacks moving up have engaged in a propaganda blitz to change attitudes toward the reasonable intent of affirmative action programs. Actually, the concept of an American "reverse discrimination" is absurd and a contradiction in terms. Never in history has a majority population in power engaged in programs or written laws to discriminate against itself. The only thing whites give up because of affirmative action is privilege—something to which they are not entitled in the first place.

The resolution of the race question in this country would liberate us to liberate others around the world. For until white America is what it ought to be, black America cannot be what it ought to be. And until black Americans are no longer prohibited by race from achieving their potential, all Americans will be poorer.

These words that Martin Luther King Jr. spoke more than a decade ago are as vital a statement today as then:

"We will either learn to live together as brothers and sisters or we shall surely die apart as fools."

Explanatory analogies, particularly if they are provocative or strange, can capture the attention of an uninterested audience. But their very strangeness often limits their effectiveness as arguments; any dissimilarities become too apparent. If you use such an analogy—something like Raspberry's comparison of making a purse to making a law—limit it. Refer to it briefly and use it only to capture and focus attention. If you open your essay with an explanatory analogy, you may, of course, refer back to it in your conclusion to give your reader a sense of having come full circle. While explanatory analogies stimulate interest, as Jackson's track-meet comparison does, they cannot provide the basis for a complete argument. Sophisticated audiences will tend to be skeptical of analogies in general and will question whether or not the comparison actually holds. They will complain that Jackson's comparison of racial discrimination to a rigged foot race is no different from the comparison of the president to a ship captain. If you hope to use a logical analogy with a sophisticated audience, make sure the similarities are strong and clear, as is Raspberry's comparison of the Davis admission program to the one at Harvard. Lacking such a logical analogy, almost any argument—even one by a debater of Jesse Jackson's ability—will fail.

EXERCISE 6

In the following explanatory analogy argument, underline those sections in which the author provides a purpose and outlines the features he will compare. Then underline the key words and make connections between the topic sentences in the body paragraphs and the sequence outlined in the introduction.

Don't Pass the Poison, Please!

Recently the Department of Health, Education, and Welfare's antismoking campaign has come under sharp attack. Led by the tobacco companies, opponents of the campaign claim that it threatens the freedom of choice of Americans. They argue that, whatever the consequences, people should have the right to choose whether or not they will smoke. But suppose you are in a restaurant, and the man at the table next to you pulls a vial of something out of his pocket and asks you, "Excuse me, do you mind if I poison myself?" Then he pours some of the liquid out of the vial and prepares to drink it. You would probably do one of two things: attempt to stop him or brush it off as a joke. If you brush it off as a joke, you will be very upset when he drinks the liquid and falls over dead. Now just suppose you are in the same restaurant and rather than poison himself our guest wants to poison you too. Would you be restricting his freedom of choice if you stopped him from pouring the liquid into your glass?

Tobacco smoke is a poison. The evidence documenting its connection with heart disease and lung cancer is overwhelming. The Surgeon General of the United States has estimated that smoking a pack of cigarettes takes three minutes off a smoker's life. But tobacco smoke is a poison with an extra dimension. As it spreads, and others inhale it, the poison affects not only the smoker, but those around the smoker. If the person at the table next to you in a restaurant is smoking, you will probably say nothing; you will breathe the smoke-filled air. In this situation you have lost your freedom of choice. Even though you choose not to smoke, by breathing the poisoned air you are, in effect, smoking. By putting up with the smoker, you are saying, "Sure, go ahead and poison me too."

Since smoking takes its toll over the course of years, people sometimes do not realize that tobacco smoke is a kind of poison as deadly, in the long run, as arsenic. Even though they admit that in general a smoker will not live as long as a nonsmoker, many smokers still refuse to believe that the cigarette they smoke today or tomorrow will affect them thirty years from now. They continue to light up and continue to poison others. In doing so, they exercise shortsightedness, not freedom of choice.

Americans expect their government to protect them; they would expect the authorities to arrest and detain anybody who walked about a restaurant trying to pour poison into people's drinks. The Department of Health, Education, and Welfare, through its antismoking campaign, is trying to protect American citizens from a poison—it is doing its job. The tobacco companies may be right to argue that freedom of choice is the issue, but they are clearly wrong to overlook the freedom of choice of nonsmokers. The Department of Health, Education, and Welfare must be allowed to protect the freedom of every American to say, "Don't pass the poison, please." When the Department of Health, Education, and Welfare helps them to say it, then, and only then, is the Department living up to its name. (This essay was written in 1978 before the Department of Health, Education, and Welfare became the Department of Health and Human Services.)

APPEAL TO AUTHORITY

The greatest problem facing anyone who wants to write a deductive argument is establishing a premise. The audience must accept the premise or else the entire argument fails. One way to overcome this problem is to have an authority establish your premise for you. Appeal to authority is one kind of argument you, as a college student, will have considerable opportunity to use in your writing. If you master the basic form of this kind of argument, you will greatly simplify some of the assignments you face.

In an appeal-to-authority argument, you cite the opinion or conclusion of an authority—whether an individual or a group—and then apply it to the issue at hand. An argument by appeal to authority will be only as good as the authority it cites. To establish an authority's legitimacy, you must first establish the authority's *relevance*. You must show that the authority's expertise includes the field you are discussing. In an argument about American foreign policy, you might do well to quote some remarks of Henry Kissinger's. In a debate over the relative merits of movie directors, a reference to an opinion of Kissinger's would be less effective; his authority is not relevant in that field.

Our example may seem farfetched, but we live in a culture that has spawned a wide array of bogus authorities. You can and should question the relevance of any authority a writer or speaker cites to support an argument; often this can bring the entire argument into question. Consider, for example, the debate over whether or not race determines intelligence. William Shockley, who champions the idea that differences among races on IQ tests indicate a genetic factor, is a Nobel Prize winner and bills himself as such. He has used the authority of his Nobel Prize to win supporters. But Shockley won the Nobel Prize for research in physics, not for research in genetics—a field he has turned to only recently and in which his expertise is not as great. Shockley's authority, then, is not totally relevant to the field he has entered—a fact many of his opponents have pounced upon.

EXERCISE 7

Below is a list of famous people who use their authority to endorse a wide variety of products and causes. Draw a line between the authorities and the field in which their authority is relevant. Then list the fields in which these people speak, even though their skills and accomplishments are not relevant to those fields.

	fashion design
	insect killers
Muhammad Ali	men's clothing
	auto racing
Jack Nicklaus	hair spray and shampoo
	Southeast Asian politics
Dorothy Hamill	football
	boxing
Gloria Vanderbilt	golf
	TV talk shows
Phyllis George	ice skating
	automobiles
A. J. Foyt	food processors
	panty hose
Ed McMahon	acting
	moviemaking
Jane Fonda	car rentals
	TV sportscasting
Juliet Prowse	motor oil
	dog food
O. J. Simpson	grass seed
	sunglasses
	nuclear energy
	watches
	dancing

Besides *relevance* to the field you are writing about, your authorities must have established *reputations.* You must be able to cite their works and accomplishments and indicate why they have won respect in their fields. If you are using one specific work by an authority, you should mention its title, and, if possible, summarize its reputation. When you establish your authority's reputation, you should always be on the lookout for questions about your authority's integrity. If your authority has a financial interest in a question, few will accept his or her word. The best, the most unimpeachable authority will have no direct personal or financial interest in the question you are arguing, although such an authority is often difficult to find.

Once you introduce an authority and establish reputation and relevance, you must fairly and accurately summarize the authority's views and then make them the basis of a premise. After you establish your premise, you can proceed deductively. Depending on the amount of detail and elaboration you use, relevance, reputation, and summary may come in three separate paragraphs or in one. In some cases the relevance of the authority is so clear that you need not state it.

EXERCISE 8

Here is an introduction to a successful appeal-to-authority essay on the topic of whether the Green Bay Packers should fire head coach Bart Starr. Find the statements of relevance and reputation, and find the summary.

> The decision to fire a football coach is always difficult. Almost every coach will have supporters and detractors, and amid all the clamor that both groups create, a rational decision may be almost impossible. The confused athletic director or university president, however, may find some help in the teachings of Paul W. "Bear" Bryant. Bryant was the coach with the most wins in the history of college football. His University of Alabama team won thirteen Southeast Conference and four national championships. In his autobiography, *Bear,* Bryant claims that a successful coach must recruit superior athletes, must make those athletes play up to their potential, and must win the big games—games that determine conference titles and national rankings.

Appeal to authority will work with any audience, as long as the audience accepts your authority. Sometimes you can win over members of a hostile audience by citing an authority they respect and using this authority to float a premise that leads to a conclusion they would otherwise reject. During the Vietnam War, for example, antiwar groups made frequent appeals to the authority of those military men who spoke out against the war and described it as misguided. With conservative, promilitary, and hostile audiences, this kind of appeal was much more likely to succeed than appeals to counterculture heroes like Jane Fonda or Benjamin Spock.

If you decide to use statistics in your essay, one final note about appeal to authority is worth considering. Each time you cite a statistic, you, in effect, appeal to the authority of the person or group that provided it. If your argument is to be honest and aboveboard, then, you should give the source for your statistics and establish the reputation and relevance of this source. If the statistics are part of an inductive argument, you may make this appeal to authority brief—as brief, in some cases, as a footnote. But you must always be sure to cite sources, no matter how briefly. The more you argue, the more you will see how crucial the authority for a statistic is. Opponents in an argument will almost always have different data; your job, as a listener, is to discover the statistics that are true and relevant. As a writer, you want to make sure that your reader has the opportunity to check your data—you must be clear about your sources. If you look back to the body paragraphs of the essay on the Florida Functional Literacy Test (pp. 199–200), you can see an example of this brief appeal to authority for statistics.

Working Toward the Longer Essay: Three Models for Combining Arguments

When you argue with someone out loud, you rarely use only one type of argument. Rather you launch a multiple attack, hitting your opponents with authorities, analogies, and illustrations and offering premises they cannot refuse. Similarly, when you write an argumentative essay, you should not necessarily use only one model. When you combine models, you follow the practice of most good writers. If you look at essays that are famous and widely reprinted, you will soon learn that very few of them are perfect definition, illustration, or comparison-contrast essays. Fine writers do not set out to follow a model; rather they set out to make a statement in the most convincing and effective manner possible. They incorporate different types of organization and argument as they strive for an overall effect. When writing argumentative essays, you can imitate the best writers by trying to come up with effective combinations of your own. In shorter essays you may follow a step-by-step model, but the ability to make combinations will determine your success in longer assignments. The permutations, of course, are endless—this is what makes writing an enterprise that ultimately cannot be systematized. But we can introduce you to several combinations and hope that they will prepare you to devise your own.

As we pointed out in Chapter II, your body paragraphs should always be complete—that is, they should analyze, document, or illustrate in some detail the claim you are making. In any argument you write, whatever its overall structure, the body paragraphs can and should include different types of arguments. In a deductive argument, for example, you may use inductive examples, authorities, and logical and explanatory analogies. Since these arguments are in a subordinate rather than a central role, the requirements upon them are less rigorous. The introduction of your authority can be briefer, your sample of inductive examples can be smaller, and your explanatory analogy can be less cautious. In the following essay, we have noted the variety and number of supports the writer has found for her claims.

Rifles Only

For several days Roy Larrabee had been hunting white-tailed deer unsuccessfully in a North Florida game preserve. He had not seen a deer during his entire hunting trip and was anxious to get a shot at a buck. After walking down an old fire trail, Roy caught a glimpse of a large buck sneaking through the underbrush some distance away. All in one motion, he shouldered his old twelve-gauge shotgun and squeezed the trigger, letting loose a load of buckshot. The animal was hit by only a few pellets and ran off to some distant thicket to die a slow, agonizing death. Roy never found that deer and through this experience learned the grave inadequacy of a shotgun in deer hunting. He now supports the game laws that ban stalking deer with firearms other than rifles—laws that he once felt were unnecessary and stupid.

Narrative

Conclusion

Expert bowman Fred Bear, one of the world's most famous hunters, has pointed out that deer are among the most elusive animals—hunters must be prepared when they have the rare opportunity to shoot one. Fred Bear also emphasizes another fact which Roy should have been aware of: the musculature and anatomy of deer are such that unless a projectile (bullet or arrow) penetrates deeply into a vital area, the animal will not die right away. The pellets in Roy's buckshot were not heavy enough to bring down the deer directly after contact. A rifle, however, is very different from a shotgun. A rifle's small-diameter, high-velocity bullet has unsurpassed penetration and expands on contact, delivering consistent and immediately fatal blows if the hunter fires accurately.

Authority

Another thing hunters should consider is the presence of the underbrush they commonly encounter when hunting deer. Rick Banning, a park ranger at the Ocala National Forest,

Authority

has observed white-tailed deer for years and has reached a conclusion that most veteran hunters share: the thicker the brush, the better the deer like it. Odds are, the hunter who finds a deer is also going to find vegetation in the line of fire. The pellets in a buckshot load are small and easily deflected by vines and twigs. The rifle projectile, on the other hand, easily punches through the surrounding cover with more than enough killing power to bring the deer down. Analogy

The final and most important consideration is the range at which the weapon is effective. The shotgun is at best a short-range weapon. A survey of hunters by the Florida Department of Wildlife in 1976, however, revealed that in most cases (72%) deer were sighted at long range, one hundred fifty to two hundred feet. At this range an attempt with a shotgun will result only in a complete miss or, as in Roy's case, a crippled deer never to be recovered. A rifle handles the long-range shot with plenty of power. This power means the rifle bullet penetrates deep enough to insure a fast, clean kill. Statistics Authority

Hunters tend to be an independent lot, and many have criticized and mocked the law that requires that deer be stalked with rifles. But every hunter has the duty to insure as painless a death as possible. In order to bag deer humanely and consistently, the bullet must penetrate deeply in a vital area, go through twigs and vines without being deflected or slowed down, and perform well at long range. The small-caliber, high-velocity rifle bullet meets all these requirements and is the best weapon for this type of hunting. Rather than scorning the state law, hunters should understand its motive and heed it. Roy Larrabee does. Premise; Inductive Example

We will now discuss three general combinations that work in long essays: induction-deduction, deduction-analogy, and induction-analogy. Use them as a guide to create successful combinations of your own. By combining argumentative models to create an overall effect, you will be emulating the practice of most successful writers.

Induction-Deduction

When you open an essay with a compelling inductive example—a narrative—you often gain the attention and sometimes gain the sympathy of your audience, but you do not set up a clear sequence for your body paragraphs. When you open an essay by setting up a premise, you establish a clear sequence, but you necessarily speak in general terms whose immediate relevance to your subject may not be apparent. You risk losing all but the most sophisticated and sympathetic of audiences. You can, however, both hold attention and establish sequence if you are astute enough to have your narration lead to a premise; in this way you combine the inductive and deductive models. The following example is not a complete success. The writing is melodramatic and overwrought. But it does show how to set up an inductive-deductive combination.

> Paul Benoit and his family moved to the Midwest fifteen years ago because of better job opportunities. Now he wishes they had never left New England. The auto parts factory where he found a good-paying job has been closed for thirteen months. "I'm sorry, man," his supervisor told him, "the factory's got to close 'cause no one's buying American cars." These words churned in Paul's mind as he walked along Detroit's snowy sidewalks. Paul did not mind walking; it gave him time to delay facing the inevitable—walking into a cold, dark apartment and facing six whimpering kids pleading for food. With empty pockets, Paul trudged up the steps to his building and wondered how much longer his meager unemployment checks would last.
>
> The story of Paul Benoit may become a grim reality for many Americans if we do not wake up and face the fact that our industrial landscape is changing. The United States is moving from a smokestack to a high-tech economy; the only choice we have is to retrain our workforce.

Once the writer uses Paul Benoit to establish the premise (we must retrain our workforce), the writer can go on to his real subject, which is the need for the federal government to establish a retraining program for displaced industrial workers. He can proceed deductively and focus in his body paragraphs on how specific parts of the program will retrain workers. But he cannot forget Paul entirely. To give the essay a sense of completion, he should return to Paul in the conclusion and show how the job retraining program would have helped the Benoit household.

Deduction-Analogy

As we have mentioned, analogy argument is basically comparison-contrast with a purpose. One of the best ways to create a sense of purpose is to introduce a premise before you move into your analogy. This is precisely what the essay on Chuck Taylor All Stars does (pp. 191–193). By first defining what an athletic shoe should be and should do, the author turns the contrast between

All Stars and European shoes into an argument. Consider the essay in Chapter III (pp. 121–123) which compares *Jaws* to *The Exorcist*. To become an argument, the essay requires a premise about what movies—particularly sensationalistic movies—should be and should do. We added the underlined sections below to the introduction and conclusion to turn the original expository essay into an argument.

The Devil Is Scarier

Introduction

Movies may not be better than ever, but they do seem to be scarier than ever. The horror film continues to flourish, and recently filmmakers have discovered new ways to shock their audiences. With the public's appetite for this kind of titillation at an all-time high, the question of what actually makes a film scary has become important to the movie industry. For some producers, shocking and grotesque monsters seem to be the answer. But movies with huge, scaly, deformed creatures do not usually develop mass appeal; they attract juveniles, not their parents. The actual key to deep and profound terror—the kind that brings adults into the theaters—is not grotesqueness, but invisibility. The evil force that we cannot define or know is what truly scares us. We can test this generalization by applying it to two great box-office successes—*Jaws* and *The Exorcist*.

Widely separated in their locale, characters, and theme, both films portray an uncontrollable evil force that arbitrarily preys upon unsuspecting victims. Both films celebrate the exceptional men who overcome it, although the resolution they bring about is only temporary. But in *Jaws*, the evil force takes on a physical shape, and the movie, despite some superb special effects, is less frightening. Although both films are so scary that the distinction may seem academic, filmmakers seeking the key to box-office success may want to consider why *The Exorcist* is scarier.

Conclusion

When "Bruce" strikes his first victim in *Jaws*, we do not see him. We see only a young girl's puzzlement, her horrible recognition, her helplessness, and her terror. The shark, though a fearful physical specimen, does not terrify us so much as his mystery does, a fact the makers of *Jaws* recognized and exploited by not letting audiences see Bruce until the second half of the movie. In *The Exorcist*, audiences never see the devil, but only his influence. Despite the thousands of dollars spent constructing Bruce, he ultimately makes *Jaws* a less scary movie than it might have been. Once we see him, we can deal with him. Unseen, he is as horrifying as the devil, and only the bravest of us dare challenge him. In both *Jaws* and *The Exorcist,* the combination of mysterious evil, brave heroes, and partial resolution of their conflict produced long lines and record box-office receipts. Both movies are scary, but *The Exorcist,* with its invisible, unknowable, unspeakable evil, is scarier.

INDUCTION-ANALOGY

Sometimes your data may include two compelling cases. If so, you may open with two narratives and then either compare or contrast the features common to them. This combination can be particularly effective when you are asked to make a fine or difficult distinction between two cases. In the following essay, the writer faces an extremely difficult question, a question with which many great thinkers—Henry David Thoreau, Mohandas Gandhi, and Martin Luther King, Jr., among them—have wrestled. The writer was asked to distinguish between legitimate political protest and acts of terrorism. Working within a time limit, she had little opportunity for extensive research and thus her account is not entirely accurate. Beginning with her own knowledge, she took two specific incidents with which she was familiar and contrasted them. Her combination of induction and analogy led to an argument that treats a difficult topic with precision. As you read her essay, note the two narratives, find where she establishes the sequence for her body paragraphs, and find where the analogy argument begins. Note also that one weakness in this essay is its vague use of authority; the writer never tells us whom she refers to when she mentions "political scientists." Another weakness is the inapt explanatory analogy comparing an act of political terror to a domestic quarrel.

Legitimate Political Revolutions Versus Acts of Terrorism

The year is 1917. The Russian people have endured centuries of czarist oppression. After months of diplomatic negotiation with the czar, the people decide that they have had enough of the czar's idle talk; the time has come for action. Led by Vladimir Ilyich Lenin, the people stage a march on the Winter Palace and end centuries of oppression. The Union of Soviet Socialist Republics is born.

In another part of the world, at another time, another people stage a revolt of sorts. Their story takes place in Munich, West Germany, at the 1972 Summer Olympics. This particular Olympiad has a special significance, since the Israelis are competing in the same country where Hitler killed six million Jews. But now Germany is quite hospitable, and everyone thinks that the games will go off without a hitch. Suddenly, terror strikes when Palestinian Arabs invade the Israeli athletes' quarters. In the end, twenty-two men are dead, and the murderers have only achieved the feat of killing a few human beings. The motive for their act is entirely forgotten.

Both legitimate political revolutions and acts of terrorism have evolved from people's desire to find a better way of life. Because both acts spring from the same idea, most people cannot distinguish between the two. But lately, political scientists have attempted that feat. These scientists carefully examine all their data before they label any incident, for they know that often only a fine distinction exists between a legitimate political revolution and an act of terrorism. To determine whether an incident is indeed a legitimate political revolution or an act of terrorism, political scientists observe, among other things, the basic motives behind the incident, the role violence plays in it, and the popular support for it.

Primarily, political scientists distinguish between legitimate political revolutions and acts of terrorism by determining the basic motive behind the incident. Usually, before a legitimate political revolution occurs, the people have endured years of oppression. That oppression motivates them to search for a freedom they have never known. This burning desire for freedom helps the revolt to succeed, as in the 1917–18 Bolshevik Revolution.

On the other hand, acts of terrorism are not usually motivated by a burning desire for freedom. More often, their only motive is pure, irrational anger. Acts of terrorism are often analogous to domestic quarrels—the people involved in a domestic quarrel may have a knock-down, drag-out fight, but days later, they only remember the fight itself, not its cause. The truth is, the cause of the fight was probably too insignificant to remember. The same situation exists in many acts of terrorism. For instance, people will always remember the 1972 Munich incident because twenty-two men died, but the average person cannot remember why those men died.

Political scientists can differentiate between legitimate political revolutions and acts of terrorism in another way. Through years of study, they have found that if they know the role that violence plays in the incident, they can better determine whether the act is a legitimate political revolution or an act of terrorism. For instance, the participants in a legitimate political revolution characteristically think of violence as a secondary means of achieving their goals.

Usually, they try to make changes in their present government through extensive, peaceful talks. They will resort to violence only when they have exhausted all peaceful possibilities for a reform of their oppressive government. The Bolsheviks followed this procedure to the letter; they used violence only when they felt it was absolutely necessary.

Terrorists, on the other hand, use violence as a primary means of achieving their goals. In their reliance on violence as a means of change, they often do not think through the repercussions of the situation carefully. Other people see only the violent act—not its causes—and think that terrorists are just irrational beings who do not know what they want. Even when terrorists have legitimate goals in mind, their use of violence overshadows those goals and hides them from public view forever. Even though the Palestinians may have had legitimate goals in mind at Munich, their use of violence eliminated any chance they had of getting their point across.

Both the motive behind it and the role violence plays in it contribute to the amount of popular support an incident receives. When distinguishing between legitimate political revolutions and acts of terrorism, political scientists note the presence or absence of popular support. The general population is usually behind a legitimate political revolution; the Bolshevik Revolution was no exception. In a revolution the majority of the people are affected by the basic motive behind the revolt. They try to bring about change through peaceful methods but become frustrated when they see their present government will not relinquish power. As a last resort, they take up arms to achieve their goal of a new and better society.

Terrorist acts almost never have the popular support of the people. The Palestinian terrorists can surely attest to that fact; even the rest of the Arab world did not support the Munich attack. Since they cannot understand terrorists' motives for using violence, the public cannot identify with terrorists. The majority of the public cannot condone the use of violence as a primary means of achieving a goal. They feel that people who use violence to prove a point render the point meaningless because the violence overshadows everything else. Terrorists have little, if any, general support for their actions.

Through years of research and study, political scientists have noticed certain historical patterns that help differentiate between legitimate political revolutions and acts of terrorism. By observing the basic motive, the role of violence, and the degree of popular support, they can determine the incident's legitimacy. However, as political scientists have frequently pointed out, these categories are very broad. Although researchers

> have made some headway, they feel that years may pass before they can clearly draw the line between revolution and terrorism. In fact, the possibility exists that political scientists will never be able to completely distinguish between the two.

After this student captured your attention with two examples, she listed three features by which she could contrast them: the basic motives, the role of violence, and the popular support. She set up a sequence for the rest of the essay so that you always knew where you were and where you were heading. Her conclusion brought the essay full circle by summarizing the similarities and differences and reasserting her central statement.

The combinations we have described are only three among many. We offer them to spur your own creative powers. Remember that combinations will often depend on both the data you have and your estimation of your audience. These factors will vary, so we can offer you no final, all-purpose model. Instead you must treat the models as parts that you will combine and vary to form wholes. The topic, as well as your information and your audience, will always shape your essay.

Anticipating Objections

At some point in any successful argument (and successful essay), you must anticipate and defeat objections. Experienced debaters always try to guess their opponents' strongest argument and try to defeat it before the other side even raises it. This ploy makes sense for several reasons. First, you do better to state the opposing case and deal with it on your own terms than to leave it out there somewhere in the audience. Second, if you anticipate an objection, you also give your audience the sense that you are fair-minded—that you have looked at the question from both sides. Third, by anticipating and dealing with objections, you will show that you have mastered your subject in some depth. Finally, your determination to make a clever argument will require you to be well informed. In general, expository writing does not require anticipation of an objection; argumentative writing does. Once again, argumentative writing requires an extra step of you, but, once again, that step leads to clear and important benefits.

Obviously if you spend your entire essay dealing with potential objections, you will never get to the point. If possible, you should find the single strongest potential objection to your view, deal with it, and then proceed with your case. Fortunately, the type of argument you make largely controls the type of objection you can expect. If you consciously shape your argument, you can deal with objections very systematically.

Refutations in Deductive Arguments In a deductive essay, you know that your premise is crucial; as you introduce it, you must appear tolerant and undogmatic. This is difficult to do, particularly if you are using a single premise. Consider, for example, the paragraph about composition teachers (p. 186). A reader might complain that the premise about the importance of enthusiasm overlooks the importance of subject knowledge, diligence in commenting on student work, and willingness to set high standards. Of course, the writer of this paragraph could argue that a teacher must have enthusiasm to have these other virtues. The key point, however, is that this argument will be stronger and more convincing if these objections are raised and then dealt with openly. In a deductive argument, then, you should anticipate objections to your premise. Usually your refutation will come in a separate paragraph, after you state your premise and before you begin your sequence of body paragraphs. The refutation will require at least a paragraph because you must state the objection fully and fairly and then show how your premise is more valid than the one you are refuting. In the following two paragraphs, you can see quite clearly the connection between offering a premise and anticipating objections to it.

> When baseball fans rate major league players, they usually apply fairly basic and common criteria. They look at the batting average of a player, at his fielding statistics, and perhaps recall a few of his great plays. But when they rate catchers, fans should change their standards, for the catcher's job requires more than physical skills. Of all nine positions on a baseball team, only the catcher looks out on the entire diamond. From this command point, he must run the team and dictate strategy in crucial situations. The catcher must also handle pitchers; as he tells the pitcher what to throw, he must outthink opposing hitters and managers. The real determinant of greatness in a catcher is his knowledge of the game and his intelligence. Without these, even the finest athlete will not be a successful catcher.
>
> Of course, some may object that intelligence is not all that a catcher needs. Teams expect their catchers to hit and throw like any other player. A catcher who hits for power is the

> object of every general manager's search. All this is true enough, but the catcher's mental skills are of preeminent importance. The Cincinnati Reds often kept a slumping Johnny Bench in the lineup because, hitting or not, he was too valuable behind the plate. Duffy Dyer never replaced Jerry Grote on the New York Met teams of the late sixties and early seventies. Although Dyer was a better hitter, Grote called a better game and helped the young Met pitchers remain composed. These are only two examples; hundreds more could be cited in support of the basic point. A catcher's thoughts are even more important than his deeds. While the catcher remains an athlete—a man who must perform physical feats—greatness as a catcher awaits only those who think as well as they hit or throw.

Refutations in Inductive Arguments Illustrations and examples are at the heart of an inductive argument. When you proceed inductively, then, you must anticipate particular cases that might seem to contradict the conclusion toward which you are leading. You must look for exceptions to your rule and convert them to exceptions that *prove* your rule. At the very least, you should minimize the importance of the exception. For example, in the past thirty years a wide variety of studies time and again have linked cigarette smoking with several health hazards. The generalization "Cigarette smoking is hazardous to your health" is based on the accumulation of thousands of particular cases. One response on the part of tobacco companies and growers has been to find very old people who have smoked all their lives. They point to these people as proof that smoking is not as hazardous as the government claims, or, at least, that the evidence against smoking is not as clear as it might seem. Of course, one long-lived smoker does not outweigh thousands of smokers who have become cancer victims. But if you want to argue for government antismoking programs, you should bring those old smokers into your essay and dismiss their importance rather than leave them to the tobacco lobby.

In an inductive essay, then, you should anticipate objections—that is, exceptions to the rule—as you introduce your illustrations in the body paragraphs. Whereas the anticipation of an objection in a deductive essay usually comes in a very specific place, in an inductive essay you may raise objections anywhere within the body paragraphs. The following selection addresses a topic we've discussed before—Levi's jeans. Note how the writer uses an exception to prove the rule.

If durability is one quality by which shoppers can judge jeans, then Levi's once again stand above all other jeans. Levi Strauss manufactures its jeans with such care and confidence—double stitching all seams and reinforcing them with rivets—that the company will replace for free a pair that tears or rips. Some other jeans can last a long time, and one national chain store has recently televised commercials in which happy customers claim that the chain's jeans outlasted Levi's. But these exceptions do not disprove the rule. If the chain store has such confidence in its jeans, it should imitate Levi Strauss and replace them for free. The managers of the chain store will not do this because they know people can destroy any but the strongest jeans. Levi Strauss knows this too and probably replaces quite a few jeans that undeserving owners have destroyed. Levi Strauss, however, can risk this loss because the superior durability of its jeans means that such cases are relatively rare. Television commercials to the contrary, the return policy on Levi's proves that they remain the most durable of jeans.

Refutations in Analogy Arguments When you write an analogy argument, you must anticipate the objection that your analogy is not truly logical—that the cases you are comparing are not similar. Your refutation can come immediately after you introduce the comparison or later, after you have worked through the comparison and just before you state the conclusion. Where you decide to place your refutation should depend on your audience. With an unsophisticated audience, you may wait; its members are less likely to question a comparison. With a hostile audience, you should raise the objection immediately. It will probably be on the tips of their tongues anyway. Anticipating a hostile response, the author of the argument for the University of Florida's Halloween Ball tried to make a refutation in her second paragraph (p. 126). She is not very successful because her statement of the objection is brief. Nevertheless, her argument is stronger because of her attempt to deal with at least one potential objective—football games make money for the university, while the Halloween Ball does not. The following selection shows how the writer of the *Jaws-Exorcist* comparison could have anticipated an objection after he introduced his analogy.

Some fans may claim that comparisons between *Jaws* and *The Exorcist* are unfair—that one film's villain is real, the

> other's supernatural. But this is to overlook the first half of *Jaws,* in which Bruce is virtually supernatural; he is invisible, unknowable, and omnipotent. The producers of *Jaws* clearly had the same insight as the producers of *The Exorcist*—the way to really scare people is to make evil unknowable, to make people imagine evil rather than see it. The producers of *Jaws,* however, perhaps fascinated by their remarkably lifelike facsimile of a shark, did not follow this insight as faithfully as did the producers of *The Exorcist.*

Refutations in Appeals to Authority When you appeal to an authority, you want the authority to be unimpeachable. However, in some cases, your authority may be a controversial figure. If so, deal with potential blots on your authority's record after you establish relevance and reputation. If your authority has a personal interest in an issue, admit it, but argue that this does not disqualify him or her. If your authority is unobjectionable, of course, you can proceed as you would in any deductive essay and anticipate objections only to your general argument not to your authority. In the following introduction, the author uses a controversial authority, anticipates an objection to her, and then vindicates the authority.

> Jane Fonda has gained fame as an actress, having won two Academy Awards. She also became famous for her political views during the Vietnam War. She championed the antiwar cause long before it was popular and risked her acting career to speak out against a government policy she felt was immoral. Today as Americans debate the question of nuclear power, Ms. Fonda is once again in the news, criticizing nuclear power plants and the nuclear power industry. Many may feel that she has no right to use her fame in this way and that she has no knowledge in this field. In the sixties, many felt that her lack of expertise in Southeast Asian politics should have disqualifed her from speaking out against the war. But as a woman of intelligence, conscience, and accomplishment and as a woman who was right once before (even Richard Nixon, during his interviews with David Frost, described American policy in Vietnam as misguided and mistaken), Ms. Fonda deserves respect and attention. She argues against nuclear power on the basis of one very simple but important premise. A source of energy must be safe. If it is not, then Americans should not risk it.

First-Person Writing and Argumentative Writing: Establishing Personal Authority

At the end of Chapter I, we urged you to write in the third person. In school and in work situations, people rarely ask for your personal responses or feelings; they want you to provide information that is impersonal and objective. If you think of your papers as arguments, you will clearly see the limitations of the first person. You do not want your readers to say, "Yes, but that's only your opinion." A hostile audience will use that expression to avoid dealing with what you are saying if you do not set up a premise, a series of illustrations, an analogy, or an authority.

The first-person essay, then, is largely inimical to successful argument—largely but not totally. If you have expertise in a field, if you can introduce *yourself* as an authority, then you may use the word *I* quite effectively. But this "I" can only command respect if you put yourself through the same tests that you use for any authority—that is, only if you establish your relevance and your reputation. Here is an introduction to an essay on a topic we have encountered before—athletic shoes. Note how the writer effectively establishes personal authority.

> I am not a great athlete. In high school I lettered in basketball, but only because I clawed and scratched for offensive rebounds and forced my way ahead of better shooters and leapers. I tried to play in college but found that hustle cannot compensate for lack of ability. Still, I like to keep in shape and enjoy competition. I play racquetball and tennis regularly and am on a basketball team in a YMCA league. Because I am so active, my athletic shoes are very important to me; my wife estimates that I spend more than twenty hours a week in them. As the shoes have gotten more and more expensive, choosing a pair has become more important and more difficult. I cannot afford to pay $60 for shoes very often. So I look first for low cost and durability. Then I look for comfort and traction. If the shoe meets my other standards, I may then look for style.

Summary Argumentative writing, then, is more difficult than expository writing. It requires you to define your audience, to combine models, and to anticipate objections. But in doing all these things, you will usually create a more comprehensive, convincing, and precisely organized essay. By thinking of your papers as arguments, you will increase your chances of communicating effectively in both the academic and business worlds. The step from exposition to argumentation is not easy, but if you make it successfully, you will become a better writer.

In the following essay, study how the author uses different arguments within her body paragraphs, combines models, and anticipates objections.

Long Live the Ball

Leslie, a first-quarter freshman at the University of Florida, had been cramming all week for midterms. She had missed at least one meal a day, was feeling weak, and insisted on gnawing her fingernails until they bled. Seeking relief from the mounting tension inside her, she glanced at the school newspaper on her desk and saw an advertisement for the Halloween Ball. Leslie wondered briefly about the Halloween Ball, picked up her psychology book, and continued to study. She thought it a bit ironic that this class caused her so much anxiety and pressure, because chapter five described mental tension and the necessity to find outlets for it. She understood that jogging, tennis, and meditation were all tension relievers, but she had no time during the day for jogging or tennis, and she had no idea how to begin meditating. Leslie became even more nervous when she realized she had absolutely no outlets for her tensions.

Just then, the phone rang; it was Scott and Matthew. They asked Leslie if she wanted to go to the Halloween Ball around ten that night. She insisted that she had to study, but they persuaded her that the time away from her studies would be good for her. They told her to be ready by 9:45 sharp and to wear a white leotard with tights. By nine-thirty Leslie was worn out. If she read anything else by Dr. Jacob Katz, famous psychologist at the University of Michigan, about the importance of tension-relieving activities, she would go crazy. Matthew and Scott were at her place a little before ten o'clock. Both were wearing black shirts and pants and were holding onto the handles of black garbage-can tops. When Matthew and Scott placed Leslie between them, she said she felt like an Oreo cookie, and everyone burst out laughing. She was right: they were an Oreo cookie, and they were on their way to the Halloween Ball.

At the ball they saw some of the weirdest costumes ever imagined. People were dressed as mummies, cameras, bandages, toothpaste tubes, and hamburgers. Anything and everything was at the Halloween Ball. Leslie was glad she was safely sandwiched between Matthew and Scott because she noticed how strangely people were acting. Some staggered instead of walked, some were barely able to stand, and many hung onto each other. The smell of alcohol was everywhere. The glazed eyes of Halloween Ball revelers suggested heavy drug use. Broken bottles were scattered for yards. But despite the confusion, Leslie thought that everyone was relaxed and having a good time. She was home by one in the morning. The next day she felt refreshed and ready to continue her intense studying. She reviewed chapter five and realized that the Halloween Ball had been her "tension-breaker."

Leslie is an example of a student who benefited from the controversial Halloween Ball. University officials and police protest that "the ball fosters extensive alcohol and drug use, free-form sexual activity, and physical violence." For these reasons they want to discontinue the ball. No one can deny that the ball encourages some bizarre behavior, but many other well-accepted festivals in our country have much worse side effects than the Halloween Ball. Because its benefits outweigh its drawbacks, the ball should remain a part of university life.

As Leslie discovered in her textbook, students need "tension-breakers" to prevent depression and fatigue. Tests performed on one hundred University of Michigan students showed that when they studied intensely at least three hours a day without mental relaxation, they became depressed and/or fatigued. But when mental relaxation followed their studying, they were invigorated. Mental relaxers include meditation, jogging, movies, sports, carnivals—anything that takes one's mind off a problem or a stressful situation.

The Halloween Ball is one type of stress reliever. People can momentarily take their minds off the midterm grind by thinking up creative costumes to wear to the ball. But whether students attend the ball in costume or not, simply watching the parade of odd characters and assorted products is a respite from midsemester tension and anxiety. And of course, people can dance, socialize, or just sit in a corner, listen to the band, and relax.

Those opposed to the ball say it is dangerous because of the presence of alcohol and illegal drugs. Leslie's impression of staggering, bleary-eyed people was realistic. At the ball students do consume large quantities of alcohol and drugs. But if the administration wanted to cancel every event attended by drunk and stoned people, they would have to cancel most of the activities on this campus, including some classes. One might better argue that excessive alcohol and drug use is proof that students are looking for relief from pressure. The Halloween Ball provides that relief and allows students like Leslie to return to their schoolwork with vigor and motivation.

Another complaint about the ball is that people lose all sexual inhibitions; the story of one young woman "taking on all comers" in front of Library West has become a campus legend. Most students would agree that sex should be kept private, but some of our most socially accepted establishments openly promote sex. Disco dances are more sexually suggestive than most behavior at the ball; the university's dormitory councils sponsor such dances. The play *The Norman Conquests* revolves around various seductions and acts of adultery, some represented in quite explicit detail; the university's theater department has produced it. One does not have to condone the free-form sex at the ball to argue that these acts should not lead to its cancellation. The point, rather, is that the ball is not the only event that encourages open sexuality—people who enjoy this event should not be punished for something that has become increasingly common on campus and in our society.

A third argument against the ball is that it "fosters physical violence and immoral behavior." But people who criticize the ball should think of the conduct of fans at sporting events. The National Football League's records show an average of twenty-seven arrests per game because of "unruly conduct." The National Baseball, Basketball, and Hockey Leagues boast similar statistics. Popular bars and clubs in Gainesville report at least five arrests a week. The University Police Department reports an average of twenty arrests at the Halloween Ball, a one-night affair. The number of arrests at one sports event alone is likely to exceed the number of arrests at the ball, and in one week more people will be arrested at a bar in Gainesville than are arrested at the ball. Does this mean that football, basketball, baseball, and hockey games should be cancelled? Should bars and nightclubs close down? People criticize the Halloween Ball because its problems come all on one night, but actually the problems are relatively few.

Opponents of the ball also claim that a riot could easily start. But this is true anytime large numbers of people congregate. Authorities have worried about riots at the Republican and Democratic National Conventions (a riot did take place at the 1968 Democratic Convention), Billy Graham Crusade gatherings, sporting events, Mardi Gras, and even the Olympics. Who wants to cancel these events?

Of course, two wrongs do not make a right. The fact that some things that happen at the ball also happen at other events does not vindicate the ball. But the ball should not have to meet special standards either; its drawbacks should not cause university officials to overlook its great virtues. It provides one night in the year when students like Leslie can release internal pressures and relax creatively. Before they cancel the ball, administrators may want to study Leslie's psychology text. For despite instances of drug abuse, free-form sex, and rowdy behavior, the ball remains a celebration important to the mental and physical well-being of students. The benefits it offers are worth the risks it entails.

Exercise 9

Read the following essay, which argues for experimentation with laboratory animals. Analyze the argument in the following ways.

1. Where does the author anticipate objections? How extensive and fair is his treatment of these objections? Does he tempt you to dismiss them?
2. To what types of authorities does he appeal? How does he establish reputation and relevance?
3. What is the premise on which the author's argument relies? Does he state it?
4. What is the generalization that he hopes to prove? How effective are his illustrations?

An enduring controversy surrounds the use of live animals for scientific experimentation. Despite the passage of several animal-protection laws throughout the years (most notably HR 13881 of 1967, a federal law that set standards for the use of laboratory animals), well-intentioned but ill-informed antivivisectionists continue their efforts to have state and national legislatures enact additional legislation restricting the use of animals in experiments. Many scientists fear that such legislation will hamper scientific investigation by forcing the scientific community to deal with government bureaucracy. Although real benefits for humans have been derived directly from animal experimentation, antivivisectionist groups contend that all animal suffering, and therefore most animal experimentation, should be prohibited.

Most readers are familiar with the emotional, sentimental tone of most antivivisectionist literature. Advertisements that consist of grainy photographs of sloe-eyed puppies staring dolefully out of strange, painful-looking devices are a familiar sight in many newspapers. Replete with poorly documented horror stories of sadism and cruelty in the laboratory, these ads, in their appeal to the emotions rather than the intellect, understandably provoke the ire of many animal lovers. "Oh, no, we don't believe in the use of animals for medical research at all," claims Mrs. Helen Winger, president of the vocal and influential California Animal Defense and Antivivisectionist League. She goes on to elaborate: "Scientists are just being cruel and bloodthirsty when they use animals." Such short-sighted sentiment may seem almost laughable to the dispassionate reader, but the very emotionalism implicit in statements such as Mrs. Winger's prompts many Americans to write to their legislators to voice opposition to animal experimentation. But additional legislation regulating the use of animals for scientific research could adversely affect the quality of human life by slowing scientific progress in the fight against disease.

Many antivivisectionists fail to realize the integral role that research animals play in the continuing refinement of medical techniques. According to Harold C. Dodge, professor of medicine at Rochester College, "There is no way to find solutions to biological problems except to study biological systems. It should be obvious that laboratory animals played a part in nearly every important advance in modern medicine." Among those advances are the development of drugs to combat diabetes and hypertension. Many thousands of people are alive today as a direct result of these two developments alone. Noted neurosurgeon Robert White described in a recent article the successful surgical removal of a large tumor from the brain of a young child. This surgery, contends White, was made possible by similar surgery performed experimentally on monkeys. New methods for the treatment of severe burns and shock, electric pacemakers for cardiac patients, and nearly all new drugs and vaccines are but a few of the medical advances made possible by animal experimentation.

Significantly, humans are not the sole beneficiaries of animal experimentation. Some years ago, medical researchers performed experiments on dogs and cats in an effort to discover new immunological agents for human diseases. The researchers were unsuccessful in accomplishing their primary task, but a vaccine for canine distemper and panleucopenia (a similar disease afflicting cats) resulted from their efforts. The suffering and death inflicted on the animals involved in this particular experiment actually allowed a far greater number of animals to escape a slow and painful death. Domestic animals afflicted with diseases common to humans (heart disease, cancer, hemophilia, diabetes, for example) have also shared the benefits of animal experimentation.

Obviously, when live animals are used as experimental subjects for tests investigating the effects of burns, stress, new drugs, or surgical techniques, the animals may suffer pain, and many may die. According to Carl F. Schmidt, Professor Emeritus of Pharmacology at the University of Pennsylvania, this suffering is alleviated whenever possible through the use of anesthetics. Dr. Schmidt candidly admits that many experiments causing pain to the subject animal are not amenable to the use of pain-dulling agents. Among such experiments are those testing stress adaptations, drug reactions, and brain functions. The pain and death inflicted on experimental animals must be weighed against the medical advances made possible only by the use of these animals. The suffering and premature death avoided in both humans and animals by the use of new medical techniques is incalculable.

Most antivivisectionists concede the value of medical research but insist that such research can be accomplished without the use of animals. They believe that modern alternatives—tissue cultures and mathematical models programmed through computers—render the use of experimental animals obsolete. Nearly all scientists, however, agree that these alternatives are imperfect replacements for experimental animals. Neurosurgeon Robert White states flatly: "The technological advances and expense necessary to accomplish such a program (computer simulation of an animal) to replace present day animal research facilities are unachievable." Tissue cultures (cells stimulated to divide in a nutrient solution, forming tissues and, in some cases, organs) are similarly limited as replacements for animal research. According to one scientist, "Tissue cultures are not legal for use in vaccines in this country. Aside from economic impracticality, there is the fear of hidden viruses in the cultures. Would you want to inoculate anyone with such material?" Research animals are so indispensable to scientists that Dr. Virgil H. Moon of the Jefferson Medical College was prompted to remark: "The test animal is to biological science what the test tube is to chemistry."

Despite feeble arguments to the contrary, animals provide a basic, important, and irreplaceable tool for scientific research. Such research has provided, and will continue to provide, useful advances in the quality of life—as long as future legislation does not stifle scientific progress in a morass of red tape. Some proposed legislation would empower the federal government to regulate the use of animals for experimental purposes and would require scientists to seek the approval of a government agency before conducting experiments involving animals. One scientist testifying before

Congress stated, "It is a fantasy to suppose a Washington coordinator could appropriately determine the number and species of animals to be used." Adds another, "All the best things I've done were done on just a hunch, and usually in the middle of the night." The potential harm in forcing scientists to deal with a notorious federal bureaucracy is obvious. Science has made significant progress in the struggle against disease and suffering; however, cancer, heart disease, and other ailments continue to take human lives. To implement measures that could very well slow the rate of progress against such implacable foes would be to court disaster, both for ourselves and our children.

Conclusion

In Samuel Johnson's *Rasselas,* a group of characters embark on a quest for happiness. They fail to find a magic formula for that much-sought feeling, and the book ends with a "Conclusion, In Which Nothing Is Concluded." In this book we have sought something perhaps as rare as happiness—good writing—and we too have discovered no magic formula to produce it. Good writing remains the product of struggle and revision, of anxiety and, occasionally, despair. No literary equivalent to the "no-wax floor" exists. And so this book also must end with a "Conclusion, In Which Nothing Is Concluded."

This does not mean that the book leaves you at a dead end. Rather it leaves you at a beginning. If you can recognize and write agent prose, then you give yourself a chance to develop your ideas effectively. Questions about motive and means, scene and action become possible once the agent is in place. As you work through those questions, you can begin to write good prose—prose that specifies a point at issue and cogently comments on it. Agentless prose, while easier to write, opens no opportunities for development. (This is why it is so popular with political leaders who have something to hide.) It leaves you in a world of abstract and ready-made phrases—"our fast-paced modern lifestyle," "the contingencies of reinforcement"—phrases that fill paper but say nothing. It leaves you in the world of the "*D*—lacks specifics" essay.

When you write agent prose, you give yourself the opportunity to say something, the opportunity to make an argument. How that argument turns out will depend on the quality of your research and the quality of your thought. In the end, agent prose can only be a beginning, and the conclusion of this book waits for you to write it.

Appendix: A Short Guide to Sentence Basics

In this section we return to the basic component of all writing: the sentence. We will discuss ways to make connections within sentences, ways to make sure all the parts of a sentence agree with one another, and ways to punctuate various sentence elements for clarity. This appendix is not meant to be an extensive guide to sentence structure, usage, and mechanics. Rather we hope a brief discussion will point out some basic ways to achieve well-structured, well-punctuated sentences in which all the components agree. Once again, as in our presentation of agent prose, our underlying purpose is to help you achieve writing that is clear and direct.

Building Sentences Properly

Sentence Types

In Chapter I we introduced you to three basic word groups—the phrase, the independent (or main) clause, and the dependent (or subordinate) clause. As we pointed out, a phrase is a group of words that forms a thought or a distinct part of a sentence but does not have a subject and a verb. A clause is a group of words with a subject and a verb. An independent clause can stand alone;

a dependent clause cannot. These word groups can combine in many ways to form many kinds of sentences, but all sentences have at their core an independent clause.

Simple Sentences Simple sentences consist of one independent clause alone, but they are not necessarily short. They can contain multiple subjects and verbs and a variety of phrases that complement the independent clause. Consider these examples of simple sentences.

> The quarterback completed the pass.
>
> Under pressure from the defensive line, the quarterback completed the pass.
>
> The quarterback completed the pass and jogged off the field.
>
> The quarterback, playing in his first game, completed the pass to the veteran wide receiver.

Compound Sentences Compound sentences consist of two or more independent clauses, which can be joined in four ways. Consider the following examples:

> The baby clutched her teddy bear, and her father carried her to bed.

In this first example, a comma and a coordinating conjunction (*and*) link the independent clauses. Coordinating conjunctions are *and, but, or, yet, for, nor,* and *so.*

> Either Philip will drive us to the concert hall or Art will walk there with us.

These independent clauses are joined by the correlative conjunction *either . . . or.* Correlative conjunctions are conjunctions that come in pairs. Others are *both . . . and, neither . . . nor, whether . . . or,* and *not only . . . but (also).*

> The band played the fight song; the fans chanted "Go Tigers."

A semicolon joins these independent clauses. You cannot use a comma alone to join independent clauses.

> Their cook specializes in Italian food; however, he prepares fresh seafood too.

A semicolon and the conjunctive adverb *however* join these independent clauses. Note that the conjunctive adverb is followed by a comma. Other common conjunctive adverbs are *conse-*

quently, furthermore, nevertheless, therefore, then, moreover, likewise, also, accordingly, besides, still, namely, and *hence.*

Complex Sentences Complex sentences consist of one independent clause and one or more dependent clauses. Depending on what you wish to emphasize in the sentence, you can choose to place the dependent clause before, within, or after the independent clause. Consider the following examples in which we have underlined the dependent clause.

> Because I dislike Mexican food, we ate at McDonald's rather than Taco Bell. (Here you emphasize your dislike by placing the dependent clause first.)
>
> We are continually late for classes because our alarm is broken. (Here you emphasize your tardiness by placing the dependent clause last.)
>
> The chain saw that Peter purchased at Sears was superior to the one he had previously. (Here the dependent clause is introduced by a relative pronoun; it is an adjective clause and must follow *chain saw.*)

You link dependent clauses to independent clauses with a subordinating conjunction or a relative pronoun. Depending on the meaning of the dependent clause, subordinating conjunctions may require commas, or they may not; the same is true for relative pronouns. There are many subordinating conjunctions. Typical ones are *after, although, as, because, before, if, since, unless, when,* and *while.* The relative pronouns are *who* (and its forms), *which,* and *that.*

Compound-Complex Sentences Compound-complex sentences consist of two or more independent clauses and one or more dependent clauses. Consider the following examples:

> When the game had ended, the fans poured onto the field; however, they were soon ordered off by campus police.
>
> The exam contained several essay questions, but since our teacher had prepared us so well, we were able to answer them.

The independent clauses in a compound-complex sentence are joined the same way they are in a compound sentence. Dependent clauses connect to one of the independent clauses just as they do in a complex sentence.

You make major structural errors when you do not correctly join the basic word groups to form your sentences or when you try to make a phrase or a dependent clause stand alone. Once you clearly understand the ways to form sentences, you should be able to recognize and avoid those errors, which are commonly called fragments, comma splices, fused, or run-on, sentences, and unbalanced sentences.

FRAGMENTS

You form fragments—incomplete sentences—when you allow a phrase or a dependent clause to stand alone. Remember that all sentences contain at least one independent clause that states the central idea. Phrases and dependent clauses give additional information about a central idea, but they do not themselves contain complete thoughts. Note how fragments result when the writer makes phrases stand alone.

> Swimming smoothly across the lake.
>
> After a lunch of canned ravioli.
>
> In the library next to the rare book room.
>
> Having opened the door.

These phrases do not contain both a subject and a verb (an agent and an action), and they do not present complete thoughts. By joining phrases to independent clauses, you can eliminate fragments.

> I saw Jenny swimming smoothly across the lake.
>
> After a lunch of canned ravioli, I began feeling ill.
>
> In the library next to the rare book room, the student met his girlfriend.
>
> Having opened the door, the man followed us into the hall.

Fragments also result when writers make dependent clauses stand alone.

> If the team wins this game.
>
> Although I do not usually enjoy dancing.
>
> That the boat's sail had caught the wind.
>
> Which he did not like as well as the original *Godfather*.

Although these dependent clauses contain both a subject and a verb, they do not express complete thoughts. Because they are introduced by the subordinating conjunctions *if* and *although,* and the relative pronouns *that* and *which,* they must be joined to an independent clause that will contain the central idea of the sentence. You can eliminate fragments by joining dependent clauses to independent clauses to form complex sentences.

> If the team wins this game, it will receive a bowl bid.
>
> I had a pleasant evening with Rick at the Zone, although I do not usually enjoy dancing.
>
> I knew we would win the race when I saw that the boat's sail had caught the wind.
>
> Bill was disappointed when he saw *The Godfather, Part II,* which he did not like as well as the original *Godfather.*

Of course, as a way of avoiding sentence fragments, you can also change all the dependent clauses to simple sentences.

> The team wins this game.
>
> I do not usually enjoy dancing.
>
> The boat's sail had caught the wind.
>
> He did not like *The Godfather, Part II* as well as the original *Godfather.*

EXERCISE 1

Identify the following word groups as fragments (F) or sentences (S).

____ 1. Coming upon suddenly.
____ 2. In the time that it took us to walk from the library to the dorm.
____ 3. However much time it takes.
____ 4. Cycling at a steady pace, we finished the race ahead of most of the others.
____ 5. Studying at the library allows me to use the unabridged dictionary.
____ 6. Which I did not enjoy at all.
____ 7. That the pass was off target and the kick short.
____ 8. Because Seth sent the letter early in the week.
____ 9. Upsetting me very much.
____ 10. The path that winds around the stadium.

Exercise 2

Correct the following fragments by joining them to independent clauses or deleting subordinating conjunctions.

1. Because the apartment was on the other side of town.
2. Struggling through the vague prose.
3. While we were in the store.
4. In the parking lot under the brown car.
5. After we finished the pizza.
6. Whereas Jules was friendly.
7. Since the weather looked foreboding.
8. Which we didn't know at the time.
9. Casually suggesting that Jan run for president.
10. The feeling that I was being followed.

Comma Splices

You form comma splices when you join the independent clauses of a compound sentence with a comma. In our discussion of compound sentences, we noted that independent clauses can be joined by a conjunction preceded by a comma, a semicolon alone, or a conjunctive adverb preceded by a semicolon. While the comma performs many important functions, which we will discuss in the following section on punctuation, a comma alone cannot join independent clauses. Consider the following examples of comma splices.

> When we saw Manuel, we called to him, he did not hear us, however.
>
> Miles gathered the branches, Eric cleared the site for the fire.
>
> Michelle, who has attended every concert this season, purchased our tickets, she also arranged to take us out to dinner.

You can eliminate the comma splices by joining the independent clauses correctly.

> When we saw Manuel, we called to him; however, he did not hear us.
>
> Miles gathered the branches, and Eric cleared the site for the fire.
>
> Michelle, who has attended every concert this season, purchased our tickets; she also arranged to take us out to dinner.

Exercise 3

Identify and correct the sentences that have comma splices.

1. The candidate spoke to the proponents of a new city bikeway yesterday, promising them that she would support their recommendation.
2. The musician spoke to the workshop participants, he assured them that they could learn to improvise.
3. Television news reports seem unnecessarily glum, they center on violent crimes and government scandals.
4. Because they focus mostly on technology and adventure, early science fiction novels seem shallow compared to those of today.
5. Paul, my roommate, accompanied us to the game, however, he did not sit with us.
6. Contrary to my prediction, Ohio State did not accept my application, but I hope to apply there again next year.
7. Feeling bored by the topic of the lecture, Marcie left the meeting early, she should not have come at all.
8. Because they had been friends in high school, Cora and Martha decided to room together in college, they signed up for many of the same courses as well.
9. The drivers started their engines, the gun sounded to begin the race.
10. However much I like Benjamin, I cannot give him the job.

Fused Sentences

Like comma splices, fused sentences occur when you form a compound sentence incorrectly. You create comma splices when you use only a comma to join independent clauses, and you make fused sentences when you run clauses together without placing any punctuation between them. Consider the following examples of fused sentences.

> Tom went with his friends to the dance he left with Nina.
>
> Even though I have written to Gene frequently, he has never answered I will not write to him again.
>
> The class was canceled the professor was caught in a blizzard in Chicago.

In order to correct these fused sentences you must identify the independent clauses in each and decide on the method you will use to join them correctly. We have underscored the independent clauses separately.

> Tom went with his friends to the dance he left with Nina.

Since both independent clauses tell of Tom's actions, you should probably not divide them into separate sentences. You can form a correct compound sentence by joining the independent clauses with a coordinating conjunction or conjunctive adverb.

> Tom went with his friends to the dance, but he left with Nina.
>
> Tom went with his friends to the dance; however, he left with Nina.

You could also place a subordinating conjunction before one of the independent clauses, changing it to a dependent clause and forming a complex rather than a compound sentence. We have italicized the dependent clause and underscored the independent clause.

> *Although Tom went with his friends to the dance,* he left with Nina.

In the following sentence, the dependent clause is again italicized and the independent clauses are underscored separately.

> *Even though I have written to Gene frequently,* he has never answered I will not write to him again.

Since the first independent clause is introduced by a dependent clause, you may want to make the second independent clause a separate sentence. If you want to keep the sentence compound-complex, you might join the independent clauses with a semicolon, an appropriate conjunction, or an appropriate conjunctive adverb.

> Even though I have written to Gene frequently, he has never answered; I will not write to him again.
>
> Even though I have written to Gene frequently, he has never answered, so I will not write to him again.
>
> Even though I have written to Gene frequently, he has never answered; therefore, I will not write to him again.

Once again, the first step is to identify the independent clauses.

> The class was canceled the professor was caught in a blizzard in Chicago.

The most logical way to connect these clauses might be for you to make one clause dependent and write a complex sentence. You could also link such closely related clauses with a semicolon.

> The class was canceled *because the professor was caught in a blizzard in Chicago.*
>
> *Since the professor was caught in a blizzard in Chicago,* the class was canceled.
>
> The class was canceled; the professor was caught in a blizzard in Chicago.

EXERCISE 4

Correct the following fused sentences by forming proper compound, complex, or compound-complex sentences.

1. Knowing that half the students failed the midterm, the professor offered special tutoring sessions before the final she thought the students needed extra help.
2. The kicker missed two field goals the coach cut him from the team.
3. Josh carefully prepared the roast duckling he had never had anyone over to dinner before.
4. The kidnappers left the ransom note in the mailbox the girl's father found it there.
5. Because Connors overpowered McEnroe, the match was over quickly it had lasted less than two hours.

UNBALANCED SENTENCES

When you form simple, compound, complex, and compound-complex sentences, you join phrases, dependent clauses, and independent clauses in the ways we have discussed. You should also balance these sentence elements by making sure they are grammatically similar. Phrases should parallel phrases; clauses should parallel clauses. Multiple nouns, verbs, adjectives, and adverbs should be in similar forms as well. If you do not parallel related words or word groups, you will produce unbalanced sentences that will distract your reader and obscure your ideas. Consider the following examples that demonstrate unbalanced sentence parts.

> Students need to attend class regularly and taking notes carefully.
>
> I enjoy tennis, golf, and to play racquetball.
>
> Considering its low gas mileage, the car is a bargain even

though it has a broken radio, the front end needs alignment, and new windshield wipers must be purchased.

The coach told them either to concentrate during practice or that they should quit the team.

The artist chose to paint landscapes, and they were always painted in vivid colors.

Below we will identify the unbalanced sentence parts and explain how to rewrite the sentences in parallel form.

Students need to attend classes regularly and taking notes carefully.

Here we can change the gerund *taking* to the infinitive *to take* in order to parallel the infinitive *to attend.* In this way, the two phrases become balanced.

Students need to attend classes regularly and to take notes carefully.

I enjoy tennis, golf, and to play racquetball.

Here we can eliminate the infinitive phrase *to play racquetball* and replace it with the noun *racquetball,* which is parallel to the other two nouns in the list.

I enjoy tennis, golf, and racquetball.

Considering its low gas mileage, the car is a bargain even though it has a broken radio, the front end needs alignment, and a new windshield must be purchased.

Here we add an agent, *we,* and begin each phrase with a verb that agrees with this agent. In this way, the verbs are in similar form, and the sentence is balanced.

Considering its low gas mileage, the car is a bargain even though we must fix the radio, align the front end, and replace the windshield wipers.

The coach told them either to concentrate during practice or that they should quit the team.

Whenever correlative conjunctions join phrases or clauses they must be followed by similar word patterns. Here we see that the conjunction *either* is followed by the verb phrase *to concentrate during practice* and so we place a similar phrase after the conjunction *or—to quit the team.*

The coach told them either to concentrate during practice or to quit the team.

The artist chose to paint landscapes, and they were always painted in vivid colors.

In compound sentences, the independent clauses should parallel each other. Since the first independent clause has an agent and a past tense verb, we can provide the appropriate agent and past tense verb for the second independent clause.

The artist chose to paint landscapes, and he always used vivid colors.

EXERCISE 5

Many times you will create unbalanced sentences because you are writing hurriedly. You should be able to recognize and correct such problems when you revise your rough draft. Practice this process by rewriting the following samples to improve the balance between sentence parts.

1. Because I like Eileen and having no problems with her nonstop talking, I accepted her offer of a ride to Pittsburgh.
2. The dance hall was so crowded and warm that you could either be sweltering inside or find refuge on the porch.
3. To play tennis once a week and running daily are my forms of exercise.
4. We were both tired of standing in line and to the point of being upset because the plane was late.
5. Early registration allows the university to computerize the registration process and avoiding a confusing scramble for courses.
6. I enjoy going to the beach not only because I like to swim but also because of surfing.
7. Grandmother prepared a ham and a turkey, and the dishes were placed at either end of the table.
8. The Shovelheads won the conference championship last year, but this year they have been plagued with injuries to key players and their coach quitting.
9. She could either study law, politics, or be a doctor.
10. During the summer months, the wildlife society loses many volunteers and is faced with the cancellation of its nature walks for children.

Making Sentence Parts Agree

Besides connecting sentence elements properly and making sure they are parallel, you must see that all the parts of your sentences agree with one another. You should be concerned with subject-verb agreement and pronoun-antecedent agreement. The sexist use of pronouns is another problem you will encounter when you attempt to make all your sentence parts agree. We will address these topics in this section.

SUBJECT-VERB AGREEMENT

In all acceptable sentences, the subject agrees with its verb in number. Note these two examples.

> The boy runs.
>
> The boys run.

Complicated sentences can contain multiple subjects or complex noun phrases as subjects, in which case the appropriate verb form is not always obvious. For instance:

> Fine acting and elaborate scenery are characteristic of our high school plays.

In our example you should recognize that there is a compound subject that calls for a plural verb.

> Nervously trying to talk to Gloria while quickly eating my lunch so as not to be late getting back to work causes indigestion.

The subject of this sentence is the gerund *trying,* which takes a singular verb. You can see that by employing such a complicated gerund phrase you run the risk not only of making agreement errors but also of blurring the sentence idea. As we have pointed out before, whenever you employ a gerund phrase as the subject of your sentence, you are writing agentless prose.

If you begin sentences with a form of the expletive *there is,* you risk agreement errors. *There* stands in the place of the subject, but you must search through the sentence to discover the "true subject," or agent, that *there* replaces. For example, you might write the following sentence.

> There was disease, famine, and death throughout Turkey after the earthquake.

Yet *were* is the correct verb because the true subject of the sentence is *disease, famine, and death.* To avoid such confusion, you should avoid using expletives.

Certain words that serve as sentence subjects (agents) require certain verb forms. *Each, one, either, neither,* and all words ending in *-one* or *-body* take a singular verb. Words such as *few, both, many,* and *several* take plural verbs. Note the following examples in which we underline subjects and verbs.

> Everyone in the dormitories has a stereo.
>
> Few of the students in my dorm have cars.
>
> Several of the injured were from our town.
>
> Neither of the drivers was hurt.

In the sentences above the subjects *everyone, few, several,* and *neither* are followed by prepositional phrases. These phrases give additional information about the subjects, but they do not affect the form of the verb. You can delete these prepositional phrases without changing the central statement of the main clause: "Everyone has a stereo" and "Neither was hurt" remain independent clauses with the prepositional phrases deleted. Many times students mistake the last word in the prepositional phrase for the true subject and consequently make agreement errors. Note the first and last sample sentences. You must be careful to identify *everyone* and *neither* as the true subjects and to realize that the plural nouns *dormitories* and *drivers* are part of prepositional phrases and do not affect agreement.

We should mention two additional rules. When you use the correlative conjunction *both . . . and,* the subject is always plural. For example:

> Both excellent hiking trails and an exquisite view of the lake attract visitors to the state park.

When you use the correlative conjunctions *either . . . or, neither . . . nor,* or *not only . . . but (also),* the noun following the second conjunction determines the verb form. For example:

> Neither Troy nor his parents like milk.
>
> Neither Troy nor his son likes milk.

In these sentences the nouns *parents* and *son* determine the form of the verb *like.* It must be in plural form to agree with *parents,* a plural noun, and in singular form to agree with *son,* a singular noun.

The other rule concerns collective nouns. Collective nouns refer to a group of people or things. Some common collective nouns are *audience, army, committee, company, couple, crowd, family, faculty, group, herd, jury, majority, school,* and *team.* When you try to determine which verb form agrees with a collective noun subject, you can often become confused. Collective nouns can be either singular or plural. Consider the following examples.

> The faculty defends the president's action.
>
> The faculty defend the president's action.

If you consider the collective noun subject *faculty* as a unit, you will use the singular form of the verb, *defends.* If you are thinking of the individuals that make up the faculty, you will use the plural form of the verb, *defend.* Remember that you must determine whether you are treating the collective subject as a unit or as individuals before you can decide on the correct verb form. Consider one more set of examples.

> The couple are taking separate vacations.

EXERCISE 6

Underline the correct verbs.

1. Against my advice, Janine and her sister (watches, watch) television every night until midnight.
2. There (is, are) many possible candidates.
3. Either of the two girls (is, are) able to apply for the scholarship.
4. The task of assembling a bicycle in a short time without waking Robbie and Marie (await, awaits) me on Christmas Eve.
5. Neither he nor his daughters (was, were) willing to sell the property.
6. At every Michael Jackson concert, the crowd (surges, surge) into the stadium as soon as the doors are opened.
7. Each of the flowers (was, were) awarded a blue ribbon.
8. Anybody who likes éclairs (is, are) welcome to come over for dessert.
9. The committee (is, are) having trouble agreeing on the budget.
10. Both the pilot and the copilot (is, are) uninjured.

Here the collective subject is considered to be two individuals, and the verb form is plural.

> The team is still in the locker room.

Here the collective subject is considered as a unit, and the verb form is singular.

Pronoun-Antecedent Agreement

In all acceptable sentences, pronouns agree with their antecedents. As we discussed in the section on subject specificity, the term *antecedent* refers to the noun that you replace with a pronoun to avoid repetition. Consider these sentences: "The mayor called the meeting to order. She read from a prepared statement." *The mayor* is the antecedent for the pronoun *she.* Notice that since the noun *mayor* is singular and, in this case, feminine, the pronoun must be singular and feminine as well. You can apply many of the rules that govern subject-verb agreement to pronoun-antecedent agreement. Remember that words ending in *-one* and *-body* along with the words *each, one, either,* and *neither* always take the singular form of the verb. You can then assume that these words take singular pronouns as well. Consider these sentences in which we have underlined the personal and possessive pronouns and italicized their antecedents.

> *Neither* of the swimmers thinks that she will lose the race.
>
> *Everybody* loves a burger if he or she can have it fixed the right way.
>
> *Everyone* was hoping that he or she would be chosen.
>
> *Each* of the girls carried her equipment off the field.
>
> *Nobody* had his speech prepared, so the teacher dismissed the young men.

Words such as *few, both, many,* and *several,* which take the plural form of the verb, also call for plural pronouns. Consider these sentences:

> *Both* of the youngsters like their burgers without onions.
>
> *Many* of the new golfers chose their clubs hesitantly.
>
> *Several* of the players were told that they could not make the trip.

You can also apply the rules for subject-verb agreement when determining what pronoun to use following a correlative conjunction. When you use *both . . . and,* the subject is always plural, so the pronoun replacing the subject is also plural. With the correlative conjunctions *either . . . or, neither . . . nor,* and *not only . . . but (also),* the number and gender of the noun following the second conjunction determines the number and gender of the pronoun. Note the following example sentences.

> *Both Sharon and Germaine* take <u>their</u> vitamins daily.
>
> *Neither the chairman nor the committee members* have completed <u>their</u> reports.
>
> *Not only my sisters but also my cousin* has <u>her</u> own car.

When you determine which pronoun to use for a collective noun, you should again follow the rules that determine the verb form. If you are considering the collective noun as a unit, you will use a singular verb form and singular pronouns. If you are considering the collective noun as a group of individuals, you will use the plural verb form and plural pronouns. Consider the following sentences with collective nouns and related pronouns. We have underlined the pronouns and italicized their antecedents.

EXERCISE 7

Cross out the incorrect pronouns and verbs and substitute the correct pronoun form and verb form.

1. Each of the boys in the play have their speech memorized perfectly.
2. Neither of the teachers allow their students to use books during the test.
3. Many in the class has decided his or her fate was unjust.
4. The family has their reunion at Mount Washington each spring.
5. Either the president or several officials will pay his respects to the slain leader by attending the funeral.
6. Everybody on this hall have their own radios.
7. The team has lost their first game of the season.
8. Few of my friends in the country has planted his or her garden yet.
9. By a continued increase in sales, the company hopes to reach their goals.
10. Both the horse and the jockey is recovering from his injuries.

The *army* was moving into position and preparing to commence its attack.

The *family* disagree among themselves on minor issues but they agree on important ones.

The *jury* have elected their foreman.

The *company* gives its executives holiday bonuses.

Pronoun agreement errors can frequently distract and confuse your readers. You must locate the antecedent carefully, remember certain special rules, and determine the correct pronoun form.

PRONOUNS AND GENDER: AVOIDING SEXIST USE OF PRONOUNS

As we have mentioned, when you test a pronoun by locating its antecedent, you note whether the antecedent is singular or plural and then choose the appropriate pronoun. In the following sentences, the nouns and pronouns do not agree in number.

The typical doctor feels that they deserve some help with malpractice insurance. (*Doctor* is singular; *they* is plural.)

A university professor often believes they are underpaid. (*Professor* is singular; *they* is plural.)

Any student will tell you that they have a hard time making ends meet. (*Any student* is singular; *they* is plural.)

These sentences lead to one other important point about noun-pronoun agreement. Recently, many people have suggested that the English language is sexist, particularly in its tendency to use the masculine singular pronoun (*he*) to replace singular nouns that are not gender specific. For instance you might write:

The typical doctor feels that he deserves some help with malpractice insurance.

A university professor often believes that he is underpaid.

The average student feels that he has too little time for his social life.

But doctors, students, and professors may be either women or men; the assumption of masculine dominance and importance that underlies these sentences is both unjust and discriminatory. Yet our language offers no substitute for *he;* English has no gender-neutral personal pronoun. So what can you do to avoid sexism in your writing? One solution is to use both the feminine and masculine singular pronouns to replace singular nouns that are not gender specific.

> The typical doctor feels that he or she deserves some help with malpractice insurance.
>
> A university professor often believes that he or she is underpaid.
>
> The average student feels that he or she has too little time for his or her social life.

As you can see in the last sentence, using both singular pronouns can sometimes lead to wordy constructions. Many times, however, you can simply delete some pronouns to make the sentence flow more smoothly.

> The average student feels that he or she has too little time for a normal social life.

Another practical solution is to make your nouns that refer to general classes plural and then replace those nouns with the plural (and sexually neutral) pronoun *they*. Many times the result is smoother than a sentence that uses both *he* and *she* to replace nouns that are not gender specific.

> Most doctors feel that they deserve some help with malpractice insurance.
>
> University professors often believe that they are underpaid.
>
> Students generally feel that they have too little time for their social lives.

EXERCISE 8

Revise the following paragraph. Avoid the sexist use of pronouns, and be sure that all pronouns agree in number and gender with their antecedents.

> A first-year law student must work long, hard hours if he is to succeed. The demands on him are great; assignments include hundreds of pages of technical reading each night and frequent ten- to fifteen-page briefs. The student is under great pressure to do well; they hope to earn high grades and extra-curricular honors, on the law review and in moot court competitions, for example. Only the most intelligent and diligent student can hope he will survive his first year of law school, their first step on the way to a career in law.

Punctuating for Clarity

If you connect sentences properly and make sure that all of their parts agree, you will be adding to the clarity of your writing. Another element that contributes to clear, direct writing is punctuation. In this section we will outline the use of commas, semicolons, and colons.

THE COMMA

As we have mentioned, commas are often used to help create compound, complex, and compound-complex sentences. In this section, we want to show how commas can be used in particular ways to link phrases, dependent clauses, and independent clauses.

Commas in Compound Sentences You should place a comma before a conjunction that links independent clauses. The comma signals to readers that the sentence is compound and allows them to read the sentence correctly the first time. Note the following examples:

> The men lifted the cement blocks and the boys collected the smaller bricks.
>
> I could call Rosa or Bob could call Carol to find out about the class.
>
> Mel likes hotdogs and Lionel likes hamburgers.

In these examples, the omission of the comma before the conjunction might cause readers some confusion when they first read the sentences. In the first sentence, readers might think that the men are lifting both the blocks and the boys. A comma before the conjunction *and* signals readers that the sentence is compound and that another independent clause will follow the conjunction. The same type of misinterpretation is possible in the second sentence. *Bob* is the agent of the second main clause, yet without the comma before *or, Bob* could be mistaken for a second object of the verb *call.* The third sentence exemplifies this same confusion. *Mel* and *Lionel* are the subject-agents of the two main clauses, but without a comma before the conjunction readers might at first think "Mel likes hotdogs and Lionel." Not all compound sentences with commas omitted will be as ambiguous or misleading as our example sentences. You should nonetheless always use a comma before the conjunction in a compound sentence to make things as clear as possible to the reader. A comma before a coordinating conjunction signals that one clause has ended and another is beginning.

EXERCISE 9

Place commas before conjunctions linking independent clauses.

1. He performs well on stage but in rehearsal he never excels.
2. The rain pounded against our car and the engine started making screeching noises.
3. Rachel is going to France this summer but Marina is going to Germany.
4. I rented a car and Len and I drove through the city.
5. Faith healers seem phoney to me yet they attract many followers.
6. I will give the money to Saul or Beverly will give it to his wife.

Commas with Phrases and Dependent Clauses In general, you should place a comma after an introductory element (a word, a phrase, or a dependent clause) in order to separate it from the the rest of the sentence. If you follow this comma rule, your readers will understand the sentence on first reading. Also, the subject or agent of the independent clause usually follows the introductory phrase or clause; therefore, by separating the introductory element from the clause with a comma, you focus attention on the important agent (doer) of the action. No comma is necessary, however, after an introductory word or a brief prepositional phrase if the word or phrase does not cause a break in the continuity of the sentence. Note these examples:

> After talking at length with Ray Karen left for the airport.
>
> In the morning fog hangs over the city.
>
> Because I wash my hair each day Wes thinks I need special shampoo.

In these examples the omission of the comma after the introductory phrase or clause blurs the focus on the agent of the independent clause. In the first sentence, readers will have to read carefully if they are to understand at what point the introductory phrase ends and the independent clause begins. A comma after the word *Ray* separates the sentence parts and focuses the readers' attention on *Karen,* the subject, or agent, of the independent clause. The second sentence is even more confusing without proper punctuation. Readers will at first think that something occurs "in the morning fog." A comma placed after the introductory phrase will signal readers that *fog* is the subject, or agent, of the independent clause. In this way readers can understand the sentence meaning immediately; they will not have to search for the agent. In the last sentence, the introductory dependent clause runs into the independent clause so that readers might have trouble sorting out the sentence parts and sentence meaning. By using a comma to divide sentence parts, you can place the focus on the agent (*Wes*) and his action (*thinks*). Also, the reader can recognize the dependent clause and clearly understand the total statement made by the complex sentence.

The same is not necessarily true when a phrase or dependent clause occurs elsewhere in the sentence. You need to decide whether the phrase or clause is restrictive or nonrestrictive. A nonrestrictive phrase or clause gives additional, nonessential information about the word it modifies; you can therefore delete a nonrestrictive phrase or clause from a sentence without changing the basic meaning of the sentence. You should use commas to set off such nonrestrictive modifiers from the rest of your sentence. On the other hand, a restrictive phrase or clause adds essential information to the word it modifies; you cannot delete a restrictive phrase or clause from a sentence without changing the meaning of the sentence. You *do not* set off restrictive modifiers with commas. Note the following examples:

> Only fans who hold season tickets receive special parking permits.
>
> The fans, many of whom had stood for hours in the rain to buy tickets, were jubilant when the Bears won their first game of the season.
>
> Harold chose the red and black tie, which was unfortunately the most expensive.
>
> The girl whom I was planning to ask to the dance broke her ankle.
>
> The girl, whom I was planning to ask to the dance, broke her ankle.

In the first sentence, the clause *who hold season tickets* modifies the word *fans,* which is the subject, or agent, of the sentence. The clause provides essential information about the word *fans;* it is not fans in general who receive parking permits but only fans *who hold season tickets.* If you try to delete the clause from the sentence you change the meaning of the sentence completely. This clause is a restrictive clause—it restricts the meaning of the word it modifies (*fans*); you must not separate the clause from the word it modifies. In the second sentence, the modifying clause does not provide information essential to the meaning of the sentence. If you delete this clause from the sentence, you are missing some additional information, but the basic meaning stays the same. You should set this clause off from the rest of the sentence with commas since it does not restrict the subject. In the third sentence, the dependent clause introduced by *which* is nonrestrictive; you should set it off from the independent clause since it could be omitted from the sentence without altering the main thought of the sentence. We include the remaining two sentences to show you that you must consider the context of your statements before deciding if the modifier is restrictive or nonrestrictive. In the fourth sentence the essential information about the agent is not just *the girl* but *the girl whom I was planning to ask to the dance.* The modifier is restrictive, so it is not set off with commas. In the last sentence, *the girl* has been

---

EXERCISE 10

Place commas where they are needed.

1. By hurrying into the bank the teller attracted everyone's attention.
2. Because I was dating Jason Rico decided to ignore me.
3. Mr. Reed who is the chairman of the meeting called us to order.
4. The player who screamed at the referee was evicted from the game.
5. Stopping abruptly the candidate left the podium.
6. Furthermore these two men had never attended our meetings before.
7. The Chamber of Commerce has suggested widening Maple Avenue which is the town's main thoroughfare.
8. The car that he bought at Art's Car Center ran better than the one he had bought at Auto City.
9. By writing to the principal Mrs. Bernstein hoped to clear her son of the charges.
10. Dogs that do not have tags must be picked up by the dogcatcher.

---

previously identified, and *whom I was planning to ask to the dance* is nonessential information which could be deleted without changing the meaning of the sentence. Because this modifier is nonrestrictive, it is set off with commas.

Transitional words and phrases, whether they occur at the beginning of the sentence or not, should be set off by commas, since they interrupt the flow of the sentence. Note the following examples.

> On the other hand, Tina prefers historical fiction.
>
> Dr. Davis believes, however, that the plan was poorly conceived from the beginning.
>
> We all agreed that the performance was a success, all things considered.

Commas in Compound-Complex Sentences Remember that a compound-complex sentence consists of two independent clauses and one dependent clause. Of course, you will need to place a comma before the conjunction joining the independent clauses (if indeed that is how they are joined). If the dependent clause is introductory, you should place a comma after it to signal the start of the independent clause. If the dependent clause falls in the middle or at the end of one of the independent clauses, you must decide if it is restrictive or nonrestrictive. In other words, follow the basic rules applicable to compound and complex sentences. Study the following examples:

> My financial situation is dismal, and I will not be able to enter law school if I do not get a scholarship.
>
> John has studied diligently since he entered medical school, and his professors expect him to be a fine doctor.
>
> Because students are on vacation and have time to seek such entertainment, Hollywood producers aim summer movies at younger audiences, but, as a result, adults face a limited summer fare at the box office.

Exercise 11

Insert commas where they are needed in the following sentences.

1. Unless Dale Murphy begins to hit more home runs the Braves will not have a chance to win their division.
2. The first semester of college can be trying for students because they are away from home for the first time and colleges should provide some counseling.

3. I entered the marathon with high hopes but I finished in last place because the course was much tougher than I expected.
4. When the United States declared war on Japan the whole country was united but the armed services were unprepared for war.
5. My mother has been a wonderful golfer since she was quite young and I hope I take after her.

Minor Comma Rules The comma rules we have just discussed all direct you to use the comma in certain situations to clarify your meaning. Other comma rules are important as well. We will outline them briefly in this section.

Use commas to separate elements in a series. We suggest that you place a comma before the conjunction *and* that signals the last element in the series. This comma is sometimes considered optional.

> The campers carried tents, knapsacks, and firewood into the clearing.
>
> Two years ago I had a new job, a young family, and ambitious plans for the future.
>
> Kayaking, playing squash, and dancing are my favorite forms of exercise.

Use commas to separate major elements in dates, addresses, and names of places. Note the following examples of correct comma placement.

> The Japanese bombed Pearl Harbor on December 7, 1941.
>
> June 17, 1948, is the day Leo was born.
>
> Abraham Lincoln was born on February 12, 1809, in Kentucky.
>
> Tacoma, Washington, is a port city on the Puget Sound.
>
> Judy's address is 89 Woodlawn Street, Jamaica Plain, Massachusetts.

Use commas to set off directly quoted material from any other element of the sentence.

> "Come in right now," said the children's mother.
>
> I said, "Roland has total responsibility."
>
> "I do not believe that Henry committed the crime," Perry Mason said, "and I intend to prove that he is innocent."
>
> "Tomorrow," I said, "is the day we begin our trip."

An *appositive* is a word or phrase that identifies the immediately preceding word or phrase. The appositive could be substituted for the preceding word or phrase without changing the meaning of the sentence. As with modifiers, appositives can be either restrictive or nonrestrictive.

> For many years the artist Norman Rockwell illustrated the covers of the *Saturday Evening Post.*

In the sentence above, *Norman Rockwell* is a restrictive appositive; without it the reader would not know which artist did the illustrations. No commas are necessary or appropriate to set off a restrictive appositive.

> Ms. Hogan, the head of the committee, will appoint three members to the subcommittee.

In this example, *the head of the committee* is a nonrestrictive appositive. Ms. Hogan is sufficiently identified by her name alone; the appositive adds additional, nonessential information to the sentence. Nonrestrictive appositives should always be set off from the rest of the sentence by commas. Consider the use of commas with nonrestrictive appositives in the following sentences.

> Dean, the boy next door, never came to play with us.
>
> My brother treasured his new car, a speedy Corvette.
>
> The pilot, a ten-year veteran, had flown two hundred combat missions.
>
> Our primary concern, that mother get enough rest, did not seem to be shared by our father.
>
> I would recommend that she see Mrs. Owen, the school nurse.

The Semicolon

The semicolon is a more powerful link than the comma. Remember that you can use a comma followed by a conjunction to link independent clauses, but you can use a semicolon alone to perform the same task. In fact, the primary task of the semicolon is linking independent clauses. Do not use semicolons at random, however. You should first consider the independent clauses to decide if you need to indicate their relationship with a certain conjunction or conjunctive adverb. If, however, the independent clauses are strongly related in meaning and their relationship needs no qualification, a semicolon will be an appropriate link. If you decide to use a conjunctive adverb such as *however, therefore, consequently,* or *moreover* to join the independent clauses, you will need to place a semicolon before the conjunctive adverb and a comma after it. Consider the following examples.

> Sophie enjoys sledding; therefore, she was excited when snow began to fall this morning.
>
> We gathered the firewood; the girls cleared the space for the fire.
>
> The film reflects the director's primary interests; it tells of patriotism and faithful love between a man and a woman.
>
> The publisher asked us to hire an experienced candidate; therefore, we interviewed a long-time foreign correspondent, an associate editor of a national newsmagazine, and the managing editor of the city's largest newspaper.
>
> At the battle at Antietam Creek, Union troops under General McClellan lined up on one side of the creek; Confederate troops under General Lee faced them on the other side.

You can use the semicolon for one other task—to separate elements in a series when these elements contain internal commas. Consider the following examples.

> We elected the following officers: Mrs. Stephanie Jones, president; Miss Emily Sorrentino, vice-president; Mr. Ford Gray, treasurer; and Ms. Alice Du Bose, secretary.
>
> We have finally settled on our travel plans: we will drive to Disney Land on Saturday and proceed to Los Angeles; we will stay in Los Angeles for a week, visiting family and friends; and the next Saturday we will return home.

Exercise 12

Insert commas where they are needed. If they have been inserted unnecessarily, circle them to indicate that they should be omitted. Replace a comma with a semicolon if necessary, and circle unnecessary semicolons.

1. Finding that I had lost my way I asked a policeman for help.
2. I lost my keys and my car had to remain in the parking lot.
3. Onyx, Sandy Shep and Maxine were our dogs a mangy bunch.

4. I like Jay therefore I asked him to the game.
5. Fern the new student in French class was consequently embarrassed by her accent.
6. We spotted the three scouts who had come from Arkansas on the sidelines; staring at Glenn the team hero.
7. On November 22, 1963 John F. Kennedy was assassinated.
8. The old construction site was unsafe, nails and broken glass were everywhere among the rubble.
9. Because David had lied to Margo and had gone out with Phillipa Richie thought David was unfair, Richie felt David should have been honest with the women.
10. Furthermore I think Craig is unqualified.
11. After the turn of the century my grandfather came to America and first settled in New York.
12. He did not want to wake up, he had to finish his term paper run a few errands do the laundry and buy some groceries.
13. As my friend and I walked down the street; he saw Sean and we both confronted him.
14. After taking Modern British Poetry I have decided to major in English.
15. "Gretchen" said her mother "take out the garbage soon."

THE COLON

Like the semicolon, there are two main ways to use the colon. First use a colon to introduce a list or a quotation. Do not use the words *for example* before a colon; the colon alone is sufficient.

> Many interesting flavors of ice cream were available at the new restaurant: cookie cream, peanut butter fudge, melon sherbet, and raspberry swirl.
>
> We decided on the following men for the mission: Jared Greene, Clarence Pauling, and Randy Burns.
>
> The following items were missing: a typewriter, a fur coat, and a pair of earrings.
>
> Churchill made this dramatic statement: "I have nothing to offer but blood, sweat, toil, and tears."

Second you may use a colon before a clause that clarifies the preceding clause or illustrates a point in the preceding clause.

Consider these examples:

> Jim Brown is an exceedingly lucky man: very few football players have gone through their careers without serious injury.
>
> Television movies are generally poor: they are made quickly with little attention to credible story lines or consistent characters.
>
> Most creative cooks don't follow recipes exactly: they substitute ingredients and add spices to suit their individual tastes.
>
> The director of the film paid careful attention to authenticity: most scenes were shot on location in Papua New Guinea and Australia.

It is also appropriate to connect the independent clauses in these examples with either semicolons or dashes. A colon indicates a greater break in the continuity of the sentence than a semicolon; a dash indicates a greater break than a colon. As you become adept at writing agent prose, you can choose the punctuation that best clarifies what you want to say.

EXERCISE 13

Insert semicolons and colons wherever they are needed in the following sentences. If necessary, change commas or other marks of punctuation to semicolons and colons.

1. It is the best of times and the worst of times, increased prosperity for some, extreme poverty for others.
2. The steps in replacing spark plugs are as follows, remove the terminal wires, take out the spark plugs, use the proper size spark plug wrench to screw in the new plugs, and connect the terminal wires to the plugs, making sure they are connected to the same cylinder as before.
3. The project was proceeding well on the whole, however, there were a number of problems, and the project manager always seemed to have a disturbed frown on her face.
4. It is very late, I must go home immediately or I won't be able to get up for work tomorrow.
5. There were three reasons for his success, integrity, industry, a good personality.
6. As Neil and Tanya walked down the street, he saw only shop windows, she saw only people's faces.

7. Reasonable rules in grammar have to be based on the way people use the language, there is really no other standard.
8. Some people believe success in life requires intelligence, industry, and honesty, other people believe that only personality is important.
9. One by one, the children tiptoed in, Jackie with a wilting flower, Cathy, with a glass of ice, and Steven, with a get-well card.
10. He did not wish to go, besides, the weather was miserable.

INDEX

E

F

G

H

I

Q-R

S

T

U-V